25.00

D1009843

DATE DUE

oct. 0			
10/22/02			

DEMCO 38-297

3 1215 00092 5377

A Gift to the

LIBRARY

of

MISSION COLLEGE

Donated by

Dale Pifer

THE
LIVING TRUST
REVOLUTION

THE
LIVING
TRUST
REVOLUTION

WHY AMERICA IS ABANDONING WILLS AND PROBATE

■

Robert A. Esperti
and Renno L. Peterson

VIKING

VIKING
Published by the Penguin Group
Viking Penguin, a division of Penguin Books USA Inc.,
375 Hudson Street, New York, New York 10014, U.S.A.
Penguin Books Ltd, 27 Wrights Lane,
London W8 5TZ, England
Penguin Books Australia Ltd, Ringwood,
Victoria, Australia
Penguin Books Canada Ltd, 10 Alcorn Avenue, Suite 300,
Toronto, Ontario, Canada M4V 3B2
Penguin Books (N.Z.) Ltd, 182–190 Wairau Road,
Auckland 10, New Zealand

Penguin Books Ltd, Registered Offices:
Harmondsworth, Middlesex, England

First published in 1992 by Viking Penguin,
a division of Penguin Books USA Inc.

1   3   5   7   9   10   8   6   4   2

A NOTE TO THE READER

The authors are not engaged in rendering legal, tax, accounting, or similar professional services. While legal, tax, and accounting issues covered in this book have been checked with sources believed to be reliable, some material may be affected by changes in the laws or in the interpretations of such laws since the manuscript for this book was completed. For that reason the accuracy and completeness of such information and the opinions based thereon are not guaranteed. In addition, state or local tax laws or procedural rules may have a material impact on the general recommendations made by the authors, and the strategies outlined in this book may not be suitable for every individual. If legal, accounting, tax, investment, or other expert advice is required, obtain the services of a competent practitioner.

LIBRARY OF CONGRESS CATALOGING IN PUBLICATION DATA
Esperti, Robert A.
Living trust revolution : why America is abandoning wills and
probate / Robert A. Esperti & Renno L. Peterson.
p.   cm.
Includes index.
ISBN 0-670-84714-3
1. Living trusts—United States.   2. Wills—United States.
3. Probate law and practice—United States.   I. Peterson, Renno L.
II. Title.
KF734.E85   1992
346.7305'2—dc20
[347.30652]   92-16375

Printed in the United States of America
Set in New Baskerville
Designed by Victoria Hartman

For Liz, Rob, and James, and
for Karen, Andy, and Eric—
Your love and patience make
all our work worthwhile

Acknowledgments

We have had the opportunity to work with many special people in creating this book. It is impossible to name them all, but we would like to give particular thanks to a handful of our friends and colleagues who gave their time, expertise, and support. First and foremost, we would like to thank Lisa Kane DeVitto, Esq., who devoted so much time, energy, and thought to the research for this book. Her work was invaluable from start to finish. We also want to thank William D. Kirchick, Esq., of the law firm Bingham, Dana & Gould in Boston, Massachusetts. Bill reviewed all of our chapters on the after-death income issues of probate estates and trusts. While he didn't agree with all of our conclusions, he offered important input and a good point of view. His comments are much appreciated. Special thanks to Peter Lampack, our agent and friend, who has given us wise counsel and who has worked so well with our publisher.

We also would like to thank the many lawyers and other professionals who reviewed the manuscript of this book in its various stages. They shared wonderful insights and edits that were important in refining our research and writing.

Lastly, we want to thank the attorneys who are members of the National Network of Loving Trust® Attorneys. With their support and their willingness to advance the principles in this book, we will change the way Americans plan for their future needs and for those of their loved ones.

Contents

x • *Contents*

PART TWO

Living Trust–Centered Planning Compared to Testamentary Trusts and Joint Tenancy

PART THREE

Why America Is Abandoning Wills and Probate

APPENDIX A

Analysis of the After-Death Income Tax Issues

APPENDIX B

1991 Probate Survey of Four States

Introduction

The United States is experiencing a wealth transfer the likes of which has never been seen in history. Some $6.8 trillion worth of assets will soon pass from parents to children, grandchildren, friends, charities, and others.[1] The enormity of this wealth transfer will have an impact on virtually every family in America.

Who is going to control how this immense wealth will pass? A growing number of lawyers, accountants, financial advisers, and life insurance professionals believe that this wealth should not be controlled by wills and probate, but rather should pass by revocable living trust planning. These professionals believe that wills and probate do not serve the needs of their clients, and they often question the motivations of probate lawyers. They believe that will-planning/probate is an outdated, anachronistic system that does not serve the public's best interests even though it is being practiced by most lawyers throughout main-street America. The argument of advocates of revocable living trust planning is powerful in its simplicity: The revocable living trust works better and costs less than wills and probate.

Lawyers who practice probate law disagree. They believe that this wealth should pass as it has traditionally passed, by wills and probate. These probate lawyers denounce the living trust as a gimmick that is oversold and unfairly challenges the will planning and probate status quo. They consider living trust advocates as more P. T. Barnum than Oliver Wendell Holmes.

Some probate lawyers are more subtle in their attack on living trusts. They take the position that there is no definitive right or wrong when it comes to living trusts and will-planning/probate because "it all depends." They want the public to believe that it is senseless to debate the issues because the specifics of each client's situation must first be analyzed before a proper lawyerly decision can be made. This calculated "nonposition," more often than not, is used as an excuse for writing yet another will-planning/probate estate plan.

The will-versus-trust debate is a consumer issue that will involve many billions of dollars in planning fees and over $400 billion in probate fees in the next two decades. However, the debate is about more than money. It is also a battle over professional power and prestige that calls for an assessment of how the public's interests should best be served.

The controversy over living trusts has been fueled by articles in magazines and newspapers in recent years. In their attempts to inform the public, these articles have created more confusion than enlightenment. For example, in 1987, *The Wall Street Journal* published an article entitled "Revocable Living Trusts Become Popular Option in Estate Planning," which cited some of the many advantages of revocable living trusts.[2] Four years later the same reporter wrote, "Living Trust Hoopla Bears a Close Look."[3] In this article, several estate planning experts gave diametrically opposite views on the uses and abuses of the revocable living trust. Various opinions were quoted that left the reader speculating about which lawyer was telling the reporter the truth. That same week, *Fortune* magazine featured an article entitled "The (Financially) Perfect Death."[4] It contained several professional testimonials extolling the virtues of living trusts.

There has been a rash of popular books about living trusts that have added to the turmoil, leaving most readers confused and bewildered. Most of these books tell the reader in sweeping generalizations that a living trust is good and then turn to particular planning strategies that have nothing to do with why living trusts are better than wills and probate. These books raise the planning expectations of their readers without giving them the ammunition to counter their lawyers, who use their own sweeping generalizations to denigrate living trusts.

The American public is relying on joint tenancy planning and fill-in-the-blank estate planning forms in the mistaken belief that these techniques will totally avoid probate and lawyers. Unfortunately, these approaches cannot begin to meet the public's planning expectations and will create serious problems for them and their family members in future years.

The public is beginning to learn more about the controversy over living trust–centered planning versus will-planning/probate and is asking questions that demand frank answers:

- Why are the benefits and the mechanics of the living trust such a mystery to most lawyers?
- Are lawyers ignoring the living trust for monetary reasons?
- Does a living trust have drawbacks that lead practitioners to recommend against its use?
- Is a living trust so different from a trust created within a will?

These questions prompt additional difficult questions about the behavior and attitudes of a great many lawyers.

Why do lawyers who practice will and probate law blame trust lawyers and other professionals for stirring up a needless controversy? Why does the living trust provoke aggressiveness, hostility, and fear among many lawyers? Is there a probate conspiracy?

It is because of these questions and the tremendous amount of misinformation that permeates the debate that we decided to write a definitive book on the pros and cons of living trusts that would directly compare them to wills and probate.

In Part One, "Living Trust–Centered Planning Versus Will-Planning/Probate," we address and analyze each of the major issues that differentiate living trust–centered estate planning and will-planning/probate. For each issue, we determine which camp has carried the burden of proof. The evidence conclusively proves that a living trust should be the core document of every estate plan.

In Part Two, "Living Trust–Centered Planning Compared to Testamentary Trusts and Joint Tenancy," we examine why living trust–centered planning is markedly superior to trusts that are created by wills and to joint tenancy.

In Part Three, "Why America Is Abandoning Wills and Probate," we summarize all of the issues in the debate and definitively demonstrate that living trust–centered planning is far superior to will-planning/probate. We also come to grips with why more lawyers are not using living trust–centered planning as the mainstay of their estate planning practices.

The trust debate is about changing the way America plans. It involves planning for trillions of dollars by an industry that will charge billions of dollars for that planning. It will affect almost every family in America in some way.

PART ONE

Living Trust–Centered Planning Versus Will-Planning/Probate

· 1 ·

A Probate Perspective

Probate has become synonymous with the public's frustration with the legal complexities, delay, and expense associated with the death of a loved one. The concept of probate avoidance was popularized in the 1960s and, since that time, has become the rallying cry for advocates of the revocable living trust. Professor James Casner, a legal pioneer in the field, wrote one of the first and most influential articles for attorneys in 1960.[1] Norman F. Dacey's *How to Avoid Probate!* was one of the first widely read books attacking the probate system.[2] Today, probate epitomizes the differences between will-planning/probate and living trust–centered planning.

The Will-Planning/Probate Process

A rudimentary understanding of the mechanics and origins of the will-planning/probate process is a prerequisite to understanding the benefits of a living trust. Let's begin with what probate is.

The term *probate* has more than one meaning. Technically, probate means to prove the validity of a will in a court, a process which can take a short time if no one contests the legitimacy of the will. *Probate* is commonly used in a much broader sense to describe the process of passing an owner's title to property after the owner's death. The technical term for this administrative court process, which can be very lengthy, is really *administration.*

In administration, a decedent's affairs are inventoried, and creditors are identified and paid. There are a host of other administrative procedures which ensure that the estate's lawyer, executor, and various taxing authorities will be paid before the balance of the estate is distributed to rightful heirs.

Although probate and administration are, strictly speaking, two different processes, the term *probate* is used for both probate and administration. Even lawyers and judges use the term in this manner. Probate has been described as "encompassing the transfer of property on death and guardianship"[3] and "our court-operated system for transferring wealth at death."[4] *Black's Law Dictionary* describes the term as follows:

> In American law, now a general name or term used
> to include all matters of which probate courts have
> jurisdiction.[5]

Probate is also the name of the court that has jurisdiction over probate and administration. The names of these courts vary from state to state. Courts with jurisdiction over probate and administration are sometimes called common or surrogate courts, but in a majority of states they are referred to as probate courts. In addition to probate and administration, probate courts usually have jurisdiction over the guardianship of minors and mentally incompetent adults.[6] Guardianships, because they are under the jurisdiction of the probate courts, are often referred to as "living probates."

Administration occurs both when a person dies *intestate*

(without a valid will or will-substitute) and when a person dies *testate* (with a valid will). Contrary to the widely held popular opinion, if a person dies owning property in his or her own name, and that owner executed a last will and testament, that property *will go through probate.* A will that is executed will inevitably be probated.

If valid will-substitutes are employed, probate will not be required. Commonly used will-substitutes include living trusts, joint tenancy ownership, and beneficiary designations such as those ordinarily used for life insurance and employee benefit plans.

The ultimate goal of the will-planning/probate process is to transfer title to property from a decedent to the decedent's heirs. There are, however, numerous interim administrative steps that must be performed and discharged before that event can occur.

While the statutes that govern wills and probate vary from state to state, the process usually begins with the preparation and filing of a petition for probate or Letters of Administration (legal terminology for the commencement of the probate process). If a person dies with a will, the executor who is named in the will files the petition as soon as possible after the decedent's death. If a person dies without a will— intestate—then usually an heir files the petition.

When the petition is filed, an initial hearing date is set. The purpose of the hearing is for the court to formally approve the executor (executrix, if female) who is named in the will. In some states, the executor is called a personal representative. In an intestacy, the court must appoint an administrator (administratrix, if female). An administrator is usually a bank trust department or a trust company but may be a professional administrator or an heir.

No matter whether called executors, personal representatives, or administrators, these court-approved or appointed agents basically have the same functions. We will use the term *executor* because of its familiarity to most people.

In addition to the executor, the probate process requires the services of a lawyer. The lawyer is retained by the executor to guide the estate through the complexities of the probate system by preparing the filings, speaking at hearings, drafting petitions to the court, and filling in the myriad kinds of paperwork that probate and administration require. Probate without lawyers would be a contradiction in terms.

The executor and the lawyer perform the tasks required during the probate process. It is usual for first-time executors to rely totally on the knowledge and expertise of the estate's attorney.

In the initial probate hearing, the validity of the will is established. Probate statutes often require that, in order to prove a last will and testament, its witnesses must testify with regard to the technical validity and niceties of its signing. This is not, however, required in all states. Under modern probate statutes such as the Uniform Probate Code, many states now allow a self-proving clause, which allows a will to be admitted to probate without the testimony of its witnesses. The subscribing witnesses sign an affidavit at the time the will is signed attesting to its correctness in lieu of in-person testimony down the road.

The executor notifies creditors as soon as possible after the commencement of the probate proceeding. Notices are also mailed to heirs and beneficiaries. The process of ascertaining the scope, nature, value, and location of the decedent's assets is started concurrently with the notification of creditors. Depending on the jurisdiction, appraisers are appointed by either the probate judge or the executor.

Creditors must file their claims against the estate in the precise manner and within the exact time prescribed by local statutes, usually two to six months after probate has begun. During this legal hiatus, distributions cannot be made from the estate except for certain family allowances prescribed by state law or approved by the court.

Once the period for submitting creditors' claims has ended, and assuming there are no disputes, a petition for a judgment of final distribution can be presented. Once this petition is approved, the executor can distribute the remaining property to the heirs.

The length of probate varies from a few months to many years, but averages from about one year to eighteen months. In Chapter 4, "Delays in Administration," we discuss the length of probate in depth.

The probate process can be extended if disputes of any kind arise. If a federal estate tax return is filed, an estate may remain open until such time as the audit period expires, or until an audit is actually concluded, which can be three years or more. An estate may very well remain open for a period of up to fourteen years if it elects to pay federal estate taxes on the installment method. Litigation, whether initiated by taxing authorities, creditors, or interested parties, may delay the closing of the estate for many years or even decades.[7]

During the entire period of administration the estate will be under the control and supervision of the probate court. Most transactions, especially monetary ones and those dealing with the specific disposition of assets, are subject to court approval.

In the eighteen states that have adopted some version of the Uniform Probate Code and those that have instituted "streamlined probate procedures," informal or unsupervised probate is allowed. An informal probate is not directly supervised by the court, although the usual procedures for creditor notification and other administrative procedures must be strictly observed.

With an informal probate administration there is far less paperwork and contact with the court. However, informal probate does not relieve the executor or the attorney of fulfilling the routine steps that characterize formal probate proceedings.

The probate and administration process is frequently and harshly criticized by both professional and lay commentators who feel that it is an antiquated remnant from a bygone era that serves few, if any, useful purposes. They believe that probate is not necessary and that it creates horrendous aggravation, delays, and expense.

A Brief History of Probate and Probate Reform

Probate, as we know it today, did not appear suddenly as the result of an act of Congress or a consortium of states passing a probate statute. After the Revolutionary War, the thirteen original states adopted probate from the English common law and English statute. As America grew more complex, probate evolved from a very informal proceeding to a much more complicated process. The move away from informality in after-death transactions unquestionably corresponded with the change in the nature of our national wealth, a transformation that went from the ownership of land and personal effects to more complicated commercial holdings. One writer has observed that state and federal inheritance tax laws made government a significant factor in determining the direction of probate policies and practices.[8]

As the economy became even more commercial and less agrarian in the late nineteenth century and into the twentieth century, and the pace of communications and life in general accelerated rapidly, the simple probate systems devised in each state during the early and midnineteenth century were no longer effective. In 1937, a noted law school professor made it clear that probate reform was necessary:

> Yet, one who seeks to find a solution to the problems of dispensing with or shortening the administration of decedents' estates is literally a voice crying in the wilderness.[9]

Probate reforms began as early as 1946 when the American Bar Association (ABA) promulgated the Model Probate Code to encourage more uniform probate laws. This Model Code influenced legislation in only thirteen states.

In the 1960s, the ABA and the National Conference of Commissioners on Uniform State Laws worked to consolidate the Model Probate Code with other uniform laws relating to probate and guardianship. As a result, the Uniform Probate Code (UPC) was drafted by a group of ten legal scholars in consultation with the ABA and the banking industry and was approved by the ABA in 1969. Some of the primary goals of the UPC were to

- Achieve uniformity of state laws
- Simplify and streamline the probate process through less reliance on the court system
- Simplify ancillary administration (multiple probates in different states for property owned in those states by the same decedent)
- Provide for resolution of conflicting claims of where a decedent lived for legal purposes (domicile)
- Provide for the validity of transfers by payable-on-death accounts that automatically bypassed probate

These proposed changes to probate law and procedure were timely because in the late 1960s probate was considered a national scandal because of its high cost and long duration.

A large part of the recognition by the public of probate's problems in the 1960s was the publicity generated by books and articles on the subject.[10] The costs of probate in America were even more egregious because, in contrast to the American system, the British had developed a system that relied less on courts and lawyers and more on the efforts of a personal representative. In 1968, one commentator found that, on average, it took 17 times longer and cost 100 times more to transfer a person's property to heirs in the United States than it did in Great Britain.[11] The European civil law system did not use a personal representative or extensive court proceedings; property was transferred by a system of "universal succession" in which heirs inherited property subject to a decedent's debts.

In the 1960s and 1970s, popular literature in America abounded with criticisms of the cost and delay of probate. A survey published in a prominent legal periodical reported that from 4 to 10 percent of the gross value of an estate was consumed in combined fiduciary and attorney fees.[12] While use of minimum fee schedules for probate services imposed by local bar associations was recognized as a common and reputable practice,[13] some members of the legal profession candidly acknowledged that antiprobate criticisms were well founded.[14]

In the early 1970s, radical probate reform legislation was proposed in three states that would have exempted from probate all estates of less than $60,000 (then the minimum amount for reporting purposes under federal estate tax laws.)[15] It was clear that probate reform was a major consumer issue, and that only a few states were attempting to satisfy the demands of their public's outcry.

A University of Michigan professor, Richard V. Wellman, a drafter of the Uniform Probate Code and one of its strongest proponents, tirelessly urged judges, lawyers, and legislators to support the UPC. Probate lawyers were outraged and vocal in their opposition to this simplification attempt, evidently feeling that simplification would adversely affect their role and compensation in the probate process.

In the early 1970s, Wellman's writings warned judges and lawyers to support probate reform or risk losing their probate business altogether. Numbers of lawyers and judges joined the chorus, but, instead of advocating reform, they urged greater efficiency in the probate court system and better service at lower fees by probate lawyers. As a result, not many fundamental reforms in the probate system were made.

Probate in the 1990s

As of 1992, the goal of achieving uniformity among state laws has not been met, as only eighteen states have adopted some version of the Uniform Probate Code.[16] Even states that adopted the UPC have changed the code to such an extent that there are wide variations among them.

But the UPC has, nevertheless, had a positive influence on the statutes and case law of other states. At least twenty-three more states have adopted specific portions of the UPC,[17] most commonly the following:

- Simpler, more modern provisions for intestacy
- The augmented estate for purposes of spousal rights (making sure that a surviving spouse receives some guaranteed portion of the deceased spouse's estate)
- Ancillary administration (multiple probates due to owning real property in more than one state)
- Multiple-party and payable-on-death accounts (attempts at incorporating beneficiary designations for certain property)

The UPC's least commonly adopted provisions are those that establish informal probate and succession without administration. These provisions attempt to cut much of the red tape for which lawyers and executors charge, and they have not been popular with lawyers. Probate critics cite this lack of enthusiasm as proof of the unwillingness of attorney-controlled state legislatures to achieve real and meaningful probate reform. The evidence is fairly strong that, in the traditional areas of probate and administration, reforms have not met the hopes for modernization of their many professional crusaders.

Some of the most widely accepted provisions of the Uniform Probate Code have been in the area of nonprobate transfers, such as payable-on-death accounts which avoid probate altogether.[18] A noted legal scholar has documented that in the latter half of the twentieth century the United States is experiencing a "nonprobate revolution," and that the probate system is, for all practical purposes, becoming less and less important in the transfer of wealth at death.[19]

This is because much of the nation's wealth is owned in nonprobate property such as pension funds, life insurance policies, joint accounts, and revocable living trusts. In addition, creditors do not rely on probate because of its delays and complexity. They find that they get paid without having to suffer through the probate process. This is a facet of probate that, interestingly enough, many lawyers point to as justification of its very existence. In Chapter 8, "Protection from Creditors," we show why creditors do not necessarily like probate either.

The Perception of Probate

In spite of the number of attempted probate reforms, some commentators believe that little has changed. One writer states, "The reality is that the cost, time, and complexity [of probate] have been little affected."[20] Another says, "In the great majority of cases, however, administration is a needless expense."[21]

Advocates of will-planning/probate take the diametrically opposite point of view and believe that "the probate process has been simplified considerably in recent years" and that delay and expense have been reduced accordingly.[22]

At times, lawyers in the same state, all of whom presumably understand the probate process and its inherent costs, argue among themselves as to whether probate is something to be applauded or avoided and disagree about the costs of probate, its duration, and even its degree of complexity.[23]

The numerous changes in various state probate statutes have not altered the public's negative perception of its value or the attacks by its critics. In 1989, the American Association of Retired Persons (AARP) issued a report on probate.[24] The report includes a number of powerful and scathing comments and quotations that are not kind to the will-planning/probate tradition. John McCabe, the legislative director for the National Conference of Commissioners on Uniform State Laws, is quoted as saying, "The probate process has been a cash cow for attorneys. Small law firms pay their basic office expenses with probate fees."[25] Another comment comes from an attorney writing in a bar journal who is quoted as stating, in part, that probate practice traditionally has been a "guaranteed retirement annuity program for attorneys."[26]

The AARP report arrives at the following conclusion:

In conclusion, probate as generally practiced in the United States is an anachronism. Probate's procedures and protections, even with recent reforms, are inappropriate for all but the most exceptional cases. And, to the extent that the probate system is unreasonable, attorneys' fees in connection with probate work are unreasonable.[27]

We agree with this conclusion, and we believe that probate avoidance is a primary reason why the American public is abandoning wills and probate in favor of living trust–centered planning.

A Brief History of the Revocable Living Trust

The living trust is an ancient and venerable legal concept developed in the tradition of the English common law over a thousand years ago. It predates the modern concept of wills, which was established in England by the Statute of Wills in 1540. The living trust, in its earliest form, was used by members of the English nobility to ensure that their property passed the way they wanted without unnecessary interference by the government.

Living trusts are valid in all of our states, including the state of Louisiana, which bases its legal structure on the French Napoleonic Code. The living trust has been analyzed, studied, and favorably written about by legal scholars in definitive legal treatises.[28] It has been used successfully by specialist practitioners for a very long time.

Unfortunately, the living trust has been identified as a planning technique only for the wealthy. It would appear that because the living trust started with the legal maneuvering of English nobility, it has always been associated with the rich. This perception is also due to the fact that in the past lawyers were reluctant to spend time planning for smaller estates because they could not justify a large enough current fee to cover their effort. Neither of these reasons has any basis in fact today.

The advent of consumerism in the law and the increasing prosperity of Americans have led to a new interest in living trust planning. Now, more than ever, living trusts are mentioned in the media and in estate planning literature. More and more professionals and laypersons alike are nodding their heads affirmatively when asked whether they are familiar with the living trust as a substitute to will-planning and probate. Lawyers are learning that living trust planning can be priced so that it is affordable for almost everyone. The living trust is becoming popular as the core estate planning document of choice for many Americans.

The Fully Funded Revocable Living Trust as a Will Substitute

A revocable living trust, also known as an *inter vivos* trust (from the Latin phrase meaning "between the living"), is created by a trust maker who transfers property to a trustee for the benefit of a beneficiary.[29] A revocable living trust can be established either by declaration, when the trust maker is the sole trustee, or by a transfer of property in trust to other trustees, who can include the maker.[30] A revocable living trust can be revoked or amended by the trust maker at any time prior to death, allowing it to be changed as the planning needs of its maker change.

Revocable living trusts sometimes can be difficult to conceptualize, especially for people who have not read one or seen one actually work. In our book *Loving Trust*, we used an analogy of "baby-sitter instructions" to describe a living trust. Over the years, we have found that this is the easiest way for most people to understand how a living trust works.

If we and our wives are going away for a weekend, our baby-sitter receives a full twenty minutes of instruction. We leave several pages of instructions detailing everything that needs to be done for our children. Scattered all over the house are little gummed stickers with notes on them, both to the boys and to the baby-sitter. We will be close to a phone, and, of course, we will call at least twice a day.

A properly drafted living trust is a set of baby-sitter instructions for the care of loved ones. Our instructions tell our trustee—the baby-sitter—how to care for our beneficiaries—our children. The instructions are as detailed as possible, to cover all of the expected—and unexpected—events that might occur. Not only do these instructions tell our trustee about how to use our money and property to care for our beneficiaries, they tell our trustee why we left certain instructions and how we want them carried out.

The most important feature that a revocable living trust has that a will does not have is its ability to care for its maker. A revocable living trust is valid the day it is signed. If the trust maker becomes sick or incapacitated, the living trust can care for the maker without the intervention of the court. A will can function only after the death of its maker and it is subject to probate; a living trust can care for its maker immediately and avoids both a living probate and a death probate.

A living trust has a number of other characteristics that set it apart from will-planning/probate and other will-substitutes:

- A trust is created by a person or persons whom attorneys call a settlor, trustor, creator, or grantor.
- The person responsible for following the trust maker's instructions is called a trustee.
- Trustees can be individuals or licensed institutions. The maker can also be his or her own trustee in most states. If more than one trustee is serving, they are referred to as co-trustees.
- Trusts can be created by more than one maker. Joint makers are called co-makers.
- Living trusts can be created for the benefit of the maker and for the benefit of other people. The people for whose benefit a trust is created are called its beneficiaries.
- Living trusts can accomplish just about any objective of the maker as long as that objective is not illegal or against public policy.
- The beneficiaries who have the first rights to the trust property are called primary beneficiaries. If the primary beneficiaries die or become disqualified by the terms of the trust, then the property will go to contingent beneficiaries.
- Trusts should be in writing and are effective even if they are not signed by a trustee.
- Any number of separate trusts can be created in a single trust document.
- When the maker puts property in a trust, the maker "funds" the trust.
- Trust makers can be primary or contingent beneficiaries of their own trusts.

A revocable living trust has been referred to as "a will substitute that has come of age."[31] As you will see as you read the chapters that follow, the revocable living trust has even more features that make it the most versatile and effective estate planning technique that is available. When a living trust is used as the foundation of a properly drafted estate plan—we call this living trust–centered planning—there is no better way to care for the needs of an individual and his or her loved ones.

The Costs of Will-Planning/ Probate Versus the Costs of Living Trusts

Questions for Discussion

- Do lawyers have to charge differently for wills and living trusts?
- What are the costs of probate and administration of a will?
- What are the costs of funding and maintaining a revocable living trust?
- What are the costs of the after-death administration of a fully funded revocable living trust?
- Do living trusts cost less or more than will-planning/probate?

Advocates of the fully funded revocable living trust argue that will-planning/probate should be avoided because of its costs. They view these costs as excessively high, and, in many cases, totally unnecessary. Trust advocates believe that *all* costs associated with the probate process can be substantially, if not totally, eliminated with a fully funded revocable living trust and that after-death administration costs can be substantially reduced.

Trust advocates believe that even when the costs of creating, funding, and administering living trusts are taken into consideration, the living trust–centered estate plan represents a significantly more economical planning device than the will-planning/probate alternative.

Will-planning/probate defenders believe that the probate process is not particularly expensive. They frequently make the argument that the costs of probate, at least where attorneys' fees are concerned, are not related to the probate process at all, but rather to the routine after-death administration expense that they believe is incurred in an identical manner when living trust planning is used. They further contend that minimal, if any, cost savings can be achieved by choosing a living trust over the traditional will-planning/probate alternative. They base their position on what they allege are the disproportionately high costs of creating, funding, maintaining, and administering a trust.

There is little consensus among professional and lay commentators as to what the related costs of probate and administration really are. Nor is there agreement on what costs are common to both probate and administration and the after-death administration of revocable living trusts. Economic differences among geographic regions also muddy the water. The disparity between the legal fees charged in Last Chance, Idaho, or American Fork, Utah, and Boston, Massachusetts, or New York City is obviously significant.

The controversy over the relative costs of will-planning/probate versus the costs of preparing, funding, and operating revocable living trusts is permeated with uncertainty because of a lack of centralized, concrete information. It is also laden with differing degrees of emotionalism. The very nature of attempting to compare costs that cross socioeconomic and geographic lines is difficult. In the material that follows, we examine this issue on the basis of the very best empirical evidence available.

Do Lawyers Have to Charge Differently for Wills and Living Trusts?

There are many different kinds of wills and trusts. There are simple wills and simple trusts. There are wills that create testamentary trusts for purposes of federal estate tax planning and for purposes of people planning. Likewise, there are revocable living trusts that create subtrusts used for federal estate tax planning and for personal planning.

Because of the many differences among the types of wills and the types of trusts and between wills and trusts in general, it is difficult to compare the costs of will-centered plans with those of living trust–centered plans unless a will and a living trust that contain the same provisions are compared.

First, let's consider a simple will and a simple trust. The definition of a simple will, for our purposes, is a will that makes an outright distribution of property to heirs. It is used purely as an instrument to determine who gets the will maker's property. A simple trust is a trust that is used to avoid probate. It too distributes the trust maker's property outright to beneficiaries.

The time required of an attorney to prepare a simple will versus a simple trust is not significantly different. The documents are similar in terms of content, although the trust usually contains additional standard legal language and may be somewhat lengthier. By using computer technology, most lawyers can create documents quickly and efficiently, especially when drafting the standard, repetitive clauses that are commonly referred to as legal boilerplate.

If will-planning/probate attorneys and trust practitioners wish to give their clients the opportunity to select either the will-centered approach or the living trust–centered approach, necessary time must be spent outlining the relative merits and drawbacks of each. Thus there should also be little, if any, difference in the actual time the practitioner spends with the client regardless of which approach is selected.

Both will-planning/probate and trust practitioners must take the time in each planning situation to determine the client's specific assets and how each is titled. This is absolutely necessary for any estate planning practitioner. It is simply not possible to do responsible estate planning without accomplishing this task, and any attempt to shortcut this step can be catastrophic. For example, if a client owns property in joint tenancy with right of survivorship and that asset is not addressed by the practitioner as part of the estate plan, it is possible that the dispositive provisions of the client's will or living trust could *not* be carried out with respect to that property.

A will can only control property if the property is titled in the will maker's name or if it is payable on death to the will maker's estate. A living trust can only control property that is titled in the name of the trust or made payable to the trust at the trust maker's death.

In our example, neither estate planning approach would control an asset that is titled in joint tenancy. The estate planning attorney has the unequivocal obligation to review evidence of title to make sure that property ownership and beneficiary designations are consistent with the client's desires in the overall estate plan.[1]

Except for the actual task of funding a revocable living trust, the process of explaining and ascertaining title should not vary between will-planning/probate practitioners and trust practitioners.

Generally, the same ancillary documents are prepared for both the simple will-centered plan and the simple trust-centered plan. Competent estate planning attorneys, whether advocates of will-planning/probate or of living trust–centered planning, would agree that the use of some type of durable power of attorney, a power of attorney for health care decisions, and a living will is necessary. Each of these documents serves a distinct function in estate planning relating to a person's sickness or disability. A durable power of attorney, which we discuss in Chapter 3, "Disability Planning," is designed to be used to help manage the property of a disabled individual. A power of attorney for health care allows a person to decide who will make health care decisions if he or she is disabled and cannot make those decisions. A living will allows a person to determine, in advance, whether or not life support and other procedures should be continued if he or she is terminally ill or in a permanent vegetative state.

In the case of the simple trust-centered estate plan, a pour-over will must also be drafted as a matter of course. The pour-over will is a fail safe device. We often describe this type of will to our clients as a legal catch-all. It picks up property inadvertently left out of the trust and puts it there after death. Since a pour-over will is very simple, it can be drafted with little extra effort. It should not add significantly to the cost of a revocable living trust plan.

The same comparisons can be made when discussing more complex wills and trusts. If a lawyer is spending the time to educate clients as to their options with each approach, and each document has the same federal estate tax planning and personal planning provisions, the relative costs of the plans should theoretically be identical.

Despite this analysis, most practitioners would agree that it is common practice for attorneys to charge less for will-centered estate plans than for living trust–centered plans.

The American Association of Retired Persons has called the low fees charged by attorneys for wills "loss leaders."[2] It is their theory that by preparing a will for a very low fee, attorneys generate substantial probate fees. This theory is espoused by a number of other commentators and will-planning/probate critics. Even the American Bar Association has recognized this problem and has voiced concern over how this method of billing may increase the cost of probate and decrease the initial quality of the work performed.[3]

In reality, living trust–centered plans cost more than wills because living trust attorneys who fund those trusts spend more time with their clients. They take the time to analyze client assets completely and coordinate the title to the assets with the trust plan they are preparing.

There is little or no evidence that will-planning/probate practitioners routinely consider title to assets. We have reviewed thousands of will-centered estate plans over the years that could not possibly achieve their objectives because of the simple fact that their makers' property was controlled by other planning vehicles such as joint tenancy or beneficiary designations.

If will-planning/probate lawyers are charging less for simple will planning than living trust lawyers are for their living trust–centered plans, it is because will-planning/probate lawyers are doing far less work for far less result. It seems clear that, except for the costs of funding a living trust, there is no reason why will-planning/probate lawyers and living trust lawyers should not be charging similar fees if they are performing similar services.

What Are the Costs of Probate and Administration of a Will?

It is an indisputable fact that probate creates expense, but how much expense? In a number of articles written in the late 1980s and the early 1990s, many will-planning/probate advocates have argued that the probate process had been streamlined in many states and have either claimed or implied that the expense of probate for most families is not significant.[4]

These same will-planning/probate advocates rarely, if ever, have provided verifiable statistics to define what they meant by "not significant" or "not expensive," although a few made very rough estimates of fees.

Before we begin our analysis of the costs of probate and administration, we need to address a very important issue. Many times, probate fees—the costs of probate and administration—are expressed as a percentage figure. The legitimate question that should be asked is, A percentage of what? This question graphically demonstrates one of the most often-ignored probate inequities.

When a percentage is used to establish the amount of an estate's probate fees, it always applies to the *gross estate*. The gross estate is the appraised value of all of the assets in a probate estate without regard to any liabilities. For example:

John's assets are worth $1,000,000 and his liabilities—mortgages and other debts—total $900,000. His net worth and net estate may be $100,000 but, for probate purposes, his gross estate is valued at $1,000,000.

If the total probate fees on his estate total 6 percent (3 percent for the attorney and 3 percent for the executor), *the 6 percent is measured against the gross estate of $1,000,000.*

The probate fees are $60,000: 6 percent of the $1,000,000 he owned. This is true even though his net worth was only $100,000.

In reality, John's probate fee is <u>60 percent of his net worth</u>.

If probate fees were expressed as a percentage of net worth, a totally different picture of the real cost of will-planning/probate would emerge.

Probate's defenders argue that the "percentage of the gross estate" rationale is consistent with how financial institutions and investment managers charge for managing assets. Probate lawyers maintain that the lawyer and the executor have the same duties and risks regardless of whether creditors or heirs are being paid. And as a result, their fees are justifiably taken off the top.

Too many heirs incorrectly assume, or have the false understanding, that the percentages quoted are on the net value of the estate rather than its gross value. In the figures that we use, we are referring to a percentage of the gross estate, not the net estate.

There has been no comprehensive study of probate fees in the United States in a long time. It appears that the last nationwide study of probate fees was conducted in 1983 using 1972 statistics from tens of thousands of estates across the country. The results, which are based on the gross value of the estate before expenses and taxes, can be summarized as follows[5]:

Size of Estate ($)	Percentage of Estate For Administration (%)
$ 10,000	12.8
25,000	8.0
50,000	6.9
100,000	5.0
250,000	4.9
500,000	4.8
1,000,000	4.5
2,500,000	4.4
5,000,000	4.0
10,000,000	3.9

George M. Turner, in whose book this study was cited, stated that, even if more recent statistics had been used, the results would probably have been the same:

> It would be a difficult argument for anyone to make believe that expenses of settling estates have been decreasing over the past 10 to 15 years. That assertion would fly in the face of reality of what, in fact, has happened to all expenses, such as attorney's fees, court costs, commissions and related expenses.[6]

Turner also makes the point, based on his interviews with estate planners and trust officials, that in his opinion the study's figures are *conservative*.

Two other authorities give evidence that the probate and administrative expenses that can be expected in most estates are actually higher than those found in the 1972 Turner study.

But overall, to be on the safe side for planning purposes, probate and administration expenses of approximately 9 percent on an estate of $50,000, on down to 5.5% on a $1 million estate, and probably no less than 4.5% on the very largest estates can be anticipated, unless steps are taken to reduce the executor's and attorney's fees.[7]

Most insurance companies and other financial institutions use 5 to 10 percent of the gross estate as the estimated reduction of the estate for settlement costs. Turner states that 5 percent is the rule of thumb used by most institutions.[8]

These studies and comments make a compelling case that probate fees are in the 5 to 10 percent range for most estates. However, the one flaw in these conclusions is that they are based on national averages, which can sometimes be misleading. As more than one skeptic of averages has pointed out, if you put a block of ice on a man's head and his feet in boiling water, the temperature at his midsection will be a comfortable 70 degrees.

Because the costs of probate are in the forefront of the will versus trust debate, it is not enough to stop at this point and reach a conclusion, based on national averages and some possibly outdated studies, that probate fees must be high. It is important to understand what constitutes probate fees and to examine a number of limited, but more recent, studies so that specific conclusions can be reached as to what most Americans can expect their probate expenses to approximate regardless of where they live.

"Probate fees" is an amorphous term. The costs of probate generally include four basic components:

1. Court costs, including filing and docket fees and notice and publication expenses
2. Appraisal fees

3. Attorneys' fees
4. Executors' fees

Court Costs

Actual court costs vary considerably from state to state but are generally not very high as compared with the other costs of probate. In some states, court costs are based on the value of the estate, and in others they are fixed amounts that are charged uniformly to all estates. Fixed amounts take a higher percentage of a smaller estate's value and a lower percentage of a larger estate's value. Many states have an exemption for very small estates which eliminates virtually all of these actual court costs and filing fees.[9] However, in the majority of states, these costs will be incurred by almost all estates regardless of size.

An additional element of the court costs are fees for notice and publication. Notice must be given to potential heirs and to creditors so they can submit their claims within the prescribed statutory time periods.

Court costs, docket fees, filing fees, and costs of notice and publication can run from a few hundreds of dollars to several thousands of dollars. As a percentage of overall probate fees, these costs are small, but they represent costs that can, in the main, be avoided by the use of a fully funded revocable living trust.[10]

Even though these costs may seem insignificant, they are important to the cost comparison discussion. One of the arguments that is often raised in opposition to the use of a living trust is the cost of funding it. Yet, the cost of funding almost all living trusts is usually less than these purportedly "nickel-dime" probate court costs. A second argument against living trusts is that they are not viable planning devices for clients who have modest estates because the costs of creating, funding, and administering trusts do not justify their expense. It is those same modest estates, however, that will lose a greater percentage of their value to court costs and filing fees than their wealthier counterparts.[11]

Appraisal Fees

Valuing assets is a necessary part of the probate process for several reasons. For estates that are subject to federal estate tax or state death taxes, the estate's value must be ascertained in some valid manner to determine the amounts that are due to different taxing authorities. Property values must be established so the property can be divided among the heirs.

Appraisals also are necessary to establish the new "cost basis" of property. When a person dies, his or her property has a cost basis equal to its value on the date of the death of the decedent.[12] This concept is called "step-up in basis" and is an important income tax consideration. This is how it works:

When Sam Martin died, he owned stock in a corporation for which he had paid $10 for each share. On his death, it was worth $50 per share. Had Sam sold the stock the day before he died, there would have been a $40 per share taxable gain.

Because of the step-up in basis rules, if Sam's executor sold his stock for $50 per share, there would be no taxable gain. On Sam's death his original cost basis of $10 per share was "stepped-up" to $50 per share.

These step-up-in-basis rules apply to all assets owned at death, and they apply to all estates, even those that do not have to file federal or state death tax returns.

An appraisal is clearly necessary to determine how much is available to pay creditors, and is it also necessary so the executor and the attorney can be paid. Valuing an estate to determine attorneys' and executors' fees has created a conflict of interest argument. The attorney and executor generally are paid more as the value of the estate goes up and, conversely, are paid less as the estate's value decreases. As a result, they may be prone to influence the selection of those appraisers or the valuations which raise rather than lower the estate's valuation. At best, the attorney and a paid executor are not likely to fight very aggressively to obtain a lower valuation if a lower valuation may adversely affect their fees.

The cost of the appraisal itself varies on the basis of the number and type of assets and the purpose of the appraisal. Valuation costs, like court costs, are generally not major expenses for most estates unless taxes and fees are increased as a result of the valuation.

There should be an after-death appraisal for purposes of establishing the income tax basis of a decedent's property regardless of whether this valuation is completed through or apart from probate. A noted estate planning expert thinks that probate appraisals should be avoided. He says, "To the extent that properties do not pass through probate, it will *not* be necessary to have the value of those properties initially determined by probate court appointed appraisers (who can sometimes be both expensive and bungling)."[13]

An appraisal is also necessary when a living trust–centered plan is used. For example, if a state or federal estate tax return is required, the trust assets must be valued and a formal appraisal may be the best way to value certain assets. Also, the step-up-in-basis rules apply to property held in trust, so a valuation of trust assets for this reason is a necessity. The advantage in having a living trust—centered plan is that the *trustee,* rather than the probate court or its rules, determines who the appraiser is, what assets are subject to a formal appraisal, and what assets can be valued without a formal appraisal. Because the trustee controls these decisions instead of the rules of probate and the probate court, there is greater flexibility in the valuation process. A trustee could decide that a maker's assets could be valued by accepted methods that do not require a formal appraisal or the trustee could decide that only selected assets need to be appraised.

Because of this flexibility, the costs of appraisals are often far lower with a living trust—centered plan than they are with will-planning/probate. It is clearly better to use a living trust—centered plan to avoid a probate appraisal.

Attorneys' Fees

The largest probate fees are taken by the attorney. State statutes and, to a much lesser extent, local court rules determine how and how much an attorney may charge for probate and administration work. There are two general methods allowed: *statutory percentage fees* and *reasonable compensation.*

Only eleven states have statutory percentage fee schedules for attorneys.[14] Statutory percentage fees have been disappearing because they are perceived as windfall fees for attorneys and not proportionate to the work performed by them. Percentage fees are determined in a variety of ways. Some statutes calculate the fee on the gross value of the probate estate. California's is an example of this type of statute. In some states the percentage is taken on certain assets, whether they are subject to probate or not.[15]

Percentage fees, for the most part, are supposed to represent the maximum fee that can be taken by the executor or the attorney in most circumstances.[16] In 1987, the California Law Revision staff issued a report on California probate fees charged by attorneys.[17] According to the California study, instead of the maximum fee, the statutory fee often becomes the minimum fee with additional fees approved as a matter of course by the court.[18] This occurs because states with statutory commissions often allow the attorney to request additional fees for "extraordinary" services.[19] Extraordinary services can consist of all or some of the following:

1. Sales or mortgages of real or personal property
2. Contested or litigated claims against the estate
3. Preparation of estate, inheritance, income, sales, or other tax returns
4. Adjustment, litigation, or payment of any of these taxes (including audits of returns)
5. Litigation in regard to property of the estate
6. Carrying on the business of the decedent, including terminating it
7. Such other litigation or special services as the representative of the estate may have to prosecute, defend, or perform
8. Suit to collect assets
9. Will contest
10. Appeal to protect creditors
11. Petition for instructions
12. Preparation of agreement between estate and person contending adversely to the estate
13. Construction of the will
14. Cancellation of lease
15. Defense of account filed by executor

16. Assistance in lease negotiations
17. Determination of title holdings, evaluation procedures for valuation of property, tax decisions for death tax returns, and income tax returns[20]

It is common practice in many statutory fee jurisdictions for the courts to approve extraordinary fees.[21] There are attorneys in these states who claim that they seldom, if ever, charge extraordinary fees. However, as you will soon learn, this purported forbearance does not appear to be universal.

Lawyers sometimes take a lesser fee when a prior agreement has been made with the will maker or when the services rendered do not warrant the full fee. The restraint shown by attorneys who forego extraordinary fees is to be commended but should not be viewed as charitable in light of what are otherwise generous statutory fees.

A lawyer can charge for services with regard to nonprobate property as well. Thus, any title work on joint tenancy property, such as filing a death certificate and preparing a new deed, and any services performed with regard to property received by beneficiary designation can also be charged for in addition to the statutory percentage fee. This means that the probate-free assets may not be cost-free.

Statutory percentage fees exacerbate the attorney appraisal conflict that we touched on earlier: If an attorney is paid on the basis of the value of an estate, then the attorney has a vested interest in a higher valuation.

One of the most damning studies of attorneys' fees was prepared by the American Association of Retired Persons.[22] This study focused on three different states, California, Wisconsin, and Delaware. Of these three states, California and Delaware use statutory fee schedules. In addition, California law specifically allows attorneys to charge additional fees for extraordinary services. The AARP study found that in 33 percent of the California cases surveyed, attorneys charged additional fees for extraordinary services.[23] The AARP study also found that in the probate examples studied in San Diego, "in 85 percent of the cases, attorneys took at least the full statutory amount for their ordinary services."[24]

Delaware's statute sets a maximum percentage for fees that can be taken. However, it defines the amount that can be taken in such a manner as to include both probate and nonprobate property.[25] Here we see a state statute that counts nonprobate property as probate property for purposes of increasing the fees that can be charged.

The American Bar Association has taken a strong position against the use of percentage fees in any form.[26] It condemns "[r]igid adherence to statutory or recommended commission or fee schedules" as a frequently unfair method of determining attorneys' probate fees.[27]

While statutory percentage fees appear to be arbitrary and inequitable, they cannot be assessed properly without understanding the alternative method of determining how attorneys charge probate fees. It is called "reasonable compensation."

The majority of states allows attorneys to take a fee based on reasonable compensation.[28] One of the major difficulties of this method is defining what is "reasonable." The reasonableness of attorneys' fees can be viewed from several perspectives. The heirs of an estate may view "reasonable" as meaning a few hours of necessary legal work, while an attorney may view his or her services as of a very high calibre that has generated particularly good results for the estate. This elusive standard leaves great latitude for judicial interpretation and makes the process of defining probate fees uncertain.

Reasonable compensation is often based on the following standards:

- The time and labor required, the novelty and difficulty of the questions involved, and the skill requisite to perform the service properly
- The likelihood, if apparent to the personal representative (executor), that the acceptance of the particular employment will preclude the lawyer employed from other employment
- The fee customarily charged in the locality for similar services
- The amount involved and the results obtained
- The time limitations imposed by the personal representative (executor) or by the circumstances
- The experience, reputation, and ability of the lawyer performing the services[29]

These factors are nearly identical to those promulgated by the American Bar Association to determine fair and reasonable legal fees in general.[30]

The problem is that these nondefinitive guidelines for determining reasonable compensation must be interpreted by lawyers and courts in order to apply them in ultimately arriving at reasonable attorneys' fees. This is no small task. Practically, however, it is a job that does not ordinarily generate a great deal of concern or anxiety for the court, the attorney, or the executor. It is not uncommon for attorneys to base the reasonableness of their fees on the very same amounts that would have been traditionally charged under old percentage fee schedules. In fact, some courts in reasonable fee states issue guidelines for probate fees that use a percentage fee schedule.[31]

Most states, at one time or another, used percentage fee schedules for legal fees. For years, local bar associations published a list of "minimum" fees for almost all types of legal work, including probate and administration. Although not always enforced, these minimum fee schedules were often viewed as mandatory and were generally followed until a 1975 United States Supreme Court decision eliminated their use.[32] Minimum fee schedules have now been replaced by "suggested" fee schedules in many jurisdictions. While not mandatory or enforceable, they continue to be influential in determining the range of fees attorneys customarily charge.

A reasonable fee in any jurisdiction is likely to be a fee that is within the range of the previously used percentage fee schedule or within the local bar association's suggested fee schedule because these fees are viewed, at least by lawyers, as reasonable. Lacking any other standard, it can be argued that this approach is as rational as any other. Of course, from the perspective of the heirs, this method of determining a reasonable fee is as arbitrary as a statutory percentage fee schedule and suffers from the same inherent unfairness.

The overall conclusion of the AARP study is that attorneys' fees, no matter how they are determined, are usually 3 percent or more of the estate's gross value.[33] This is consistent with older studies and gives mounting evidence that attorneys' probate fees are not as low as probate advocates would like the public to think.[34]

Attorneys' fees are consistently the same regardless of what type of fee schedule is in effect and notwithstanding the type of probate statute under which they were calculated.[35] This point is important because, in states that have adopted so-called modern probate statutes, will-planning/probate advocates' major arguments are that probate has been modernized, that it is inexpensive and uncomplicated, and that it is still the most effective estate planning method.

Since the most recent available research lacks statistical method and reliability, we decided to conduct our own probate study as an opportunity either to corroborate or to challenge the numbers our research uncovered. We engaged a professor of mathematics to devise a scientific sampling method. The study was designed to determine the cost and duration of probate proceedings in both rural and urban areas in selected states, for decedents' estates that were closed in 1989. The survey was carried out in March and April 1991.[36]

We limited our study to four states that we felt would be representative of the differing probate administration systems throughout the country. These states are Iowa, New York, Oregon, and Texas. Iowa was chosen because it has a percentage fee statute for determining maximum attorney fees. Of those states that allow "reasonable" fees, New York was chosen because it has a traditional probate process that is not considered to be particularly progressive or modern. Oregon, on the other hand, has a "simplified" probate statute, but one that is not patterned on the *Uniform Probate Code* (UPC). Texas has enacted a version of the UPC.

The objectives of our survey were

1. To corroborate or disprove the results of several earlier surveys
2. To determine the average attorney and executor fees in the surveyed states
3. To determine the average time taken to probate estates in the surveyed states

Our study indicated that in Iowa, attorneys' fees were an average of 2.6 percent for the urban counties and 2.14 percent for the rural counties. In New York, urban attorneys' fees averaged 5.66 percent and the median was 2.83 percent; average rural attorney fees were 13.19 and the median was 5.11 percent. In Oregon, urban attorneys' fees averaged 5.06 percent and rural fees were 2.73 percent. In Texas, urban attorneys' fees averaged 5.21; the median was 1.71 percent. Rural fees averaged 2.98 percent.[37]

Our study confirms the results and conclusions of previous studies. All of the available evidence suggests that the costs of probate are not going dramatically downward. It also indicates, when read in conjunction with all of the other studies, that attorneys' fees are generally the same regardless of what method is employed to calculate them.

The evidence tells us that attorneys' probate fees are hovering around 3 percent of a gross estate, with the range extending from 1.5 percent to 4.5 percent.

Executors' Fees

By law, the executor of an estate is the person or institution who is charged with the probate and administration of an estate. In practice, however, much of the probate and administration burden is left to an attorney. The services performed by an executor and the services performed by an attorney are not easy to differentiate. Yet, even to the most uninformed critic, it seems fairly obvious that the attorney and the executor represent two people, or two fees, on a single shovel.

Sometimes, an attorney serves as both the executor *and* the attorney for the same estate. When this occurs, the attorney often collects two fees for essentially one function.[38] While taking a full fee for each function is not allowed in some states, an attorney functioning in both capacities still receives a higher fee than if serving in a single capacity.

Executors' fees are controlled by statute in most states. While there is even less information available on executors' fees than on attorneys' fees, the amount of executors' fees in general can be estimated from recent reports.

In 1989, the American College of Probate Counsel (now the American College of Trust and Estate Counsel) published a fifty-state survey of executors' fees.[39] The survey shows that thirteen states provided for statutory fees for executors based on a fixed percentage of some portion of the decedent's assets or income. The most common statute was the "reasonable fee" type. The study found that in a majority of states using a fixed percentage fee schedule, fees for extraordinary services were allowed in addition to the percentage fee.

It is difficult to compare fees charged by executors from state to state because they are calculated in many different ways. In both percentage fee states and reasonable fee states, the base upon which fee calculations are made varies widely. Some states use the probate estate value as the basis and others base their fees on the value of all property, including nonprobate property owned by the decedent. In some states, fees apply only to personal property unless real property in the estate is sold or is otherwise involved in a commercial transaction. Some states even base their fees on a combination of value and income.[40]

The American College of Trust and Estate Counsel survey provided the statutory percentage fee, or, where there was none, an example of customary local fees. For many states, it was possible to calculate approximate ranges of executors' fees for certain sizes of estates and to compare them to the ranges of attorneys' fees. For estates ranging from $100,000 to $1,000,000, executors' fees were in the range of 1 to 5 percent, with the average 3 percent.

In those states where fees were controlled by the reasonable fee standard or by custom, the executors' fees seemed to be lower than those in other states. The fees tended to be higher for smaller estates, just as attorneys' fees were.

In many states, the amount of compensation paid to an executor and an attorney, whether by custom or by statute, is identical.[41] This, along with the American College of Trust and Estate Counsel survey, leads to the logical conclusion that, on average, the combined cost of the attorney and the executor is approximately 6 percent of the value of the gross estate.

The AARP study confirms this number for those estates in which both an executor's fee and an attorney's fee were taken.[42] Our four-state study yields similar figures. Following is a table that shows the combined executors' and attorneys' fees from our survey. In several instances, one or two estates in a particular geographic area were unusually expensive or lengthy, causing the average to be skewed. Rather than showing only the average in these counties, which may be misleading, we have also shown the median figures. They tend to be a much better measure of reality than averages when there are statistical aberrations because the median figures show the percentages charged that are exactly in the middle of the range of all fees. The median figures are not affected by numbers that may be unnaturally high or low.

	Executor's Fees		Attorneys' Fees		Combined Fees	
	Average	Median	Average	Median	Average	Median
IOWA						
Urban	2.00		2.60		4.60	
Rural	2.00		2.14		4.14	
NEW YORK						
Urban	3.10	2.71	5.66	2.83	8.76	5.54
Rural	3.67	1.96	13.19	5.11	16.86	7.07
OREGON						
Urban	2.29	2.28	5.06	2.40	7.35	4.68
Rural	1.41		2.73		4.14	
TEXAS						
Urban	2.10	1.40	5.21	1.71	7.31	3.11
Rural	9.60	2.11	2.98	2.56	12.58	4.67

If these executor fees look familiar to you, they should; they clearly approximate the figures that our research developed for attorneys' fees. Their similarity tends to prove the validity of each, and it confirms the trust camp's critique that probate is expensive.

On the basis of the weight of the evidence, it would appear that the real cost of probate, where there are a paid executor and attorney, is approximately 5 to 6 percent of a decedent's gross estate, and that this is true regardless of how a state regulates its fees.

Advocates of the probate process rightly contend that in many family situations a member of the decedent's family acts as the executor of an estate. If this occurs, especially where the surviving spouse is named as executor, the executor's fee may be waived. This potential waiver of the executor's fee is used as a justification by the will-planning/ probate camp that probate fees are not so bad.

The argument that most executors waive their fees makes assumptions that may not be true. Relying on future events that cannot be controlled is not particularly good planning. The fact remains that an executor *can* take a fee and often does. There is no assurance that the executor named in today's last will and testament will be the executor named upon the death of the will maker; just like will makers, executors become disabled, they die, or they just refuse to serve. It is intellectually impossible to justify the cost of probate by making the blanket claim that executors' fees in family situations are nonexistent or are not a concern.

The executor fee-waiver argument does not hold water at all in those many situations where a family member is not named as the executor. It is also impractical, and potentially inequitable, to ask one child to take on the task of acting as executor of a parent's estate without compensation. If there are other children or other heirs, it is common for the executor to take a fee regardless of his or her relationship to the decedent.

A revocable living trust eliminates the need for an executor. Because the trustee of a living trust takes on the duties of an executor without the burden of probate, it follows then, that the executor's fee, or the potential for the fee, is substantially reduced or eliminated when using a revocable living trust. Since, in most jurisdictions, the executor's fee is equal to, or marginally smaller than, the attorney's fee, an executor's fee approximating 3 percent of the value of the gross estate can be eliminated by a fully funded revocable living trust.

IRS Involvement in Lawyer Probate Fees

The best statistics that exist for the real cost of probate and administration of estates greater than $600,000 are located in the records of the Internal Revenue Service. None of these statistics has been reported by the IRS, but the IRS has been active in establishing what reasonable probate and administration fees are. They have ruled that for an administration expense to be deductible the expense must be reasonable under its interpretation of state law.[43] The IRS can determine the reasonableness of administration expenses even though a probate court has already ruled that the fees are reasonable. Because of the IRS's position, the approval of fees by local probate judges does not necessarily guarantee that those same fees are reasonable for purposes of deductibility under the Internal Revenue Code.

This activity by the IRS may be indicative of nothing more than a desire by the IRS to collect revenue. It is equally likely, however, that the IRS sees a trend of higher than normal fees and that it feels it has strong justification to demand complete time and other records from those lawyers engaged in the probate and administration of an estate.

Two Probate Fees for One Generation of Property

Advocates of the will-planning/probate process neglect to address an issue that is critical in the discussion of probate fees. For a married couple there are potentially two probates for the same property: one on the death of each spouse.

It may very well be true that on the death of the first spouse, the surviving spouse may serve as executor and waive the fee. But the attorney's fee and court costs will remain. On the surviving spouse's subsequent death, there will be another probate. On this second probate, many of the same assets that passed to the surviving spouse through the original probate will be subjected to probate a second time. There will be attorneys' fees and, in all likelihood, executors' fees for the same property. This property is not property that has passed to a second generation; it is property of the same generation being subjected to a double dose of probate and a double payment of its attendant fees.[44]

A revocable living trust is designed to prevent this problem. Rather than creating double probate and double exposure to executors' and attorneys' fees, a revocable living trust eliminates these fees on the death of each spouse.

What Are the Costs of Funding and Maintaining a Revocable Living Trust?

Only assets titled in the name of a living trust avoid probate or guardianship proceedings. The process of retitling assets in the name of the trust is called *funding*.[45] A living trust that contains all of its maker's property is called a fully funded living trust. Trusts that contain most of its maker's property are called partially funded living trusts. A living trust which contains little of its maker's property is called an unfunded living trust.

The purpose of an unfunded trust, sometimes called a "standby trust," is to be available for funding in the event the maker becomes incapacitated or determines that the trust should only be funded as a last-minute predeath precaution. Unfunded living trusts are almost always named as the beneficiary of the maker's life insurance policies. Property that is not put into an unfunded living trust during the lifetime of a maker is put there after death by the maker's pour-over will. The funding and maintenance costs of unfunded trusts are by definition nonexistent or minimal.

A proper living trust–centered estate plan is fully funded. Living trust advocates view funding as an important factor in saving will-planning/probate fees. Transferring property into living trusts is not as difficult as will-planning/probate practitioners would lead the public and other professionals to believe.

When funding a living trust, title can be easily transferred while the trust maker is alive and well. It is not difficult to locate title to various properties and to understand complex business dealings when the individual who participated in the transactions is available to answer questions.

Living trust critics frequently state that the costs of funding a living trust make the cost of the trust "much higher than the fee for preparing a will."[46] These critics view funding as expensive and difficult. They base their arguments on the fact that funding is time-consuming and requires an effort that clients would rather put off until probate can do the task for them.

If probate lawyers view the titling process as complex during the clients' lifetimes, how can they possibly think it will be less difficult after their clients become mentally incapacitated or die?

Our experience is that an overwhelming percentage of clients do not initially know where their evidences of title are located, much less how title is held. As a result, funding a living trust allows clients to discern how their property is titled while accomplishing the funding task. It is relatively painless for a client to fund his or her trust.

As a general rule, a client can accomplish a good portion of the funding of his or her own trust with proper guidance. The client's attorney can review the title changes made by the client but does not have to participate in most of the administrative legwork and labor involved in locating the assets and accomplishing the transfers. The client's attorney can perform inherently complex title changes for which significant legal issues may be involved, such as deeds, business agreements, contracts, and specialized forms of securities.

If professionals such as life insurance agents, financial planners, accountants, and bankers are involved in the process, they can be of great assistance to the client's attorney.[47] People's financial affairs often become unnecessarily confused. There is frequently no investment strategy or rhyme or reason as to how title is held or how beneficiary designations are structured. Funding a revocable living trust gives the client's advisers the opportunity to examine these issues and resolve them immediately.

A well-organized law office can develop many funding aids for clients that can make the funding process considerably easier and less expensive. With the publicity that living trusts are receiving and the increasing acceptance of them by transfer agents and financial institutions, it is convenient and relatively easy to make transfers into trusts today. Financial institutions recognize a good thing when they see it and are now starting to embrace the living trust.[48]

While it is difficult to generalize, it is very likely that the total cost of funding a typical living trust usually approximates about one-fourth, or less, of the cost of the fee to prepare the documents.[49] The fees charged for preparing the documents are either a set fee or based on an hourly rate; they are not a percentage of the estate. The fee for funding a trust is not an unreasonable cost, especially when compared to the higher costs, rates, and percentages of probate.

In most instances the funding aspect of a revocable living trust makes the initial cost of creating it greater than that of a will. However, funding costs can be recouped many times over by the avoidance of probate.

The Deductibility of Funding Fees

A potential benefit of currently funding a revocable living trust is that many of the costs incurred in doing so are federal income tax deductible. Under the Internal Revenue Code, expenses for the management, conservation, or maintenance of property held for the production of income are tax deductible.[50] As miscellaneous itemized deductions, however, they are subject to the 2 percent of adjusted gross income floor.[51] For those clients who have enough expenses to qualify for the 2 percent floor, the deductibility of the fees reduces funding costs, especially for those clients with complex affairs.

The Cost of Maintaining a Fully Funded Revocable Living Trust

Once a trust is fully funded, the maintenance that it requires is minimal. A revocable living trust which has its maker as a trustee or co-trustee is not required to obtain a separate federal identification number or to file a separate income tax return. There is no requirement that would result in extra bookkeeping or accounting.

When assets are acquired subsequent to the initial funding process, the trust maker can simply direct that they be titled in the name of the trust. The procedure is much the same as if the maker were titling the property in his or her own name. The only differences are that the property is held in the name of the trust, and in some instances the client, as trustee, may have to present evidence that the trust is in existence and can own property. This generally entails an Affidavit of Trust or some other comparable document. We will discuss this and other specific trust funding mechanisms in depth in Chapter 11, "General Lifetime Consequences of Funding a Living Trust."

Trust critics often allege that a trust maker must immediately begin paying expensive trustees' fees. This argument is without merit. It universally presupposes that the trust maker will name an institutional trustee. Most people who create living trusts do not name a professional trustee. They are fully capable of operating their trust without the help of a professional manager.

Trust makers who elect initially to use institutional trustees do so for reasons that have nothing to do with probate avoidance. They are looking for professional money management, which, regardless of whether or not it is proffered by a professional trustee, generates management fees in the normal course of business.

In a properly drafted trust document, successor trustees are named. Successor trustees take charge on the death or disability of the trust maker and may receive a fee for their services. If professional trustees are named, they will most certainly charge their normal fees. If individuals are named, they may or may not charge a fee, depending on their relationship to the trust maker.

The fees charged by professional trustees vary widely from state to state, and even between institutions in the same state. Different institutions serve different sizes and types of trusts. Some institutions may have a minimum fee; some may charge a percentage of principal and income, or both, and there will be additional charges for special services, such as preparing tax returns.[52]

Fees charged by large metropolitan institutions tend to be in the range of 1 percent of assets managed, with specific hourly fees charged for special services. Every institutional trustee publishes its fees and will provide its fee schedule on request. In most instances, even these published fees can be negotiated.

If professional trustees are used on the disability of the trust maker, their fees will be in lieu of more costly guardianship and conservator fees. If professional trustees are used after the death of the trust maker, the fees will be similar to those charged for similar services under testamentary trusts created in a decedent's last will and testament. Testamentary trustee fees are likely to be higher in those states in which testamentary trustees fees are set by statute and in states in which the testamentary trust is subject to court supervision.

For people who want to eliminate the burden of managing

their assets, the creation of a living trust with an institutional trustee offers the best alternative. A person who frequently travels, an elderly person whose health or mental facilities are subject to failure, or the business person who is over-burdened with other matters often requires the services of professional money managers. These individuals can choose a trustee, or co-trustees, to manage assets, pay bills, and serve as investment advisers all within the context of a trust document. The fees charged are more than reasonable for services rendered and compare favorably to fees charged by the same institutions for lesser money management ser-vices. Professional trustee fees are reasonable and, in our opinion, provide one of the great bargains still available.

Most living trusts do not initially involve trustees' fees because clients are routinely co-trustees along with their spouses or, if they are single, with a mature child or other trusted family member or friend. And, because the trust is the alter ego of its maker, the expense of maintenance is also minimal. Operating a revocable living trust does not create an economic burden. The trust maker can manage his or her trust as long as he or she desires to do so. When the maker is disabled, the fees of a professional trustee (if one is chosen) are still less than the fees of a court-managed guardianship.

What Are the Costs of the After-Death Administration of a Fully Funded Revocable Living Trust?

Will-planning/probate advocates sometimes argue that the majority of attorneys' fees in larger estates are related to taxation and to other matters that are common in after-death work regardless of the planning vehicle used.[53] Some of the functions that are common to both will and trust planning are the following:

- Settlement of disputes among heirs
- Settlement of claims of creditors
- Federal and state tax returns and audits
- Sales, mortgages, and other transactions dealing with real estate
- Income tax planning

This list should look familiar. It contains the major elements that are considered to be extraordinary services in those states that allow statutory percentage fees for attorneys and executors. The fees for these tasks can be charged in addition to the percentage fees allowed by statute. While it is true that probate lawyers do not have to charge more for these services, the evidence indicates that as a practical matter they do.[54]

In reasonable compensation states, the task of differentiating the costs of probate and administration from after-death trust administration becomes a bit more difficult. We know of no current method for identifying where purely probate functions end and issues common to both an estate and a revocable living trust begin. However, there is evidence upon which conclusions can be drawn.

Even though some after-death administrative functions are necessary with a trust, they are not as extensive as those required in probate. Disputes among heirs and protracted creditor disputes rarely arise when living trust–centered planning is used. Most after-death trust functions are accounting or tax related and often can be performed by a competent accountant at significant cost savings.[55] Accounting fees are likely to be lower than attorneys' fees and accountants are as qualified, or more qualified, to prepare and file federal estate tax and state death tax returns and to give advice on after-death income tax planning issues.

The after-death administration of a living trust takes the place of the after-death administration of a probate estate. Both types of administration have a limited time span. The difference between them is that the after-death administration costs of a fully funded living trust are significantly lower than the costs of probate and administration.

Some trust critics contend that, since a living trust may continue for a period of time after the death of its maker, the costs of administering the trust continue, resulting in a higher cost of having a living trust. This argument is without merit. It relies on the incorrect assumption that a probate estate simply ends and that a living trust cannot end sooner than a probate estate can end. The fact is that wills often create trusts within them called testamentary trusts. These will-created trusts generate probate fees *and* ongoing fees. It is also true that simple living trusts can and do end much earlier than probate estates created under simple wills. A living trust does not have to continue long after its maker has died.

In Chapter 23, "Comparing Testamentary and Living Trusts," we demonstrate the fallacy of comparing simple will planning with living trust planning. When simple will planning is compared with simple living trust planning and when testamentary planning is compared with more complex living trust planning, living trust planning is invariably less expensive than using will-planning/probate in any form.

Retitling Trust Assets After the Death of the Trust Maker

Trust critics claim that on the death of the trust maker trust assets must often be retitled in order to distribute them either to subtrusts created in the trust document itself or to beneficiaries who take property outright. They claim that the same funding is billed twice!

To put this criticism into proper perspective, it is important to understand how the transfer of title generally occurs in probate. As probate property is identified, the executor often takes title to the property in the name of the probate estate. At times it is possible to keep the property in the decedent's name during the probate hiatus and then make direct transfers from the decedent's name to the heirs' names, but this is the exception to the rule. It is not uncommon for the probate process to require two title changes. The first transfer is from the decedent's name into the estate's name, the second from the estate into the names of the heirs.

Transfers of title within the confines of probate and administration, even if informal, are likely to be more complex because they are subject to the rules of probate. Not only do these rules often cause delay in the distribution of property, they make the transfer of title more expensive. For example, to transfer real property in many jurisdictions, the permission of the probate court must be obtained before a transfer is made. This involves a petition to the court and, at times, a hearing. Once approval is granted, court-related documents must be recorded. Title standards still must be met and strict procedures followed.

In a living trust, most of these complicated and time-consuming requirements are avoided. If a living trust provides that property is to be distributed on the death of the trust maker, then the trustee must transfer title to the beneficiary. Because the trust is fully funded, any transfers made by the trustee are not subject to the rules of probate and administration; they avoid the complications and rules of probate. This in itself may well save substantial amounts of time and money. The cost of the transfer does not usually create an extra fee because the transaction is covered by the trustee's usual and ordinary fee.[56]

When comparing transfers of title from a trust to those from a probate estate, we must not lose sight of the fact that a trustee is working with precise inventories and detailed accounting records. The trustee does not have to go through the exercise of locating, identifying, and inventorying the assets of the decedent as a preliminary step to distribution. This makes the transfer process much easier and more convenient.

Title changes for purposes of funding subtrusts created at the death of the trust maker are minimal. Many trustees, as an administrative convenience, do not make any changes in the title to assets when funding subtrusts. Assets are kept in the name of the original trust. The separate subtrusts are managed by accounting entries and internal record keeping. Generally, only when a specific transfer of an asset to a beneficiary or another third party is required is title changed.

The criticisms of probate practitioners that trusts require extensive and expensive titling fees are simply unfounded. Their critique appears to be more theoretical than practical and often has no validity whatsoever.

The Elimination of
Court Costs and Filing Fees

Both sides of the debate generally agree that where a fully funded revocable living trust is used, all traditional court costs, filing fees, and publication and notice costs associated with probate are eliminated. Probate advocates dismiss these court costs and filing fees as not particularly troublesome, especially when applied to larger estates.[57] Living trust advocates are adamant that these fees certainly can prove to be costly in smaller estates and must be considered and avoided.

Periodic Accountings

Periodic accountings are necessary for both a trust and a probate estate. In a formal probate proceeding, accounting fees are higher than those generated in an informal administration and with a living trust. Since a living trust does not go through probate and administration, it is not subject to any of the rules associated with probate accounting.

While property is in a formal probate, the executor must make periodic accountings to the probate court. These may be monthly, quarterly, or even yearly, depending on the probate statute and local court rules. These accountings must be detailed and accurate. Even in informal probates, accountings are generally required to be filed with the court at least once a year. Probate accountings end when probate ends. At this time a final accounting is rendered and the probate assets are either distributed to the heirs or to a testamentary trust. If assets are distributed to a testamentary trust, then trust accountings are required.

Periodic reports are inherent in trust accounting. If a corporate fiduciary is serving, a number of reports will automatically be produced on a monthly and/or quarterly basis as part of the trustee's fee. If a spouse or other family member is serving, accountings are likely to be informal and, at times, nonexistent. In our experience, the accounting costs associated with a trust are lower than those of a probate estate simply because they are not subject to probate rules.

Do Living Trusts Cost Less or More Than Will-Planning/Probate?

There is almost no written information on the total cost of living trust–centered planning as compared to will-planning/probate.[58] We have found, based on our extensive research, that the use of a living trust–centered plan costs far less than will-planning/probate. We believe that a properly funded revocable living trust with assets of less than $600,000 reduces after-death costs to a negligible amount that in all likelihood will be 0.5 percent or less of the gross estate. In our experience, the percentage is higher on larger estates; their after-death costs when a fully funded living trust is used may approach 0.75 percent of the gross estate.

Our Conclusion

All of the evidence conclusively proves that fully funded revocable living trusts cost significantly less than will-planning/probate!

° 3 °

Disability Planning

Questions for Discussion

- Is an adjudication of incompetency a viable alternative for planning for disability?
- What is the proper function of a durable power of attorney in disability planning?
- Does a living trust eliminate the problems created by the disability of its maker?

If we had to select a living trust's greatest virtue, the protection of the trust maker in case of his or her disability would be the likely candidate. A revocable living trust is far superior to any other estate planning technique in providing for the protracted illness or mental incapacity of its maker. The ability of the trust maker to appoint a trustee who will be subject to the terms of the trust instrument is invaluable. By leaving written instructions for the trustee, a trust maker can be comfortable in the knowledge that those instructions will provide for his or her care and that of family members in the event of the maker's disability.

Will-planning/probate advocates argue that there are disability planning techniques that may equal or surpass the revocable living trust as lifetime planning vehicles. Their arguments generally point to a court adjudication of mental incompetency, also called a guardianship proceeding, and the durable power of attorney as viable alternatives to the living trust–centered estate plan.

An Adjudication of Mental Incompetency

If a person can no longer manage his or her affairs because of a mental or physical incapacity, some very real problems arise: How can this person write and sign checks to pay bills? How can this person sign a deed to sell real estate, buy necessities, or manage the myriad other financial details that all of us face on a day-to-day basis? Who is going to care for this person and tend to these duties?

When a person is incompetent, for purposes of the law, it is almost as if that person has passed away. Like a person who has died, someone who is incompetent must have a legal agent to replace him or her. That is why, in a majority of states, the legislature has given the probate court the task of determining whether or not an individual is competent to manage his or her property or person. It is the probate court's task to ensure that an individual is properly cared for and protected if he or she can no longer care for himself or herself.

The rules for an adjudication of mental incompetency, like those for probate and administration, vary from jurisdiction to jurisdiction but are fundamentally the same. If the court rules that an individual is incompetent, it appoints a personal guardian (*guardian ad litem*) and a financial guardian (*conservator*) to act on behalf of the incompetent. The personal guardian is charged with caring for the incompetent person in much the same capacity as a parent. The financial guardian is given authority over the incompetent's property. The same person may be appointed to serve in both capacities.

A financial guardian generally has the same powers and duties as an executor. A guardianship proceeding encounters the same problems as an after-death probate. It is public, expensive, time-consuming, and filled with red tape, which is why it is often referred to as a "living probate."

For the most part, an adjudication of mental incompetency begins with a petition to the court. The petition can be voluntary, when the person agrees to the proceeding. In a voluntary petition, a person recognizes that he or she cannot function very well and asks the court to appoint a financial and a legal guardian. A petition also can be introduced by any interested person without the approval or even the knowledge of the alleged incompetent. This is an involuntary adjudication. After the petition is filed, there is often an investigation to ensure that the alleged incompetent is not being taken advantage of and that there is reasonable cause for the petition. Following this investigation, a public hearing is held. At the hearing, testimony is accepted as to the competency of the individual. In some cases, the individual is present; in others, especially when there is severe illness or injury, a physician's testimony is virtually all that is required. The proceeding has all of the elements of an advocacy proceeding. It is, in essence, a trial.

Because of the sensitive nature of an incompetency proceeding, there are few shortcuts to make the procedure less cumbersome. When there is a question of a person's incompetency, the law mandates that a full, open hearing be held to ensure the protection of the allegedly incompetent person and, of course, creditors and other interested parties.

Few commentators have anything complimentary to say about a court-imposed guardianship. One legal writer states:

Experience suggests that there is no such thing as a competency hearing without a certain element of degredation [*sic*] regardless of how carefully and skillfully the judge may handle the situation.[1]

Another legal writer cites four serious disadvantages in having an estate managed by a court-appointed fiduciary:

- Publicity
- Cost
- Inflexibility
- On the ward's death, his or her estate
  will have to be probated[2]

Other criticisms of the financial guardianship system are also of concern. One is the abuse that has crept in. Several years ago, a series of investigative newspaper reports exposed professional guardians who took their wards' money but ignored their wards. The articles pointed out several inadequacies, including the lack of court supervision, the inadequate monitoring of wards, and the method by which guardians are appointed.[3] The television series *20/20* uncovered the abuses inherent in the guardianship system.[4]

Several articles have echoed the same theme. In one of these, the writer stated, "The fact is that the dishonest guardian can steal guardianship estates right out from under the nose of the probate judge; and the ward has no more recourse in most cases than if the guardian had not been appointed."[5]

Insurance company morbidity tables assure us that in any given year an individual is far more likely to become permanently disabled than to die.[6] As America ages, disability planning looms larger and becomes more important. Foisting this medical reality on an already overloaded legal system, creating unnecessary cost, delay, and publicity, is hardly a satisfactory solution.

The American Association of Retired Persons issued an advisory booklet in 1988 that addressed disability issues.[7] This booklet advises that planning for a person's care and resources in case of disability is equally as important as the management of a person's financial assets. It describes a guardianship proceeding as "an expensive and time consuming legal process that strips you of most, if not all, your rights."[8] The booklet warns that the person whom the court appoints as guardian "could be a person you may (or may not) know and [a person] you might not want to make choices for you."[9]

A financial guardian has vast discretion as to a ward's financial matters. What expenses are paid, what property is to be sold or retained, and how to operate or liquidate a business are but a few of the decisions that are made by a financial guardian. In almost all jurisdictions, the probate judge has the full discretion and authority to appoint the financial guardian for an adjudicated incompetent. This may result in the appointment of a spouse, a grown child, or an acquaintance who has absolutely no experience or expertise in financial affairs, nor knowledge of the individual finances of the ward. It may also result in the appointment of a stranger.

The appointment of a personal guardian also presents problems. While judges attempt to name a close family member as the personal guardian, and under some statutes are required to do just that, this is not always possible.[10] In fact, a report by the Committee on Tax and Estate Planning of the Section of Real Property, Probate and Trust Law of the American Bar Association cautions that the court-appointed fiduciary may not be the person the ward would choose!

Under circumstances where a close family member or

friend cannot be appointed, a stranger will be making highly personal decisions on behalf of a ward that he or she does not know. By substituting his or her judgment for the ward's, a personal guardian may be doing exactly the opposite of that which the ward would want.

A financial guardianship presents little risk to the person or "friend of the court" who initiates the proceeding. In most jurisdictions, the ward's estate pays the expense of the proceeding. A disgruntled family member or creditor can initiate a court proceeding that can be expensive to the potential ward without shouldering any responsibility for the ultimate result.

Undoing a guardianship is more difficult than creating it. The guardianship process is designed to be permanent rather than temporary and is hard to reverse. In order to do so, a proceeding must be instituted to declare the ward competent. It generates cost, delay, and publicity all over again. All of the assets that were under the control of the court must be retitled in the name of the ward. The process leaves emotional and financial scars.

Some states allow a person to name a "standby" guardian. This procedure allows an individual to name his or her own guardians in the event of disability. Upon disability, the named persons are then appointed by the court to act on behalf of the ward. Appointment of standby guardians is a definite step in the right direction, but it too presents planning pitfalls because the process continues to be public and the guardian is still subject to the jurisdiction of the probate court. The expense is still there.

Taking the risk that a court-imposed guardianship will be unnecessary is a dangerous game of chance. For those people who wish to be treated with dignity upon disability, a court-imposed guardianship is not a desirable alternative.[11]

The Durable Power of Attorney

A power of attorney is a written instrument that evidences an agent's authority to a third party.[12] The agent is the "alter ego" of the principal and may act with respect to any and all matters on behalf of the principal, except for those matters that by law, public policy, or contract require personal performance by the principal.[13]

The Uniform Probate Code introduced a new legal concept called a *durable power of attorney*.[14] Ordinary powers of attorney are invalid upon the disability of their principals. Durable powers of attorney survive the disability of their principals.[15]

The durable power of attorney is one of the most creative legal innovations in recent memory. It has become a popular method for planning for disability. Among its frequently mentioned advantages, it is

- Inexpensive
- Flexible
- Simple and understandable
- All-encompassing
- Able to be used for health care decisions in many jurisdictions

On its face, a durable power of attorney is an appealing concept. Will-planning/probate advocates have readily accepted these powers as prudent planning tools and frequently recommend that they accompany will-planning/probate procedures. Their use to some extent compensates for the inability of a will to care for its maker.

Since will-planning is death planning whereas estate planning deals with lifetime issues, will-planning/probate advocates claim that the combination of a will and a durable power of attorney can match the living trust. By using these two instruments, probate lawyers claim that both death planning and disability planning can be accomplished.

Combining a will and a durable power of attorney is inadequate for most people. The biggest drawback of a durable power of attorney is that a vast majority of those drafted are general powers of attorney. Granting an agent broad powers under a general power of attorney is much like giving someone a blank check. Since general powers have virtually no constraining language, the agent has too much discretion.

When a will and a durable power of attorney are used instead of a living trust, there is no trustee to care for the maker's property. Only the agent under the durable power of attorney has this power. The agent's responsibility to his or her principal is inferior to that of a trustee. It has been said that "[t]he agent is a mere tool or instrument in the principal's hand, but the trustee is a separate responsible party."[16] Because the agent is subject to the general principles of agency law rather than trust law, the agent's discretion is not restricted: it is too broad and leaves room for abuse.

The agent's responsibilities when acting under a durable power of attorney are not well defined. The agent is not required to report or render accountings to the principal. This lack of any accountability creates an environment where the agent is free to act at will.

Advocates of durable power planning have asserted that durable powers of attorney can include complete instructions. They also claim that their agents can be instructed to account to their principals.[17]

Once a durable power of attorney becomes so extensive as to encompass a complex set of instructions, several additional drawbacks quickly arise. Perhaps the most important is that the instructions in it create a trustlike document that is still governed by the standards found in agency law rather than trust law. By attempting a hybrid between the two, legal confusion is generated as to the legal standards which apply.

Practitioners should use the living trust format to eliminate all of these deficiencies. By definition, a trust contains extensive instructions that always create a definitive fiduciary duty. A fiduciary duty is the highest duty known under our law. It makes no legal sense to substitute an inferior agency duty for well-defined trustee duty.

The success of a durable power of attorney is always dependent on its acceptance by third parties. Despite the fact that every state has adopted some form of durable power of attorney statute, the concept is not universally recognized in ordinary commerce. For example, many banks insist that in order for them to honor such a power, it must be on their approved general power of attorney forms.

This problem also applies to many brokerage companies as well. They often require that the agent's powers include maintaining margin accounts, trading in options or commodities, or engaging in other specific transactions. Unless the durable power specifically allows these powers, a brokerage company will almost always refuse to act in conjunction with the power holder. These requirements vary from company to company, making it difficult, if not impossible, for the practitioner to draft a durable power of attorney that always works.

Real estate transactions often create similar problems for an agent. A durable power of attorney which does not contain specific wording with regard to real estate may not be accepted by a title or mortgage company.

These problems of nonacceptance are often exacerbated for people who transact business in more than one state. A durable power of attorney prepared in one state may very well not be accepted in another, despite the Uniform Durable Power of Attorney Act, which is aimed at preventing these problems.[18] For purposes of interstate commerce, the durable power of attorney has not yet come into its own.

The acceptability of a durable power of attorney is likely to decrease proportionately with its complexity. At times, even a simple, straightforward durable power of attorney is difficult to use in commerce. From a practical perspective, both individuals and institutions do not readily accept such a document without significant inquiry, delay, and trepidation. It follows that the more instructions that are put in the power to protect the principal, the less effective the power will be.

When the provisions of a general durable power of attorney are inadequate or unacceptable, the agent, the maker's creditors, the maker's family, or some other interested person will have to commence a guardianship proceeding. The court will then appoint a financial guardianship to care for the maker's property, which will then be used in lieu of the durable power of attorney. Since durable powers of attorney are designed to prevent exactly this result, they fail in their mission.

A power of attorney is not easy to revoke. There are serious logistical problems associated with giving notice of revocation to persons who have relied on the power. The principal may have no way of knowing with whom the agent has transacted business. It takes time and effort for a principal to make sure that the power has been properly revoked and that the appropriate parties are on notice of the revocation.

The power's age also creates problems. The older it is, the less likelihood there is of its being accepted. A third party will want to make absolutely sure that the power is in effect and will want evidence of its current validity. This may be difficult or impossible to accomplish because the principal, who is the only person who can really vouch for the power's validity, is disabled. If the third party does some investigation and contacts the lawyer who drafted the power, the lawyer may have to disclose the principal's disability. More often than not, a third party will not go to the trouble of determining the validity of an older power of attorney. Rather than taking any risk in dealing with the agent, the third party will refuse to accept the durable power.

Another disadvantage of a durable power of attorney is that it is personal to the agent named. This means that if the agent cannot perform because of disability, death, or lack of desire, then the power is useless. Once the agent resigns, becomes disabled, or dies, the power is automatically revoked by operation of law. Under traditional agency principles, even if joint agents are named, the death of one agent revokes the agency.[19] When a durable power of attorney is revoked by any of these occurrences, there is no one left to manage the principal's financial affairs. The only alternative is the appointment of a financial guardian through court-controlled guardianship proceedings. Unfortunately, this is exactly what the durable power of attorney was created to prevent in the first place.

Some states have legislation that can effectively negate the purpose and use of the durable power of attorney. In Florida, for example, the durable power statute states that the durable power of attorney is "valid until such time as the donor shall . . . be adjudged incompetent."[20] In Colorado, a court-appointed financial guardian may revoke an agent's authority as to financial matters.[21] Other states have similar provisions. The rationale behind these statutes is that there is an inherent conflict between a financial guardian and an agent under a durable power of attorney. Rather than having each operating independent of one another and attempting to control the same assets, one or the other must prevail. Unfortunately, the one that is most often chosen is the court-appointed financial guardian, not the hand-picked agent.

Many state statutes make the durable power of attorney illusory. Anytime a disgruntled heir does not agree with the actions of the power holder, he or she can force a financial guardianship which will invalidate the power. This will almost invariably thwart the intentions of the principal and result in all of the expense, publicity, delay, and red tape that the durable power was designed to eliminate. These statutes are invitations to litigation.[22]

General durable powers of attorney are not the panacea that they have been touted to be. They have significant drawbacks when used in conjunction with will-planning/probate. That is not to say that they do not have meaningful uses in estate planning; they do, but not as a substitute for proper living trust—centered disability planning.

Limited Durable Powers of Attorney

Durable powers of attorney are most effective when they are limited to specific tasks such as funding living trusts or providing for health care.

One of the effective uses of a limited durable power of attorney, where allowed by state law, is for health care decisions. There is no more effective method of coping with doctors and hospitals than for an individual to grant a trusted friend or close family member the right to make critical medical and health care decisions. In addition, a person can grant an agent the authority to make decisions about long-term care, including nursing home and home care decisions.[23] A limited power of attorney for health care should be used in conjunction with a living trust to allow a living trust—centered plan the most flexibility.

A limited durable power of attorney is also useful for purposes of naming an agent to deal with the Internal Revenue Service and other taxing authorities upon the disability of the principal. The IRS requires a power of attorney from a taxpayer who cannot deal with it directly.[24] Without this power, the IRS may very well demand that a financial guardian be appointed and petition the court to do just that.

A limited durable power of attorney should be used in conjunction with a living trust. According to Chancellor and Probate Judge Ellen B. Brantley:

> In recent years much has been written about the use of the durable power-of-attorney. While this device has many advantages, it is not the only effective means for the management of a disabled person's property. The wonderfully flexible trust is an alternative which should be considered for use in place of, or in conjunction with, a durable power-of-attorney. . . .
>
> In addition to the trust's usefulness in property management for the disabled client, the trust is the obvious device to manage property for the benefit of a client's disabled relative.[25]

Limited durable powers of attorney can be used by their agents to put property into the disabled trust maker's trust. This gives the trust maker the opportunity to say, If I forget to put all of my assets into my trust while I am healthy, I would like you to do so for me when I am disabled so that they can be controlled and managed by my trustees pursuant to my instructions for myself and my loved ones.

The principal can name any number of agents without fear of losing control. The only power granted to the power holder is the right to fund the maker's living trust. There will be no successor agent problem, because the trust agreement will contain provisions for successor trustees within the body of the document. The disabled person's property will be controlled by the terms of his or her trust instructions. The principal does not grant an agent carte blanche authority with this kind of power. The disabled person's property and wishes will be governed by well-defined fiduciary standards and law that is designed to give maximum protection and benefits.

The Revocable Living Trust

For purposes of managing the property of a disabled individual, the revocable living trust offers clear advantages over a guardianship and a durable power of attorney:

> A living trust can also provide asset management during periods of incapacity by the [trust maker]. . . . The advantages of having a trust in effect during a period of incapacity can be appreciated by anyone who has had to set up a conservatorship to hold and manage the estate of an incapacitated person, particularly when there has been a question about whether that person is in fact incapacitated.[26]

Some of the advantages of a revocable living trust are the following:

- Its terms control the disposition and management of the property owned by it.
- It survives the death, disability, and termination of trustees and names successor trustees.
- It offers more protection against mismanagement and abuse.
- It is easier to use in transacting business with a trustee

than with an agent or a guardian because the authority of trustees is more readily accepted.

A properly written revocable living trust contains extensive instructions that the trustees are required to follow. These instructions can be as detailed as the maker desires. Oftentimes, a maker will want to provide guidelines to the trustees. These instructional statements are called *precatory statements* because they are not binding on the trustees, but rather give them general direction and perspective. The purpose of a precatory statement is to help trustees understand the intent of the maker and to facilitate many of the decisions that trustees commonly must make when administering a trust. A precatory statement might read as follows:

> *To the extent that I have given my Trustee any discretionary authority over the distribution of income or principal to my beneficiary, it is my desire that my Trustee be liberal in exercising such discretion.*

Precatory language can be much more elaborate than this example. It can include philosophy or values. Trustees generally appreciate any type of guidance that will better help them interpret the intent and the desires of a trust maker.

Trust instructions are applicable only to trust property, so it is important that the living trust be fully funded. There is always a chance that when a maker becomes disabled, not all of his or her property will be titled in the trust's name. That is why a limited durable power of attorney should be used in concert with a revocable living trust. The agent can then be relied on to transfer any remaining assets to the maker's trust without court intervention.

This is not to say that a guardianship proceeding cannot be commenced even with the existence of a revocable living trust. It can. Generally, a guardianship proceeding is initiated for one of two reasons. The first is that not all property is in the trust and no durable power exists to allow funding of the trust. The second is that health care decisions must be made and there is no durable power naming an agent to make those decisions.

In either of these cases, the property held in the trust and the authority of the trustee to manage and control it are not affected by the guardianship proceeding. The trustee's powers and authority are separate from this proceeding.

If a maker has a fully funded revocable living trust and then is adjudicated incompetent, the court appointed guardian may have the power under the particular state law to revoke the trust, thereby destroying an individual's estate plan.[27] A method to prevent this result is to make the revocable trust irrevocable on the adjudicated mental incompetency of the maker. Another is to draft the trust in such a manner as to make it clear that the right to amend or revoke the trust is personal to the maker and that a guardian or any other person shall not have the right to revoke or amend the trust.

It has been said that a trust is incapable of covering health care issues.[28] However, this is not an accurate statement. Under the durable power of attorney statutes that allow an agent to make health care decisions, there seems to be no reason why a trustee under a revocable living trust instrument cannot be named as the agent for these decisions. In fact, there seems to be no reason why a durable power cannot be incorporated as part of the provisions of a revocable living trust. The only disadvantage seems to be that the part of the trust dealing with the durable power would have to be disclosed to third parties.

A properly drafted revocable living trust document contains provisions for successor trustees, giving it continuity in the event one or more of the original trustees are unable or unwilling to serve. A revocable living trust does not terminate on the disability, death, or other termination of a trustee. In fact, even if a successor trustee is not named, a trust remains valid: a court can name a trustee without taking jurisdiction over the agreement. This is a great advantage that a living trust has over a durable power of attorney.

The law regarding the fiduciary obligations of trustees is based on centuries of interpretation; it is well-settled law.[29] A trustee will be held accountable for taking action that violates fiduciary principles. It is for this reason that the revocable living trust has much less leeway for mismanagement and abuse than the durable power of attorney. Since trustees are held to a higher standard than agents under a power of attorney and are governed by a carefully written and extensive trust document, it is likely that trustees will manage property in a much more formal and careful manner.

The use of revocable living and other trusts is becoming much more prevalent in our society. There have been a tremendous number of articles in both the popular and professional media concerning living trusts. This publicity, as well as the increasing sophistication in trust planning among financial institutions, has made dealing with a trust an almost commonplace event.

There can be no question that a trustee is far more likely to be acceptable to a third party than an agent under a durable power of attorney. The American Association of Retired Persons, in its booklet on preparing for health care decisions, has this recommendation about using revocable living trusts for disability planning:

> Do not let the formality of most trusts cause you to avoid this planning instrument. Trusts can meet certain goals and provide significant benefits which well justify the professional assistance they require.[30]

Our Conclusion

Living trust–centered estate plans are far more effective for disability planning than will-planning/probate, which relies on guardianship proceedings and powers of attorney.

Delays in Administration

Questions for Discussion

- Does probate cause delays in making immediate distributions to heirs?
- Do fully funded living trusts cause delays in making immediate distributions to beneficiaries?
- Why are there more delays with probate than with living trusts?

Advocates of revocable living trusts contend that a trust reduces, and often eliminates, the delays inherent in probate and administration. Critics reluctantly admit that probate may cause delays but argue that such delays are short, not harmful, and in many cases occur whether there is probate and administration or after-death administration of a fully funded revocable living trust.

There is little concrete evidence as to the average length of a probate and administration. Popular books sometimes make claims about the time an average probate takes, but these claims are not arrived at in any concise or scientific manner.[1] One noted legal author makes the following statement about the delays in the probate process:

The reality is that regardless of how simple an estate appears to be or actually is, it is almost impossible to close an estate through the probate system in less than one year.[2]

He then suggests that attorneys inform their clients that they should assume one and one-half to two years as the time for probate and should be aware that it is not unreasonable to expect periods of three and four years. A 1991 article in *U.S. News & World Report* states that probate takes an average of seventeen months, compared to three weeks in Great Britain![3]

It is clear that probate creates delay.[4] But does a fully funded revocable living trust reduce or eliminate this delay? To find the answer to this question, two distinct aspects of delay must be examined. The first is the delay in allowing the decedent's spouse and dependent children access to the estate's assets. These amounts may be necessary for bare subsistence or for maintaining a decent standard of living during the probate and administration period. The second issue deals with the delay in actually closing the estate and distributing all of its assets to the heirs.

Delays in Immediate Distributions to Family Members Caused by the Probate Process

One of probate's primary functions is to pass title to heirs in an orderly and proper manner after making certain that creditors are paid. Without probate or a valid will-substitute, it is impossible for assets to be retitled.

Assets titled in the name of the decedent are in legal limbo. Since the owner of the assets is no longer living, only the executor can transfer or otherwise use all or any part of the decedent's assets. For example, if a decedent has a savings account with only his or her name on the signature card, only he or she can draw funds. The same is true for the negotiation of checks made payable to the decedent or the sale of any assets. Upon a person's death, all activity terminates for property titled in the decedent's name. It is here that the delay in probate begins.

Even if the decedent left powers of attorney, they will be to no avail. Powers of attorney, except in a very few rare instances, end on the death of those who create them.[5] A power of attorney cannot be used to pass on property at death. Unless will-substitute planning is used, the probate process will be necessary to pass on an individual's property.

With formal probate, there is an inevitable delay between the date of the decedent's death and the actual hearing required to prove the will and appoint the executor. Until then, even a named executor cannot act.

This same delay occurs when a decedent dies intestate, because the court must be notified of the death and an administrator appointed. Delay is inherent in this process because of the time it takes to prepare the requisite paperwork and petition the court to qualify the administrator.

Inevitably, there is a period of emotional trauma during the period immediately after the death of a family member. After this period has passed and loved ones attempt to get back to normal, the task of organizing the decedent's affairs begins. This entails locating the original will, contacting an attorney, and finding the witnesses to the will in states that do not allow self-proving clauses.

To be accepted for probate, an original will must be filed with the probate court. A copy is not sufficient except under the most extraordinary of circumstances. Sometimes, finding the original will can be difficult. What happens, for example, if the will is stored in a safe deposit box? Some states require that these boxes be locked and sequestered for inheritance or estate tax reasons on the death of the box holder. A court order is often required to open the box, creating confusion and delay. Even in states that do not have this requirement, banks often require some type of legal authorization to allow a nonsignatory to have access to the box and the property in it.

An even thornier problem arises when a decedent leaves more than one original will. It is advisable for a person to sign one, and only one, original will. The reason for this practice is that if more than one will is signed, it is necessary to produce every original. If one of the original wills cannot be found, then the presumption is that the will was revoked.

This presumption exists because of the history and nature of wills. Wills are fragile legal documents that are subject to precise rules of law, some of which relate to the Statute of Wills passed by the English Parliament in 1540. When an original will cannot be located, a question arises as to whether a person revoked the will. Since evidence may not be available to prove that the decedent did not revoke the will—after all, the only person who really knows for sure is dead—the courts must presume that the will is invalid.

Other issues can arise when proving a will. The capacity of the maker may be questioned or the method of signing and witnessing the will may be attacked. There may be a question whether the will has been revoked because it has been defaced in some manner. We experienced an example of this:

An older woman had an attorney prepare a will that disinherited the woman's natural daughter and left all her property to another relative.

The attorney advised the woman to leave her natural child a nominal bequest of $1.00 in order to show the *probate court that the natural child had not been forgotten but was being disinherited on purpose. This nominal bequest was not required by the state's law.*

The woman reluctantly agreed to the provision but was very uncomfortable with the idea.

After the woman died, her will was examined before being entered for probate. Where the language leaving her daughter a dollar was supposed to be, there was a neat rectangular hole that had been excised from the will.

When a will is defaced, it is presumed to be revoked. Since this will had been defaced it had inadvertently been revoked. The woman was considered to have died without a will. Under the laws of intestacy, her natural child received all of her property, the opposite of her intent.

This process of proving a will can be time consuming and create significant delay. And this is only the first step in the probate process. It is only after probate reaches this point that it is even feasible for the decedent's spouse and dependent children to request an allowance from the estate's assets.

Statutes in most states provide for certain allowances for surviving spouses and dependent children.[6] For example, in Florida the family allowance is $6,000 for living expenses during the entire administration process, which may well drag on for quite some time. In Maryland, the family allowance for living expenses during the entire period of administration is $2,000 plus $1,000 for each unmarried child under the age of eighteen. In Colorado, a Uniform Probate Code state, there is a "reasonable" family allowance, which is limited to one year.[7]

Statutory family allowances are not generous and cannot,

by themselves, support a surviving spouse, let alone a surviving spouse with dependent children. This is not to imply that the court will not be more generous with the spouse on an extraordinary basis. Probate judges are likely to err on the side of generosity rather than penury, but they do not always have unfettered discretion in these matters. Other factors such as potential claims, disputes as to the validity of the will or any of its provisions, or limits in state law may make it impossible for the judge to grant more than the amounts called for in the proscribed statutory family allowances.

In addition to family allowances, states sometimes provide for exempt property or personal property allowances and homesteads. Exempt property is free of the claims of creditors and can be distributed to family members in a relatively short period. Personal property allowances enable the surviving spouse or children to take a minimal amount of personal property, such as furniture and clothing. The provisions for exempt property and property allowances are modest; amounts from $2,000 to $5,000 are common, although in a few states, the allowances are higher.[8]

Homesteads represent the value of a family residence that is not subject to the claims of creditors. The homestead allowance allows some or all of the home's value to be free from the claims of creditors. Homestead allowances do not reduce delay, although they do allow families to live in their residences during probate.

Under the probate systems of virtually every state, creditors are given a preferred position. They have first rights to the decedent's assets except for those few assets that are creditor-protected, such as exempt personal property and homestead property. It is only when creditors' claims are satisfied that distributions can be made.

A major part of probate deals with the notification and payment of creditors. Each state has some form of notice and payment statute that grants a certain amount of time for creditors to present claims. These statutes vary as to time, but the typical creditor notification period is from four to six months.[9] During this period, and often beyond it if a disputed claim is pending, the executor must be very careful about distributing assets. Since creditors who file their claims in a timely manner have a prior right to assets in a probate estate, if the executor distributes the assets and it is later determined that the claims of other creditors cannot be satisfied out of the remaining probate estate, the executor is personally liable for the improper distributions.[10] There is no liability, however, to the extent that family allowances are distributed or that exempt personal property is distributed.

The potential for liability forces an executor to exercise a great deal of caution before making a distribution of any kind from the estate. In some states, the executor cannot make *any* distributions during this period, except family allowances, and then only under certain circumstances.[11]

Delay in making distributions to immediate family members may be further prolonged if the probate estate is not liquid. If the executor must sell property in order for the estate to create cash for distributions or to pay creditors, the executor must often ask the court for permission to make these sales. This necessitates court filings and an abundance of paperwork, all of which is a matter of public record, potentially affecting the purchase price and the terms of the sale.[12] This process is time consuming in itself, and all of the details of the actual sale must be consummated before the requisite cash is generated. Because of the additional red tape and the understandable reluctance of many buyers to deal with the executor, a lengthy period may well pass before any cash is available for distribution.

In those states that have adopted the Uniform Probate Code, and in others that have initiated probate reform, an informal probate can be used. An informal probate allows the executor more discretion and latitude in making decisions, because the executor is not directly supervised by the probate court. However, even in a UPC state, the executor is governed by statute and does not have complete discretion. The executor in a UPC state may still have to petition the probate court for increases in family allowances or for other extraordinary matters. Informal probate proceedings may reduce short-term delay, but they do not eliminate it.

Will-planning/probate advocates generally acknowledge delay as a drawback of probate. Some dismiss its impact by pointing out that, in most cases, a surviving spouse seems to get by, and dependent children seem to get fed and clothed. They point out that life insurance proceeds and joint property are typically available, so the urgency of probate distributions is overstated.[13]

Their position does not take into account the trauma created by a lingering attorney-involved process that is a daily reminder of the death of a loved one. It does not address the frustration created in an already emotional situation where even a relatively minor delay is magnified many times over. Their position, like probate itself, plainly disregards the emotional aspects of the loss of a loved one. There can be no question that the results of short-term probate delay can be financially and emotionally devastating.

Delays in Distributions
to Family Members
When Using a Fully Funded Living Trust

Most literature that discusses the relative advantages of revocable living trusts as compared to will-planning/probate concedes that a fully funded revocable living trust is superior to a will for expediting distributions to beneficiaries. A legal writer has said, "It is clear that the avoidance of most of the delays inherent in formal probate administration can be just as great an incentive for using living trusts, in the proper circumstances, as is the avoidance of statutory probate fees and commissions."[14]

Why do revocable living trusts offer such a clear advantage in preventing short-term delay?

Any property held in the name of a living trust at the death of its maker is not subject to the probate process. Because of this characteristic, the trust and its trustees continue on even though the trust maker has died.

A living trust does not have to be "proved" in a probate court because its legal existence begins when it is signed. There is no delay in the operation of the trust because all court proceedings have been eliminated.

What if the trust maker signs several duplicate original trusts? It is common practice for an attorney to ask a client to sign several such duplicates. A living trust is similar to a contract. Just as duplicate originals of a contract do not affect its validity, duplicate originals do not affect the validity of a living trust. The existence of just one copy of a trust is sufficient to prove its existence. Absent a statement in writing or some other evidence that the trust has been revoked, it is valid. If only a photocopy of the trust is found, absent any other evidence, the trust can be considered valid and operable, especially if it has been funded and its trustees have been serving pursuant to the trust's terms.

A revocable living trust is very difficult to attack; we develop this concept in Chapter 6, "Privacy and Confidentiality." Even in the rare instance when a trust is contested, it is likely to continue functioning during the pendency of a lawsuit, unlike the case of a will, where everything comes to a screeching halt until such time as the validity of the will is conclusively determined.

In a will, the executor is generally *prohibited* from making distributions except as provided by statute. A trustee of a living trust is not subject to any statutory or probate-court-imposed restrictions on distributions. In a trust, the trustee makes distributions under the terms of the trust instrument itself. It is a trustee's ability to make distributions pursuant to the wishes of the trust maker which eliminates the onerous delays of probate.

A trustee is not personally liable for distributions made under the terms of the trust after the maker has died, under most circumstances.[15]

One commentator sums up the difference in the ability of a trustee and an executor to make immediate distributions as follows:

> The trustee's greater freedom from personal liability for creditors' claims, and somewhat lesser apparent potential liability for death taxes—compared with an executor or an administrator—puts the trustee in a better posture to make trust assets available to beneficiaries during estate administration.[16]

A trustee of a fully funded revocable living trust does not have to be appointed by the probate court in order to serve after the death of the trust maker. For example, in a typical living trust where the maker is married, both spouses are co-trustees. On the death of one of the spouses, the trust agreement provides for the appointment of successor trustees. They may make immediate and unfettered distributions from the trust, as long as the distributions are consistent with the terms of the trust. No time need pass for the appointment of an executor, the location of witnesses, or any of the other administrative and legal procedures required in the probate process. The trust continues as if nothing has happened.

In a fully funded living trust, the process of administering, investing, and distributing the assets is private and may be accomplished without court supervision. If the trustee chooses to sell assets, there is no court procedure for the approval of the sale nor is there a need for public notice. The sale can proceed in the same fashion as any other normal transaction.

Trustees do have restraints. They are governed by the terms of the trust. Only distributions that are consistent with a trust's provisions can be made. To the extent that trustees violate their fiduciary duty, they are liable for any losses. This is not a principle that is designed to protect creditors or to serve the probate process. Its purpose is to assure the trust maker and the beneficiaries that the trustees will perform their tasks in a responsible and prudent manner.

Will advocates sometimes take the view that living trusts prevent a spouse and a family from taking advantage of the family allowances provided in state probate statutes. This is a ridiculous argument. Family allowances are needed in probate because otherwise none of the decedent's probate assets may be available to the family. Assets in a trust are not restricted by probate at all. This argument assumes that small allowances are better than the availability of all of the decedent's property. A living trust allows a maker to care for his or her spouse and family the way he or she chooses, without state interference and with all of the trust assets.

Probate and delay are synonymous. Probate lawyers sometimes argue that such delays are often minimal if an estate is well organized or liquid or there are no creditors or disputes. It is true that probate delays may be reduced by modern statutes that simplify its procedures. However, even in the best of circumstances, probate is characterized by significant delay when compared to living trust–centered planning.

The Delays in Closing a Probate

In many estates, the executor has the legal ability to distribute assets to the heirs immediately after the statutory period for notification to creditors has expired. Since this period usually ranges from four to six months, the question arises as to why it often takes from twelve to eighteen months, or even longer, to distribute property to heirs even in relatively simple estates.

The disorganization of a client's affairs affects the time probate can take. An executor must locate all of the decedent's property. This in itself can be an extraordinarily complex and arduous task. Located assets must then be assigned a value. If the appraiser is appointed by a court, it is likely that the process will take much longer than appraisal by a person hired without court intervention.

There may be other reasons why probate is lengthy. In an article in the Connecticut Bar Association's *Estates and Probate Newsletter,* one practitioner offers his views on why probate takes so long:

> The track record of executors with respect to prompt asset distribution is abysmal, whether because of lawyer or banker procrastination or because prompt distribution makes the job look easy and makes fees based upon percentage of assets held look excessive.[17]

Estate Tax Delay

Will-planning/probate advocates often assert that long-term delay is equal for wills and trusts. They base their argument on the long-term delays encountered in larger estates as a result of federal estate tax issues.

In probate, long-term delay can be defined as that period of time that exceeds the statutory period for notifying creditors. It can further be defined as the period that must transpire before the will's heirs can receive their inheritance. For trusts, long-term delay is any delay the trustee sustains before making actual distributions to beneficiaries or to subtrusts for beneficiaries created under the terms of the trust.

Probate advocates state that since both the trustee of a living trust and the executor of a probate estate are personally liable for federal estate taxes, both must necessarily delay distributions until they are released from liability, or until the statute of limitations has run.[18] This obligation, probate advocates say, is what accounts for the same delays in distributions of probate assets and trust assets.

The Internal Revenue Code (IRC) requires that the executor and trustee pay from a decedent's estate, whether the property is held in trust or is held in the probate estate, any federal estate tax due.[19] According to Internal Revenue Code regulations, they have the duty to pay the federal estate tax even where the gross estate consists of property not in their possession.[20] While this has led some practitioners to believe that they have personal liability for federal estate taxes, this is not strictly true.[21] They are most likely personally liable only for the violation of their fiduciary duties.[22] Both can be discharged from liability for federal estate taxes under the Internal Revenue Code.[23]

Both a trustee and an executor need to exercise care in

their fiduciary duties to avoid personal liability for federal estate taxes. One way they can avoid this liability is by creating a reserve for the taxes due. Since this often leaves a substantial amount of other assets free, distributions to heirs and beneficiaries can be made from these assets.

An executor does have greater personal liability for taxes—other than the estate tax and other debts due to the U.S. government—than a trustee does. Under a separate federal statute that does not include a trustee as part of its definition of an executor, an executor has personal liability for *all* payments of any kind that are made before "all U.S. debts" are paid.[24] This means that excise taxes and other potential estate liabilities to the U.S. government must be considered by the executor before making distributions. There is no doubt that in some estates this tends to make the executor much more cautious in making distributions than his or her trustee counterpart.

Unless there is a significant valuation or other issue that creates a dispute with the Internal Revenue Service, the tax liability of most estates will be fixed on the due date of the federal estate tax return, which is generally nine months after the date of death. A trustee or executor may make distributions to heirs or beneficiaries without incurring personal liability as long as there are sufficient assets in the estate to pay the federal government.

In many estates the wholesale holding of all assets based on the principle that personal liability will be incurred on the distribution of those assets is unfounded. The argument that personal liability for taxes creates equal delay for wills and trusts is patently untrue.

Approximately 2.1 million people die each year.[25] Only about 55,000 federal estate tax returns are filed annually.[26] Federal estate tax returns are only required if a decedent's gross estate exceeds $600,000.[27] This means that only 2.6 percent of the people who die in a year file a federal estate tax return. A report by the American Association of Retired Persons, using figures from an unpublished study, estimates that the 55,000 figure represents some 10 percent of the estates actually in administration. These statistics show that, at most, only 10 percent of all estates in administration would be delayed because of liability for federal estate tax. Since many, if not most, estates do not have significant federal estate tax issues that would warrant further delay, it is likely that the number of estates that have to be delayed by liability issues is far less than 10 percent. If less than 10 percent of estates that are in administration pay federal estate tax, then how can taxes, and their attendant liability, be responsible for most of the delay? These statistics belie the arguments of will-planning/probate advocates that federal estate tax issues offer an explanation of why most estates take so long to be closed.

A second position that will-planning/probate advocates use to justify the long-term delay in probate caused by federal estate tax liability is to claim that even though an executor may not be personally liable, the estate remains liable.[28] As long as the heirs are duly informed of the continuing potential estate tax liability for the assessment of tax there is little, if any, practical reason why the estate cannot be closed.[29]

An executor may also incur liability with regard to the decedent's gift and income tax liabilities. As with federal estate taxes, an executor can be discharged from personal liability for these taxes. The Internal Revenue Code provides the procedure for the discharge.[30] Here again, there is a statutory mechanism for limiting the exposure of the executor and shortcutting the delay factor.

The same liability issues arise for the trustee of a living trust. Typically, a living trust and the subtrusts it creates at the death of its maker continue for some time. Distributions are made in accordance with the provisions of the trust, and assets are available for liabilities until they are finally distributed. The trustee can obtain a release of personal liability for estate taxes or can distribute assets with the understanding that the beneficiaries, or the property they receive, will be subject to a contingent liability. As a result, delay can be eliminated.

The law is unclear as to whether a trustee can obtain a discharge from personal liability for the decedent's gift and income taxes in the same manner as an executor. However, there should be no policy reason why an executor and a trustee should be treated differently for these matters; it is likely that a trustee could receive a discharge also.[31]

While these points may appear to be esoteric to all but the legal scholar, the reality is that executors, many of whom are inexperienced in the legal requirements of acting in a fiduciary capacity, have a tendency to act both slowly and cautiously. The delays in closing a probate estate are caused by an overabundance of caution that is founded on inaccurate knowledge or lack of understanding of how the assessment and liability statutes really operate.

The Internal Revenue Service's Concern with Probate Delay

The Internal Revenue Service is concerned with delays in the probate process and reinforces the concept that distributions of probate estate assets can be facilitated and an estate promptly closed. Its regulations state that "the period of administration of an estate cannot be unduly prolonged," and that "if the administration of an estate is unreasonably prolonged, the estate is considered terminated for Federal income tax purposes after the expiration of a reasonable period for the performance by the executor of all the duties of administration."[32] When an estate is considered "terminated," the IRS no longer will recognize its existence, allow it the status of a separate taxpaying entity, or allow it to file an income tax return. The federal fiduciary income tax return that executors of estates must file with the IRS requires a written explanation of why an estate is open after the estate's second tax year in order to facilitate compliance with this regulation.

The IRS position demonstrates the fallacy of the probate advocates' argument that much of the delay in probate is due to federal estate tax liability.

Our Conclusion

Living trust–centered planning substantially reduces or avoids the short- and long-term delays that are implicit in will-planning/probate.

Multiple Probates:
The Problems with
Ancillary Administration

Questions for Discussion

- What are the problems commonly associated with multiple probates where property is owned in more than one state?
- What methods are used to **prevent** multiple probates?
- Is a revocable living trust the most efficient method for eliminating multiple probates?

For purposes of probate and administration, each state has jurisdiction over the land real property located within its boundaries.[1] *Real property* is the legal term used to describe land, buildings attached to land, and ownership of minerals, oil, and gas. When an individual who is domiciled in state A—his or her *home state*—dies owning real property in state B, probate proceedings must generally be started in state B as well.

Out-of-state probate is often not necessary for personal property, which is all property other than real property. The likelihood and extent of out-of-state probate depend upon the type of property that the decedent owned and a particular state's probate statute.

A probate proceeding in a state other than the decedent's home state is called *ancillary administration*. The following example illustrates the ancillary administration process:

Bill and Janet Jones live in Detroit, Michigan. That is where they vote, license their cars, and belong to a church, and where Bill makes his living.

The Joneses have purchased investment properties over the years. They own a cottage in Sturgeon Bay, Wisconsin; a condominium in Miami, Florida; and several undeveloped lots near Santa Fe, New Mexico. All of these properties are titled in Bill's name.

On Bill's death, his estate will be probated in Detroit. There will also be probates—ancillary administration— in Wisconsin, Florida, and New Mexico. Each state controls the land within its borders, and each will insist that this real estate be probated by its courts.

Janet and her children will endure the time, expense, and delay of four probates!

Problems with Ancillary Administration

Because many people purchase retirement homes, vacation residences, or other investments in real estate such as oil and gas that are located outside their home state, the significant estate planning problems of out-of-state real property on the death of the owner are not uncommon.[2] However, in order for a decedent's heirs to receive own-

ership of the decedent's real property, a will must be probated in the state where the property is located.³ Almost
invariably, ownership of real property in another state by a
decedent means that an ancillary probate will be required.

Ancillary proceedings also may be required if the decedent owns personal property in another state.⁴ Ordinarily,
an executor can move out-of-state personal property back
to the decedent's home state without court action; however,
out-of-state creditors or heirs may ask the local court for
ancillary probate for personal property so that they do not
have to travel to the decedent's home state to settle their
claims.⁵

While in many instances an ancillary proceeding may not
be as formal as home-state probate, an executor is almost
always required. It is possible that the executor of the home-
state probate will be named, but more often an executor
who resides in the other state will be appointed. A local
attorney must be engaged to guide the proceedings through
that state's particular probate procedure. Generally, the validity of the will must be proved in the ancillary state just
as it must be proved in the home state.

It is possible that a will that is valid in the home state may
not be valid in the state in which the ancillary administration
is held. Having to prove the will in another state can create
complex and extended litigation, which causes the cost of
probate to skyrocket. Creditors in the ancillary administration state must be notified with all of the formality required
by its laws, and its statutory waiting periods for creditors
must be observed. This problem is more fully discussed in
Chapter 9, "Conflicts of Law."

In short, an ancillary proceeding is similar to the home
state's probate proceeding, except that it involves different
property and a different court and attorney and potentially
a different executor. As a result, probate fees are incurred

in more than one jurisdiction. And delays in any one probate may create delays in the others.

States that have adopted the Uniform Probate Code, or similar simplified probate statutes, may reduce the time and expense of ancillary administration.[6] But there is absolutely no guarantee that time and expense will be reduced.

Most will-planning/probate advocates recognize that ancillary administration proceedings are inconvenient, expensive, and time consuming. They recommend that ancillary proceedings be avoided. The question is, What is the best method for avoiding them?

Methods for Avoiding an Ancillary Administration

One of the most common methods used for avoiding ancillary administration is joint tenancy with right of survivorship. Joint tenancy avoids ancillary administration on the death of one of the owners. Unfortunately, on the death of the surviving owner, ancillary administration will be required if no additional planning is done.

Even if it is the intent of the surviving owner to institute planning that avoids an ancillary administration, it makes much more sense to plan to do so currently while both owners are living. Too many other factors can intervene that can make someone's best intent seem to be foolish procrastination in retrospect.

Joint tenancy has many more disadvantages than advantages. In Chapter 24, "Comparing Living Trusts to Joint Tenancy Planning," we take a close look at its many problems and drawbacks. For now, suffice it to say that joint tenancy has many drawbacks that are unattractive for most planning purposes. These drawbacks far outweigh any advantage joint tenancy may have in delaying ancillary administration.

Other alternatives that are used to avoid ancillary administration include creating a partnership or corporation. In most states, if property is transferred to a partnership or a corporation, it effectively converts the property into intangible personal property, which is generally not subject to ancillary administration.

The creation of these entities often entails much work and myriad tax and other complications. Separate tax returns must be filed every year for these entities. And, of course, the stock or partnership interest must still be probated in the decedent's home state. The use of a corporation might also create substantial unwanted federal income taxes on the subsequent sale of the assets during the will maker's life.

Using a Revocable Living Trust to Eliminate an Ancillary Administration

The only alternative to avoiding an ancillary administration that allows an owner to control his or her property with the least amount of expense and complication is a fully funded revocable living trust!

Property can be transferred to a living trust without excessive cost or complications. These transfers into a living trust remove the property from the state's probate system. All of the advantages of a fully funded revocable living trust apply to out-of-state property.

Our Conclusion

Will-planning/probate necessitates ancillary administration when real property is owned in more than one state. Use of fully funded living trusts avoids it.

· 6 ·

Privacy and Confidentiality

Questions for Discussion

- Why are the issues of privacy and confidentiality important in estate planning?
- Does will-planning/probate assure privacy and confidentiality?
- Are fully funded revocable living trusts private?

One of the more commonly cited advantages of living trust–centered planning is its ability to keep the affairs of its maker private. Since a trust is not subject to probate, it does not have to be filed with the probate court as a matter of public record. In contrast, a will must be filed with the probate court as part of the proceedings. As part of the public record, a will can be examined by anyone who has the inclination to visit the probate court.

Does Will-Planning/Probate Assure Privacy and Confidentiality?

Not only is a will a matter of public record, in most jurisdictions the complete inventory of the estate is a part of the public record as well. It too can be examined and copied. Petitions by heirs, creditors, and others and all of the details of the decedent's estate planning and financial affairs are typically part of the public record. Probate statutes require that public notices appear in newspapers, putting heirs and creditors on notice of pending probate proceedings. These legal announcements can have the unfortunate effect of creating significant public awareness and interest.

Will advocates sometimes dismiss the privacy issue as irrelevant and illusory. They argue that few people care about publicity. They view the public nature of probate as a non-issue. One probate defender responded to this issue with the comment "Don't flatter yourself."[1] Other commentators have taken a similar position:

> It is certainly true that the probate process involves public records while revocable trust transfers generally do not. However, is this really a concern in more than some isolated case? Despite our vanity, do we really believe that anybody is interested enough in our affairs to bother researching microfiche probate records?[2]

Obviously, a client's privacy is of little concern or importance to these writers.

Will-planning/probate advocates also make the argument that living trusts are not always private, and that they too require a great deal of disclosure. In order to determine the truth of this accusation, let's examine the facts.

Potential Heirs

People who have expectations of receiving a bequest under a will are not always privy to the terms of that will. The event that allows them to find out whether their expectations have been met is the probate of the will. If a potential heir is disappointed, a will contest may follow.

Potential heirs may not know the value of the decedent's estate, but an impatient and inquisitive heir can easily dig into the estate's public inventory of assets. With the aid of complete financial statements, an heir can ascertain the extent of his or her loss.

A trip to virtually any lawyer's office will result in detailed instructions as to how to gather this public information. This scenario can be repeated by any number of people, including the local press, creditors, jilted lovers, or unscrupulous sales people.

The Business Community

When lawyers or business people are dealing with the executor of an estate, they routinely gather all information available at the probate court. The executor's negotiating position can be significantly reduced if the facts about the liquidity of the estate, the types of assets in it, the extent of the estate's liabilities, and the individuals who have petitioned the court for distributions are known. Full disclosure is not necessarily wise in business dealings, and the side with more information usually has a decided advantage. It is not unusual for business adversaries to gather information about an estate. We offered a poignant example of our experience with this problem in our book *Loving Trust*[3]:

> *A good businessman asked his lawyer to make an offer for the purchase of significant machinery owned by a competitor who had recently passed away. His lawyer suggested that they should withhold the offer until the deceased competitor's probate file could be thoroughly investigated. The businessman agreed and the lawyer sent his paralegal to the court on a fact gathering mission.*

> *The result of the investigation more than paid for the lawyer's services. The inventory of the decedent's estate in the probate court showed that the estate was clearly in a cash-bind, and that it faced significant expenses and taxes that it didn't have the ready cash to cover. The lawyer suggested that they offer 50 cents on the dollar, which is precisely what was offered. Faced with significant bills and little cash, the estate's executor reluctantly took the low offer.*

> *The buyer's access to the records of the probate estate gave him a business windfall at the expense of the decedent's heirs.*

Guardianships

The issue of privacy is not limited to death. If an individual becomes incompetent, a guardianship is often created to care for that person and his or her financial affairs. A guardianship proceeding is usually within the jurisdiction of the probate court.

Just like probate, a guardianship proceeding is public. All of the ward's financial and medical records are fully public. There is no insulation from public scrutiny, including the degradation that often accompanies such a proceeding.

The Need for Privacy and Confidentiality

In the United States, there is a deep and abiding appreciation for keeping one's affairs private. Very few people willingly disclose their financial information to anyone except their most trusted advisers and close family members. Very few people are willing to broadcast what they own and to whom they are going to leave it upon their death or to advertise the state of their health and the amount of their property if they become disabled. Yet if a person's estate goes through probate or if a person is declared by a court to be incompetent, public disclosure is exactly what occurs. People who rely on will-planning/probate are guaranteeing that their personal affairs will be placed in the public records when they die or are declared mentally incompetent. This public disclosure is something they would not have, given a choice.

It is this very real need for privacy that contradicts the assertion "that nobody really cares whether probate or guardianships are public or not." A marketing research firm conducted a survey of over five hundred affluent family businesses in the United States to determine why their owners chose to create living trusts. They found that the issue of privacy was a major motivating reason for living trust planning:

In effect, estate settlements through a trust are appealing due to the issue of privacy. Only those individuals who are beneficiaries of the personal trust are involved in the estate settlement process. This motivation ties into the affluent family business owner's preference for confidentiality. They do not want their personal or business affairs to be public knowledge. Trust accounts [revocable living trusts] help them achieve this goal.[4]

Even if only a limited number of people look at court records, these are precisely the people who may be of concern. Presumably, the majority of those who peruse the public records are potential litigants or people who have only their own self-interest in mind.

Are Public Proceedings a Necessary Protection?

Probate advocates counter the need for privacy in times of death or incapacity by arguing that it is this public scrutiny that protects heirs from being inadvertently left out of a will. They claim that it also protects the decedent who has been unduly influenced to sign a will. The fact that the probate court offers an open forum to litigate these issues is seen as a positive factor by probate advocates. In a guardianship, will-planning/probate advocates contend that the ward gets a full hearing in determining his or her incompetence.

A fine line exists between allowing others the right to intrude in a person's affairs for their own self-interest and legitimately protecting the interests of heirs who may have a valid complaint. Offering an easily accessed forum for litigation—probate—encourages parties to litigate.

Revocable living trust planning does not eliminate a forum for just and worthy disputes. However, the nature and confidentiality of the living trust ward off people who would hope to enhance their position at the estate's expense.

In contrast, the will-planning/probate process makes gaining access to sensitive information extremely easy. Once the probate file is open, almost anyone can make a claim at little expense and risk.

The same can be said of a guardianship proceeding. Under most circumstances, there is little incentive for a self-serving person to attempt to have an individual declared mentally incompetent when a fully funded living trust is in effect. Since the trust maker's property is held in trust, a financial guardian is not necessary. Even if the court appoints a personal guardian, the incompetent person's financial affairs will be free of court intervention and intrusion. Meaningful privacy and confidentiality will continue.

With will-planning, even when a person has a durable power of attorney, a financial guardianship can be created. In some states, the court-appointed guardian can override the agent under a durable power of attorney, rendering it useless.[5] Even when there is durable power of attorney, if a guardianship proceeding is instituted, it is likely that financial information will have to be disclosed. Proper planning avoids these pitfalls.

Some diehard revocable living trust critics argue that married couples do not need to have a fully funded revocable living trust to achieve privacy in their affairs. These critics argue that joint tenancy can serve as a viable alternative. Aside from a host of other problems, privacy may only be available in joint tenancy when the first spouse dies. When the surviving spouse dies or becomes incapacitated there will be public proceedings unless the survivor implements living trust planning.

Revocable Living Trusts Are Private and Confidential Planning Documents

Privacy is far easier to retain through the use of a fully funded living trust than with will-planning/probate.

Sometimes, individuals who have business dealings with trustees are reluctant to conduct business until they have clear evidence that the trustee is acting under proper authority and within the scope of his or her authority. They are not asking to see the trust's dispositive provisions or its financial statements. They just want to know whether the trustee is empowered to do business with them. However, because of the growing public knowledge and awareness of living trusts business people and financial institutions are far more comfortable in dealing with trustees than they have been in the past.

A number of states have passed legislation that makes dealing with a trustee more convenient. For example, in Florida, a third party may rely on dealings with a trustee as long as the trustee gives limited information about the trust.[6]

When there is a need to disclose some aspects of a trust for business purposes, it is possible for the trustee to provide proof of his or her authority to act without disclosing the terms of the trust. This burden can be easily met if the trustee submits a copy of the provisions of the trust that detail the trustee's appointment and powers. In common practice, copies of the pages that name the trust maker and the trustees, the trustee's powers provisions, successor trustee provisions, and the signature page are all that a third party will need to be satisfied that the trust exists and that the trustee is duly empowered to act.

Some jurisdictions still require a trustee to "record" the trust instrument in order to comply with local title standards. When a trust is recorded, a copy of it is placed in the public records (usually in the office of the clerk of the county court), where it is indexed and is available for review by the public. Because title companies are becoming more comfortable with living trusts, this requirement is diminishing rapidly. In many cases, allowing the title company to review the document is sufficient without the formality of recording the full trust. In other instances, the trustee can submit an affidavit or certificate of trust that affirms that the trustee is duly authorized to act. It is common that certain trust provisions be attached to the affidavit or certificate.

Another method for preserving the privacy of a trust is a *nominee partnership*. The nominee partnership is a legal agreement that is created expressly for holding legal title to trust property. It shields a trust from the scrutiny of outsiders by acting as the trust's agent. This technique is discussed in Chapter 11, "General Lifetime Consequences of Funding a Living Trust." Used properly, it can preserve the privacy of the trust both during the maker's life and after his or her disability or death.

Other methods that minimize disclosure of the trust instrument include the trustees' acting directly as agents for an undisclosed trust, the use of unrecorded deeds, and the "payable on death" designations that are common to Uniform Probate Code states. All of these funding methods help to maintain the privacy of a trust. Payable on death designations are also discussed in Chapter 11.

Despite every effort to preserve total privacy with a trust, there are some states where confidentiality may not be absolute. A few states require that a state inheritance or estate tax return be filed with the probate court, even if there is no probate proceeding. This filing may be required if a state death tax lien release is necessary for real estate or other property. Generally, however, only those individuals who can demonstrate a "direct economic interest" in reviewing this information can have access to the trust.[7] There is no similar restriction for obtaining access to a will and other documents that are filed with the probate court. Probate proceedings are generally open to any member of the public who requests to see the files.

Even in those unique cases where a trust must be disclosed, the amount of information made public is much more limited. As a result, the extent of intrusion that is suffered is far less. When a trust document is disclosed, the maker's financial records and personal medical information remains private, unlike in a probate or guardianship procedure, where far more extensive information often is made part of the public record.

Our Conclusion

Will-planning/probate is a public proceeding that often discloses personal and financial affairs to the public. Living trust–centered planning is far more successful in keeping sensitive financial and personal information confidential.

·7·

Will and Trust Contests

Questions for Discussion

- What legal standing and grounds are required to attack a will and a trust?
- What standard of proof is required when attacking a will or a trust?
- What are the allowable time periods for attacking wills and trusts?
- Is it easier to contest a will than a trust?

The late Leon Jaworski, renowned trial attorney and a named partner of the major Houston firm of Fulbright and Jaworski, in an address delivered to the American College of Trial Lawyers, stated, "It has been said, and I think accurately, that a will is more apt to be the subject of litigation than any other legal instrument."[1] There is no mystery as to why will contests are so frequent. In a typical probate proceeding, potential contestants are literally invited to file objections to the will by statutes that are designed to facilitate the procedure.[2]

While there has been no formal study comparing the percentage of wills that are contested versus the percentage of living trusts that are contested, in our experience, contests of living trusts are virtually nonexistent. That there are fewer trusts than wills may account, in part, for the difference in litigation activity, but even after allowing for this, there are few reported cases of living trust contests.[3] The reason for the wide disparity in the percentage of wills and living trusts that are contested is that it is much more difficult to initiate and win a living trust lawsuit than a will contest.

Standing to Challenge a Will and a Trust

A contesting plaintiff must demonstrate some relationship to the controversy that gives him or her a legal right to bring the action in order to start a lawsuit. This right to bring suit is called *standing*. Generally, surviving spouses, potential heirs, and others who would materially benefit have the standing to initiate a will contest.[4]

Almost anyone with a relationship to the decedent who has a legitimate claim, or who thinks he or she has a legitimate claim, can contest a will by filing an objection with the probate court. This procedure is relatively uncomplicated and simple to initiate.

The risk of litigation is high in a setting that is designed to give a wide variety of people easy access to a legal forum. In our current climate of allowing plaintiffs the right to have their day in court, it is probable that most claims will be heard.

A noted estate planning professor states that a will contest "provides an opportunity for reordering the dispositive plan more to the jury's liking," and that a will contest poses a serious threat "to the client's reputation, which can be attacked unmercifully in a will contest proceeding."[5] He cites a study that indicates that when the mental capacity of the decedent was in issue, the jury found for the contestant in more than 75 percent of the cases. Yet *over half of the verdicts were reversed on appeal on grounds of insufficient evidence.*[6]

A question that often arises is whether or not the maker's heirs can challenge a revocable living trust while the maker is still living. The answer is an unequivocal *no!*

Heirs have only an expectancy to receive a gift at the death of the maker. They do not have a vested legal right in the maker's property. Since they have no vested lifetime interest in the estate, they do not have standing to bring an action challenging the trust. Only someone acting for the maker in a representative capacity, such as a guardian, can bring such an action.[7]

Disgruntled relatives could initiate a guardianship proceeding with an eye to having a "friendly" guardian appointed in order to contest the living trust of a disabled maker. However, a fully competent trust maker would most certainly dispute this action, and a guardianship would not be imposed to preserve a person's property for the benefit of potential heirs.[8] If the maker were legally incompetent, and a guardian who was friendly to the heirs were appointed, that guardian would have standing to challenge the trust. For example, the guardian could take the position that the maker was incompetent when he or she established the trust, in order to have the trust declared invalid. But even if we assume these favorable facts, the guardian would have to prove that the maker was incompetent at the time the trust was signed *and* that the challenge was in the best interest of the maker, not the relatives.[9]

After the death of the maker, "[t]he heirs . . . have no standing to set aside a revocable trust on grounds of lack of capacity or undue influence. Only the duly appointed personal representative has standing to bring suits on behalf of the decedent or regarding his assets."[10]

In almost all instances where a maker has created a living trust, the maker has also executed a pour-over will. The pour-over will is designed so that any property not titled in the name of the trust will pass to the living trust through probate. We discuss these special wills in Chapter 22, "The Pour-Over Will."

The executor named in the pour-over will has standing to challenge the trust. However, since the executor is customarily a trustee of the living trust, the likelihood of a challenge is extremely low. (We have yet to witness such a challenge in our total of forty years of experience.)

Under some circumstances, a pour-over will may designate heirs other than the beneficiaries named in the living trust. These heirs may have standing to attack the living trust.[11] This is a primary reason why it is not good practice to name any heirs in a pour-over will who are different from the beneficiaries in the living trust. Any gifts to specific beneficiaries should be included in the trust instrument itself, not in the will!

The longer a revocable living trust has been in existence, the more impervious it is to attack. If a living trust has been in existence for a period of time before the maker's death, it is exceedingly difficult for a court to find that the trust was invalid from its onset.[12] This is especially true if an "independent" trustee, such as a bank trust department, trust company, or a person who is not related to the maker, has been serving as a trustee of the maker's trust.

In a will contest, the court is facing a totally different set of circumstances. There is no operating history to overcome, just the clear-cut legal standards that have determined the validity of wills for centuries. The probate court has the easier task of applying these standards and then affirming or denying the validity of the will.

Legal Grounds to Challenge Wills or Living Trusts

Once standing is established, there has to be a legal reason to attack the validity of a will or a trust. There are several fertile areas where these attacks take place. Sometimes, the mental capacity of the maker to enter into the document is questioned. In other instances, there are questions as to whether or not the maker has been subject to undue influence or duress or has mistakenly signed the document. The technical formalities of drafting and signing the document can also be attacked.

Mental Capacity

In order for a legal instrument to be valid, a person must have the requisite mental capacity to understand the nature of that instrument. This is true of wills and trusts. However, the standard that is applied to mental capacity is not always the same for a will and for a trust.

The legal capacity to make a will varies from state to state, but the standards are relatively consistent. Generally, a person who makes a will has the legal capacity to do so "[i]f he knows his estate, the object of his affections, and to who [*sic*] he wishes to give his property, and understands the business in which he is engaged. . . ."[13]

The legal capacity required to create a valid trust is not as clear. According to a leading treatise on the law of trusts, "If an owner of property has capacity to make an effective conveyance of property, he has capacity to make an effective conveyance of his beneficial interest by declaring himself trustee of the property."[14] In other words, if a person can enter into a contract, he or she can create a trust. This standard generally requires a higher degree of legal capacity than that required for a will. However, states differ as to the legal capacity required to execute valid trusts; case law almost inevitably sets the standard in a particular state.[15]

The trend of state law is to equate the capacity to create revocable living trusts with the capacity to create a will.[16] The prevailing view is that the mental capacity required for a will and that for a trust are equivalent.

Undue Influence, Duress, and Mistake

There is no major distinction between setting aside wills or trusts on grounds of fraud, undue influence, duress, or mistake.[17] The execution of a will or a trust should be voluntary and based on an individual's wishes and desires. The longer a living trust has been in operation, the less likely it is that an attack on any of these grounds can be sustained. A trust maker who creates a living trust and places his or her property in it creates strong evidence that the trust is created according to his or her wishes. In contrast, a will is not put into use until the will maker is deceased. The courts are more likely to take a good, hard look at a contested will because they have a clean slate upon which to rule; there is no past history of actual operation to point to.

Legal Requirements for Execution of a Will

Any will that fails to conform substantially to the provisions of state statutes will be denied probate even though the denial may mean that the intentions of the will maker will not be fulfilled. This means that the will maker will be deemed to have died without a will.

Most people would agree that it is inequitable to deprive a will maker of his or her right to leave property the way he or she wished merely because there has been a technical violation of a formal will requirement. Yet the formalities required to validate wills have been developed over the centuries to protect their makers. The protection afforded by the law of wills can ultimately defeat its very purpose.

Some of the more important will formalities include a proper and sufficient signature by the maker, correct placement of that signature, publication to witnesses that the maker is indeed signing a will, capacity and qualifications of witnesses, and forms of revocation, whether intentional or not.[18]

There are many examples of these kinds of formalities. A person who makes a will in Florida must be careful to sign only at the end of the document. Signed anywhere else, the will is invalid. Some states require two witnesses, others three. The witnesses in some states can be takers under the will; in some states they cannot. In some jurisdictions the witnesses must sign in the presence of each other and the will maker; in others they need not.

The reason that a will is "executed" instead of signed is that a formal ceremony and procedure must be followed. If the formalities are not observed, the will is subject to invalidation.

One of the major reasons that trusts provide fewer legal grounds for attack is that they do not have to be executed with the same formalities as wills. In fact, a major legal encyclopedia states, "Development of the institution of the trust, and its great effectiveness in modern-day law, stems in large measure from the freedom from strict and formal requirements for its creation."[19]

Trusts are flexible in their application and use because they are not subject to the rigid rules imposed on wills. They are less vulnerable to attacks based on technicalities.

A trust can be valid, even if its maker does not use the formal words *trust* and *trustee*. For a valid trust to exist, its maker only needs to manifest an intent to create it.[20] And, as long as the trust is not for illegal purposes—like committing crimes or actions that are clearly against public policy—it will be valid.

Advocates of wills make the argument that courts protect will makers. Yet a noted authority, Professor Stanley M. Johanson, provides evidence suggesting that it is much more likely that a jury will substitute its intent for the maker's.[21] He says that *all* will contests arise in one of the following situations:

1. Where there is a second marriage and there are children by a first marriage
2. Where one child is favored over the other children
3. Where an individual has no close relatives
4. Where a nonconforming personal relation, such as a homosexual or heterosexual lover, is named in the will rather than family

If an individual faces any one of these situations, it is imperative that he or she plan with the utmost care to reduce or eliminate the possibility that the planning will be successfully attacked. Rather than rely on the courts for protection, the prudent client should use a living trust–centered plan to minimize the possibility of successful litigation.[22]

The Testamentary Nature of Trusts

Because living trusts are used to pass a maker's property to beneficiaries at the maker's death, they can be viewed as testamentary in nature. Testamentary dispositions have long been the exclusive domain of wills. Thus, living trusts have been attacked on the grounds that they were not executed in the manner specified by will statutes.

This argument is no longer valid. The modern rule of law is that where a maker creates a revocable living trust for a beneficiary but the beneficiary does not receive any interest in the trust until the death of the maker, the disposition is not testamentary.[23] Virtually all of the states have adopted statutes that generally shield revocable living trusts from attacks based on their testamentary nature.[24] In those jurisdictions where a question may remain, it appears that the trend of the courts is to uphold revocable living trusts as not being testamentary in nature.[25]

The Legal Doctrine of Merger

Another potential way to attack the validity of a living trust is to invoke the *Doctrine of Merger*. This rule states that "it is a fundamental essential of a trust that the legal estate be separated from the equitable estate or beneficial enjoyment; no trust relationship can exist where the legal title and the beneficial interest are both in the same person."[26] Under this general rule, the same person may be both a trustee and a beneficiary of a trust as long as there is not a complete identity of the trustee and the beneficiary.[27] This means that the trust maker should not be sole trustee of his or her own trust. It also means that a trust should provide for co-trustees when there is a sole lifetime beneficiary, and several lifetime beneficiaries when there is a sole trustee.[28]

Jurisdictions vary as to how they apply the Doctrine of Merger. An example of a trust successfully attacked on these grounds is a 1990 Ohio case.[29] In this case the court reluctantly held a revocable living trust to be void from its inception because the maker of the trust was the *sole* trustee and the *sole* lifetime beneficiary. In 1991, the Ohio legislature changed this law to the more modern view.

Most states have determined that the Doctrine of Merger

is an antiquated concept which is not in tune with modern times.

The Burden of Proof Required When Attacking a Will or a Trust

Who has the burden of proof in litigation is often a critical element that determines success or failure of the parties. The word *burden* in this time-honored legal phrase is no misnomer; it can truly be a burden to prove standing and specific requirements to commence an action much less meeting the legal burdens in the courtroom.

In a will contest, the person who introduces the will to the probate process generally has the burden of proving the will's valid execution and attestation.[30] The burden of proof may shift to anyone who contests the will once this burden is met. For example, the Uniform Probate Code mandates that the proponent of a will has the burden of establishing proof of proper execution. Only afterward do the contestants of a will have the burden of establishing lack of testamentary capacity, undue influence, fraud, duress, mistake, and revocation.[31]

The contestant of a living trust generally has the entire burden of proof. In this respect, attacking a trust is much like attacking a contract or a deed. This burden of proof makes it difficult for trust contestants to prevail.

The Confidentiality of Wills and Trusts

Revocable living trusts avoid probate, and the affairs they handle are not a matter of public record. The size, nature, composition, and so on, of a trust maker's estate are not available for general public scrutiny.

It is significantly more difficult for disgruntled heirs and other parties to attack a trust when its contents are not open for inspection. There is less incentive for avaricious heirs to attack a trust whose value cannot be ascertained. A noted practitioner writes:

> Contests may be avoided because inter vivos trusts are not subject to court supervision in Wyoming. There is no requirement for notifying heirs of the death of the trustor or of the commencement of post-mortem trust administration. Where the heirs are neither included in the trust nor located in the trustor's hometown, they may not hear of the trustor's death until the passage of time has barred a contest of the trust. In addition, a trust does not leave a broad trail in the public record and therefore may be more difficult to contest.[32]

Anyone who has ever played baseball knows that you cannot hit what you cannot see. The same is true for trusts. When a trust is created, its maker is not required to give notice of its existence to anyone. After the maker dies, the trustee only has to notify the trust's beneficiaries.

Challenges by dissatisfied heirs are reduced by the confidential nature of fully funded living trusts.[33] One cannot possibly overestimate the value of the confidential nature of trusts in protecting the intentions of their makers and the interests of their beneficiaries. The privacy that is endemic to a trust gives it overwhelming advantages over the traditional will-planning/probate alternative.

Limitation Periods for Contesting Wills and Trusts

Will-planning/probate does enjoy one potential advantage over a trust in terms of litigation. A person who decides to commence a will contest generally has less time to bring an action than a person who challenges a living trust. The period for contesting a will is typically less than a year. Depending on circumstances, the period for contesting a trust may extend up to several years.[34]

Because will statutes reduce the time within which a contest can be brought, the argument can be made that litigation is reduced. The opposite argument can be used against living trusts. However, all of the evidence is directly to the contrary: there are substantially fewer trust contests than will contests. Having more time to bring a lawsuit cannot make the facts of the case any better or create necessary legal standing.

The passage of time between the existence of the trust and the commencement of any lawsuit can work to the disadvantage of the plaintiff. Our law has a concept known as the *doctrine of laches*. This doctrine provides that it is inequitable to allow a lawsuit to be initiated if the plaintiff has waited too long. Laches may apply to trust litigation when a potential contestant has knowledge of a trust but takes too much time in bringing a lawsuit. This is particularly true if the contestant has accepted benefits from the trust.[35]

Our Conclusion

Will-planning/probate encourages litigation. Living trust–centered planning gives more assurance that planning efforts will be free of litigation.

· 8 ·

Protection from Creditors

Questions for Discussion

- How does the probate process limit the claims of a decedent's creditors?
- Does the living trust limit the claims of a trust maker's creditors?
- How relevant is limiting the claims of after-death creditors to estate planning?

One of the principal purposes of the probate process is to ensure that a decedent's debts are properly paid. Many states dispense with administration when an estate is insolvent or when the value of the estate is less than the amount that is exempt from creditors' claims. Some states permit heirs to bypass administration if they purchase a bond to assure the payment of a decedent's debts or expressly agree to assume the liability for these debts.

In probate, creditors have only a short time to submit their claims under certain laws, known as *nonclaim statutes*. After this period has expired, the decedent's creditors, with a few notable exceptions, are forever barred from making additional claims. The decedent's assets can then pass to heirs without being subject to any future claims.

Will-planning/probate advocates maintain that assets in

living trusts do not enjoy this advantage, because they are not subject to the probate process and are therefore not protected by its shorter claims period. Probate advocates state that this longer claims period unnecessarily prolongs exposure of the trust maker's assets to creditors.

The effectiveness and scope of probate nonclaim statutes are not as comprehensive as probate advocates would lead one to believe, and there is strong evidence that suggests that these statutes are not relied upon by creditors.

How the Probate Process Cuts Off the Claims of the Decedent's Creditors

Creditors can be secured or unsecured. *Secured creditors* have a mortgage or a lien in specific property and are protected up to the value of that property. A lender who has a mortgage on a house, for example, is a secured creditor. The death of the debtor does not affect this secured right. Secured creditors are unsecured to the extent that the amount of their debt exceeds the value of the secured property.

Unsecured creditors rely on the general assets of the debtor for the payment of their debts. Examples of unsecured creditors are credit card companies and service providers such as doctors and hospitals, who extend credit without taking a mortgage to secure the loan. Probate nonclaim statutes only cut off the claims of unsecured creditors, not secured creditors.

Nonclaim Statutes

Almost all state probate codes contain nonclaim statutes that require unsecured creditors to file claims against an estate within a specific period.[1] Claims not filed within these time periods are generally cut off as "untimely." Nonclaim statutes help assure heirs that when they receive their inheritance, it will be free from subsequent claims of the decedent's unsecured creditors.

There are two types of nonclaim statutes, *short-term* statutes and *long-term* statutes. Short-term statutes run for a short period, generally two to six months from the time probate is initiated. Long-term statutes run for longer periods, generally two to five years after the decedent's death.[2] Most states have both types of statutes.

Short-term statutes only apply to probate property. If probate proceedings are not commenced because the decedent's assets pass to the family or other heirs through joint tenancy, beneficiary designations, or a living trust, then the shorter period for probate claims is not triggered. However, claims are still eventually prohibited after the longer statutory period has expired.

The Effectiveness and Scope of Nonclaim Statutes

In the past, creditors were given notice of a decedent's death by publication in a newspaper. The publication of notice was the event that activated the commencement of the short-term time period in the probate statutes.

The effectiveness and scope of traditional probate nonclaim statutes were eroded in a 1988 U.S. Supreme Court case. In this case, the Supreme Court held that if a creditor's identity is known or is reasonably ascertainable by the executor of an estate, the due process clause of the United States Constitution requires that the executor give actual notice directly to the creditor by mail or other means.[3]

Mere publication in a newspaper is no longer effective in cutting off the claims of most creditors in a probate estate. As a result of this Supreme Court case, publication is now only sufficient for those creditors who have "conjectural claims."[4] Conjectural claims are generally claims that are not known at the time of the decedent's death.

Short-term probate statutes do not necessarily prevent the claims of all creditors. In some states, these statutes only protect the executor from late claims if distributions or payments have been made from the estate. However, heirs are not protected. Creditors can assert their claims against the heirs as long as their claims are made within the time specified in the long-term creditor statutes.[5]

Probate notice procedures sometimes may not be effective against certain types of creditors. For example, out-of-state creditors and some government agencies may have longer periods in which to file their claims. In addition, some types of claims, such as personal injury lawsuits, that arise after a decedent's death can be asserted for a longer period after death.[6]

Probate advocates frequently state that these short-term creditor statutes are very important for the protection of the estate's heirs. Their argument is essentially that a creditor is forever prohibited from making a claim if he or she does not file the claim within the statutory period. Probate advocates believe that these short-term statutes justify probate.

Short-term probate statutes are no longer as important as they have been, because of the Supreme Court's requirement that known creditors be given actual notice of a decedent's death. The fact that some state statutes do not cut off the claims of potentially important creditors and claims also weakens the creditor protection argument of probate advocates. Short-term creditor statutes are not ironclad bastions of protection from the claims of the decedent's creditors. And these short-term creditor statutes only shorten the time in which claims can be made; they do not cut off those claims that are promptly filed.

While living trusts generally cannot take advantage of these short-term creditor statutes, there is a technique that allows living trusts to have whatever advantages may be derived from these short-term creditor statutes. Living trust practitioners use a simple method to secure the benefits of the short-term probate statutes. They open a probate consisting of a minor amount of cash or property, through the use of a pour-over will. The pour-over does not control the bulk of the trust maker's property.

During this "nominal" probate, creditors are given proper statutory notice under the short-term probate statute. All creditors are paid, first with probate assets and then with assets held in the decedent's trust. Trust attorneys then take the position that proper creditor notice was given and that the creditors had access to both the probate property and the property held in the living trust. They use this technique to cut off the claims of creditors who submit claims after the short-term statutory period. Whether this technique will be effective or not depends on the particular jurisdiction and the applicable state statutes.[7] It is a commonly used and accepted practice in a great many jurisdictions.

Creditors' Claims Against the
Assets of a Revocable Living Trust

Trust makers, while they are alive, cannot create living trusts for their own benefit to avoid their creditors.[8] Creating a living trust for such a purpose violates public policy. However, on the death of the trust maker, creditors have little authority to assert claims against the assets in the maker's living trust.[9] In fact, in a great number of states a revocable living trust can offer considerable protection against a decedent's creditors.

A fundamental reason that creditors of a deceased trust maker have few, if any, rights to living trust property is the nature of the power to revoke a living trust. In 1880, the Supreme Court held that a power to revoke a legal instrument "is not an interest which can be transferred to another, or sold on execution."[10]

The *Restatement (Second) of Trusts* makes the meaning of the court's statement clear:

> Unless it is otherwise provided by statute a power of revocation reserved by the settlor cannot be reached by his creditors. If he revokes the trust and recovers the trust property, the creditors can reach the property; but they cannot compel him to revoke the trust for their benefit.[11]

Since the power to revoke is personal to the trust maker, it terminates on his or her death. Absent a statute or case law to the contrary, the creditors of living trust makers cannot reach the assets in their trusts after death.[12]

The ability of a living trust to cut off the claims of creditors is very strong. A 1987 article in the prestigious *Real Property,*

Probate and Trust Journal concluded that there are few laws that would allow a creditor of a decedent who had created a revocable living trust to obtain payment from assets held in the trust.[13]

This may seem unfair to creditors, but it is the law in most states. However, the statutes or case law of some states do provide that a trust maker's creditors may reach assets in a living trust after the death of the trust maker in certain circumstances. States in which even general, unsecured creditors may have access to trust assets are California, Massachusetts, Michigan, New Jersey, New York, and Oregon.[14] The statutes and cases that allow creditors access to living trust assets usually require that assets in a decedent's probate estate must be exhausted before trust assets can be used. This requirement that creditor claims be first paid from property that is subject to probate is an attempt to balance the rights of the beneficiaries with the rights of creditors.

There has been some erosion over the last several years in the strict rule that a trust maker's creditors are cut off after the maker's death.[15] However, there does not seem to be any significant trend by the states to embrace the concept that creditors can assert claims against a living trust after its maker's death.[16] The fact remains that in a great majority of states a living trust is far more effective in cutting off claims of creditors than probate statutes.

Do Creditors Have Rights Against the Abuse of Living Trusts?

If a maker creates a living trust with the specific intent of avoiding creditors, there are methods that allow creditors to set aside the trust for purposes of collecting their debts during the trust maker's life and after he or she has died.

Creditors can reach trust property if they can prove that the transfer was intended to "hinder, delay, or defraud creditors."[17] While proving intent is not always an easy task, the remedy exists and can be an effective tool in egregious cases.[18]

Nonclaim Statutes and the Living Trust

Most states also have statutes of limitations that apply to property that does not pass through probate. The periods in which creditors can assert claims under these statutes are longer in duration than those of the short-term probate statutes.

When probate advocates proclaim probate's superiority in protecting the estate against creditors, they are merely stating that creditors have a shorter period in which to file their claims. In those states where a living trust does not absolutely cut off the claims of a maker's creditors, the longer nonprobate claim periods still apply. Claims of a decedent's creditors are cut off under both types of statute. The nonprobate creditor statute just allows creditors a longer time in which to submit their claims.

As mentioned earlier in this chapter, it is possible to open up a nominal probate in a living trust—centered plan in order to take advantage of the short-term creditor statutes. This is an inconvenience, but it appears to be effective. While this process does not avoid probate, it limits its effect to only a minor amount of assets.

A trustee of a fully funded living trust ought to be able to give the same statutory short-term notice to creditors as an executor without the necessity to open a probate. It seems clear that the same public interest would be served whether an executor or a trustee gave notice under a short-term creditor statute. This notice would offer the same protection to creditors and to beneficiaries and could be given in the exact same manner called for in the short-term probate statute.

In at least two states, Missouri and California, a trustee can give statutory notice in virtually the same manner as an executor and assure the cutting off of creditors.[19] Given the proliferation of revocable living trusts and the trend shown by the Missouri and California statutes we expect to see similar statutes enacted in other states.

The Importance of Cutting Off the Claims of Creditors

There is a clear moral issue that permeates the whole notion of living trusts' cutting off creditors' claims. Probate nonclaim statutes are designed to satisfy claims of creditors in an expeditious manner. They limit the time in which creditors can file claims to accomplish this objective. Living trusts, on the other hand, can eliminate the claims of most creditors at the death of the trust maker, in most circumstances.[20]

In an article in the *Harvard Law Review*, Professor John H. Langbein makes the observation that creditors rarely rely on the probate process to satisfy claims.[21] He concludes, "In the late twentieth century, creditor protection and probate have largely parted company."[22] He also states that most executors and heirs pay the decedent's debts in a timely manner and that it is a matter of honor and morality that compels them to do so. He identifies a revolution in probate avoidance. He observes that vast amounts of property pass outside the probate process every year. These "nonprobate" assets include joint tenancy, beneficiary designations, and living trusts. Langbein sees a permanent shift to probate avoidance and a significant increase in the use of nonprobate assets.

His conclusion about creditors is an interesting one. He states that creditors are a powerful force in the United States and would initiate a major outcry if they were not being paid. Langbein finds little, if any, evidence that large commercial creditors such as retailers have made any attempt to control nonprobate assets. His observations are certainly true in our experience and that of our colleagues. The logical conclusion to be drawn is that creditors are being paid without the aid of an antiquated probate process.

This trend away from probate as a protection for creditors is not a recent phenomenon. It is, in fact, a well-established trend, although it has received little fanfare. The research of Professor Richard V. Wellman in urging the adoption of the Uniform Probate Code shows that the trend documented by Professor Langbein has been in existence for at least twenty years.[23]

Many current probate statutes are a continuation of long-standing laws developed in the nineteenth or early twentieth century. Unfortunately, these laws fail to take into account changes in economics and technology and are simply outdated. They do not expedite the passing of property to heirs: they only make the process unnecessarily lengthy, complex, and expensive.

The only real application of short-term probate statutes is for creditors who appear after the claims period expires. Only in a minuscule number of estates is there the possibility that an unknown creditor will turn up months or years after the decedent's death. This possibility usually occurs in professional malpractice or negligence claims. For doctors, lawyers, engineers, and other professionals who may have an undiscovered claim against them at death, there is the possibility of an after-death lawsuit. These claims are rare.

More importantly, they are almost invariably incidents for which the decedent was insured. Most professionals carry some form of liability insurance for just such claims. Generally, this malpractice insurance survives even the death of the professional.

Assuming that there might be after-death liability for a professional who is not covered by insurance, a nominal probate can be created so that statutory notice can be given under the short-term probate statute.

Our Conclusion

Living trust–centered estate planning is more effective for after-death creditor planning than is will-planning/probate planning.

∘ 9 ∘

Conflicts of Law

Questions for Discussion

- What state's laws will be used to determine the validity, legal meaning, and effect of wills and living trusts for decedents who lived in more than one state or who owned property in more than one state?
- Do the location and title to property affect how it will be treated?
- If one state has better laws than another, can those laws be used by someone who is domiciled elsewhere?
- Does a living trust work better for interstate planning than will-planning/probate?

People who own property in another state or who move to another state after their estate plans are in place must understand how each state's laws affect their estate planning. Which state's law governs their will? Which state's law governs their trust? Do the location and title to property affect how it will be treated?

These questions of which state's laws apply are known as *conflicts of laws* in legal terminology. The answers to these conflicts of law questions depend on many factors, not the least of which is what kind of planning is being used. Most lawyers and their clients fail to address these questions. Yet they have a significant impact on what kind of estate plan should ultimately be established.

Conflicts of laws can be more easily anticipated and resolved by using revocable living trusts. Revocable living trusts often can be used to "borrow" the more favorable laws of another jurisdiction. In this chapter, we explore a living trust's advantages in avoiding conflicts of laws and in facilitating interstate planning.

Conflicts of Laws and Wills

At the outset, it is important to understand that there are two types of property with which conflicts of laws for wills and trusts are concerned. The first is personal property, which is essentially all property except real property. Real property consists of land or buildings attached to the land.

The after-death disposition of personal property has been historically determined by the laws of the state in which the will maker is "domiciled."[1] The word *domicile* has a very specific meaning. It does not necessarily mean where a person resides or lives. A person's domicile is his or her *legal* home. Every person has a domicile, but reaching a legal determination of where that domicile is is not always easy. While a complete discussion of domicile is outside the scope of this book, domicile generally depends on where a person is located and his or her intent to remain there permanently.[2] A person's intent is very difficult to ascertain at times, and litigation over intent and domicile is fairly common.[3]

One of the areas in which domicile plays a large part in conflicts of law is determining the validity of a will. A basic requirement for a valid will is that the will maker possessed the legal capacity to sign it. But if a person has moved from state to state with the same will or if a person owns real property in more than one state, which state's laws determine the validity of a will?

The law of the state in which the person is domiciled at death is used to determine whether the will maker had the capacity to leave *real property* in that state.[4] If the maker owned property in more than one state, the maker's capacity to make a will to dispose of real property is determined by the law of the state where the real property is located. The law of the person's domicile is always used to determine whether the will maker had the capacity to leave *personal property* regardless of where the personal property is located.

Let's assume that a person in state A has a will which is valid in state A. Let's further assume that this person owns real property in state B, which has different signing formalities for a will than does state A. The will that is valid in state A may well be invalid in state B. If it is not valid in state B, the property in state B will pass under state B's intestacy laws.

The same issues hold true if our will maker makes a will in state A while domiciled there but later establishes domicile in state B without modifying his will. While state B may find that the will is technically valid because it was valid in state A, state B will use its own laws to interpret the terms of the state A will. It may be that state B's laws will interpret the will in such a manner as to change its effect.

Conflicts of laws issues raise problems that provide a fertile ground for initiating litigation. For example, let's say that heirs have been left out of a will. If these disgruntled heirs could convince a court to invalidate the will, they could inherit under the laws of intestacy. If the will maker owned real estate in more than one state or made a will in a state that was different from the will maker's state of domicile when he or she died, the heirs would stand a greater chance of invalidating the will because they could bring a will contest in each state in which the will maker owned real property.

In order to alleviate the inequitable results of different states' applying their laws to the same will and to reduce litigation, most states have attempted to make changes in their laws to reduce the chance that a will which is valid in one jurisdiction may be invalidated in another. There are now at least seven different statutory methods that states use to determine the formal validity of wills.[5] These statutes make it more likely that a will written in another jurisdiction will be found to be valid in the local jurisdiction. However, the interpretation of a will's terms and the legal capacity of its maker to make the will still depends on what kind of property is involved and where it is located. It is likely that these different types of statutes have made the law even more complex!

Any person who is mobile or who has real property in several states is a candidate for conflicts of laws litigation. Conflicts of laws issues arise if a person moves to a different state without changing his or her will to comply with the new state's laws. These situations make it particularly easy for aggrieved heirs to search for the most favorable jurisdictions in which to bring their lawsuits. It is therefore important to avoid these conflicts of laws problems.

Conflicts of Laws and Trusts

If a trust owns real property, the state in which the real property is located will use its law to determine a trust's validity.[6] For purposes of personal property, the validity of a trust is determined by the laws of the state where the trust is being administered or where the maker was domiciled at the time the trust was signed unless the trust maker left instructions to the contrary in his or her trust. Although these rules resemble the rules for determining the validity of wills, there are substantial differences.

In disposing of personal property, a trust maker can name which state's laws govern the validity of the trust instrument as long as the state chosen has a substantial relation to the trust.[7] For example, the state of the trust maker's domicile can be chosen, the state in which the trustee is domiciled can be chosen, or the state where the trust assets were located when the trust was created can be chosen.

There are no restrictions on the choice of law for the administration or construction of the terms of a trust that holds personal property; for these purposes, the maker can choose *any* jurisdiction's law.[8]

The trust instrument can name the law of the jurisdiction used to construe the terms of the trust; those laws must then be followed by the court that has jurisdiction over the trust, regardless of where the property is located.

> *Kathy Johnson is originally domiciled in state A and has her living trust drawn there. Her trust specifies that it is to be interpreted under the laws of state Z, where her trustee is located.*

> *Kathy later moves to state B. She owns real property in states C, D, and E. Kathy's trust will be administered according to the laws of state Z, as directed in her trust.*

Trust law does not vary as much from jurisdiction to jurisdiction as will law does. The flexibility in choosing which state's laws govern a trust makes it ideal for an individual who has property in several states or who wants certainty in how the provisions of his or her trust will be interpreted and construed. It also allows an individual to adopt those laws of another jurisdiction which may be more favorable in terms of carrying out his or her estate planning desires.

> *Dorothy McWilliams does not want to leave her husband, Fred, any more of her estate than she has to. She lives in state A; state A is a Uniform Probate Code state, so its laws provide that Fred is entitled to 50 percent of Dorothy's property. Its laws also provide that she cannot defeat his right to inherit her property by either a will or a trust drawn under the laws of that state.*

> *Dorothy has her attorney create a living trust that leaves her personal property, including all of her investments and cash, entirely to her children. Dorothy's attorney names a bank in state B as the trustee and makes sure the bank manages all of the property.*

> *State B's laws provide that trust property is not subject to the statutory claims of a spouse. Dorothy's trust provides that state B's laws must be used to interpret her trust.*

> *On Dorothy's death, state B's laws will control the disposition of the personal property in her trust. Her husband will not be able to invoke state A's law in overriding state B's law.*

By using this procedure, Dorothy can defeat her state's laws that allow Fred to take 50 percent of her property, but only as to her personal property. Fred is still entitled to 50 percent of any real property that Dorothy owns in state A. However, Dorothy has been able to meet her objectives with all her property except her real property in state A.[9]

This is only one example of how a living trust can be used to adopt the laws of other states. Because of the consistency of trust law throughout the United States and the portability of living trusts, they are much more suited to our mobile society than wills.

Our Conclusion

There are fewer conflicts of law with living trusts because the rules for determining their validity, interpretation, and construction are more liberal than those for wills.

· 10 ·

Medicaid Planning

Questions for Discussion

- What are the general requirements for qualifying for Medicaid nursing home care?
- How can a testamentary trust be used to help a surviving spouse qualify for Medicaid?
- Can a revocable living trust be designed to provide the same advantages as a testamentary trust?

Nursing home care has become prohibitively expensive for all but the wealthy, and Medicaid is the only significant government program that pays for nursing home care. However, only those citizens with low incomes and low net worth are eligible.

Most elderly individuals are interested in taking advantage of all of the governmental benefits for which they can legitimately qualify. Under current Medicaid rules, a testamentary trust by a spouse for the benefit of the other spouse is one of the few types of trust that will not disqualify the survivor from Medicaid.

Will-planning/probate advocates claim that this Medicaid advantage for testamentary trusts bolsters their case for will-planning/probate over living trust planning. A brief review of Medicaid rules will help to explain this advantage and how skillful living trust planning can potentially be used to achieve the same planning result.

Summary of
Medicaid Eligibility Requirements

Medicaid is a federally and state-funded program that provides, among other benefits, medical assistance to aged individuals "whose income and resources are insufficient to meet the costs of necessary medical services. . . ."[1] Medical services include nursing home care for persons over age sixty-five under some programs elected by a number of states.

Americans are living much longer because of scientific advances. A longer life span means that long-term care is needed more than ever before. Unfortunately, the cost of this care is high. Figures for the cost of skilled nursing care vary, of course, but the average yearly cost for 1991 ranged from $25,000 to $48,000.[2]

For an individual to qualify for Medicaid, indigence, or near-indigence, is required. Federal law mandates that to receive federal funding each state must have a medical assistance plan that determines eligibility on the basis of the income and resources that are available to the applicant.[3] A married couple is looked upon as a single economic unit for purposes of determining eligibility.

Special rules apply in determining assets and income for elderly persons seeking payment for nursing home care. A single person who is seeking nursing home benefits is generally allowed to retain only the following exempted assets in order to qualify for Medicaid:

- A home
- A total of $2,000 in cash
- A prepaid funeral
- A burial account of up to $2,500
- Term life insurance
- A limited amount of whole life insurance[4]

When a married person seeks Medicaid benefits for nursing home care and has a spouse who does not require nursing home care, a more complex evaluation is made of the assets of the couple to determine eligibility. The *institutionalized spouse,* the one seeking Medicaid benefits, is permitted to retain the same exempt assets that are allowed to a single person. The allowed amount for the *community spouse,* the spouse not seeking benefits, is larger than that allowed the institutionalized spouse to prevent the impoverishment of the community spouse.

After the exempt assets are allocated to the institutionalized spouse, the values of the couple's nonexempt joint and separate property are added together. To retain eligibility for the institutionalized spouse, the community spouse is allowed to have some of this property and still have the institutionalized spouse qualify for Medicaid. Each state sets what this community spouse allowed amount is, but the federal Medicaid law gives limits as to what a state can require. For 1991, no state can set a lower limit for allowed community spouse assets of less than $13,296 or a higher limit than $66,480.

During a specified period during the Medicaid application process, either spouse may transfer assets to the other (but not to anyone else) to divide property to meet Medicaid standards. After the assets have been rearranged to give each spouse his or her allowed amount, eligibility is determined. If the assets of either spouse exceed the allowed amount, then this excess amount must be spent on nursing home care before the institutionalized spouse will be eligible for Medicaid benefits.

Medicaid law also places limitations on income which vary from state to state. To be eligible for Medicaid, federal law mandates that the institutionalized spouse cannot have monthly income in excess of the monthly cost of the nursing home, although states can require lesser amounts. Specifying a lesser amount saves the state money because fewer people qualify for Medicaid benefits.

All income received by an institutionalized spouse is taken by the state to defray the costs of the nursing home care, after certain allowances are taken into account. Additional income may be allocated to the community spouse if needed to raise the income of the community spouse to the minimum level. The community spouse can keep all income paid to him or her individually and one-half of joint income.

This summary is not meant to present a definitive survey of Medicaid, but to describe just how little net worth and income one must have to qualify for Medicaid. If a person has more assets or income than Medicaid allows, he or she either has to use personal assets and income to pay for a nursing home or find a way to qualify for Medicaid without consuming those assets and income.

Lifetime Medicaid Planning

Most people do not want to lose virtually all of their assets and income in paying for a nursing home until they are poor enough to qualify for Medicaid. They are interested in exploring methods to protect assets and income from the high cost of nursing home care by qualifying for Medicaid. One solution that people commonly try is to give their assets to close family members. Giving away everything one owns means total loss of control over those assets. Unfortunately, once assets are given away, there is no assurance of what will happen to them. And if family members use them for the individual's benefit, these gifts can disqualify the recipient from Medicaid.

There are also federal and state gift tax ramifications.[5] The federal gift tax annual exclusion and the unified credit exemption equivalent may or may not be obstacles in making these gifts.

Sometimes, elderly people attempt to use irrevocable trusts to qualify for Medicaid and still control their property. These trusts are very limited in their use. The complex eligibility rules of Medicaid make it extremely difficult for the irrevocable trust maker and his or her spouse to have access to the principal or income of these trusts and still maintain Medicaid eligibility.

Only assets of irrevocable trusts that do not allow any distributions of trust assets to the Medicaid recipient and his or her spouse are not counted for Medicaid eligibility.[6] Limited amounts of income can be taken from these trusts by a recipient and his or her spouse, but it is very easy for the income taken to be considered income in terms of Medicaid eligibility.[7] There are also potential adverse federal and state gift tax ramifications of these trusts.[8] The irrevocable trusts cannot be effectively used by many people and should only be drafted by knowledgeable attorneys.

The government has a thirty month ineligibility period to discourage people from transferring assets in order to qualify for Medicaid. If assets are transferred by either spouse to someone other than a spouse for less than fair market value within thirty months of either applying for Medicaid or entering a nursing home facility, the presumption is that the transfer was made to obtain Medicaid eligibility, and immediate benefits are not available.[9] The thirty-month rule applies unless it can be proved that the transfer was not for purposes of Medicaid eligibility or that the transfer was to another person for the benefit of the spouse.[10] But if a transfer is for the benefit of a spouse, the rules limiting the assets he or she can have then come into play, creating yet another Medicaid qualification obstacle.

It is clear that little lifetime planning can be accomplished for purposes of Medicaid eligibility. Any planning that can be done involves giving away property with little or no hope of ever getting it back. For most people, the purchase of long-term health care insurance may well be a better solution.

There is more to Medicaid planning than the issue of qualification. A more important question has to be addressed. Does a person want to be subject to state support while living in an institution? Medicaid eligibility means that an individual is essentially at the mercy of state and federal agencies to determine the facilities offered and the minimum standard of care that will be provided. Amounts allotted to an individual for nursing home care are approved by governmental agencies that may be more concerned with budgetary constraints than with the quality of the care.

Use of a Testamentary Trust in Medicaid Planning for a Surviving Spouse

A testamentary trust for the benefit of a surviving spouse can take advantage of Medicaid benefits:

John and Mary are married. The majority of their assets are in John's name. John cannot qualify for Medicaid because of the value of his assets.

John's will places his property in trust for Mary after his death. This trust is called a testamentary trust. John's trust for Mary instructs John's trustee to care for Mary's health, support, and maintenance at the trustee's sole discretion.

On John's death the testamentary trust comes into effect. The money and property in John's trust for Mary do not disqualify her from receiving Medicaid assistance. The money and property in the trust are not counted as assets that are available to her under the Medicaid statutes.

Why this exception has been carved out is anybody's guess. One possible explanation is that assets that pass into a testamentary trust are subject to probate. Under the Medicaid statute, authorities have the right to assess Medicaid claims against an individual's estate if there are any remaining assets at his or her death.[11] The probate process offers a convenient forum to collect Medicaid claims out of undiscovered or later-acquired assets. And, of course, any amount collected in the probate process reduces the amount passing into the surviving spouse's trust.

For this technique to work, a testamentary trust for the surviving spouse's benefit must be discretionary. However, the trust can only be used to supplement Medicaid payments and cannot be used to distribute substantial income to the surviving spouse.

If a testamentary trust is designed to keep a spouse's income at reduced levels, then the federal estate tax unlimited marital deduction may be lost! To qualify for the marital deduction, the surviving spouse must receive *all* of the income from the trust annually for life.[12]

In order to qualify under the Medicaid income limitations,

the trustee may have to disqualify the trust for the unlimited marital deduction. This is a "damned if you do and damned if you don't" decision.

For those individuals whose estates are less than $600,000, this federal estate tax marital deduction may not be a concern. The unified credit exemption equivalent amount of $600,000 can be used in lieu of the unlimited marital deduction to shelter the amount left in trust for the surviving spouse.

With testamentary trust planning, there is a hiatus between the time a probate is instituted and the time that any trusts created under the will can be funded with a decedent's property. During this period, it is quite possible that Medicaid rules will determine that the property is not in trust and that it is therefore subject to Medicaid's asset and income requirements.

A Fully Funded Trust in Medicaid Planning for a Surviving Spouse

A living trust may be used to derive the same benefits as a testamentary trust for Medicaid purposes. The Medicaid testamentary trust exception does not appear to put any restrictions on how the trust is funded.[13] Therefore, it might be prudent to create a testamentary trust that can be funded by a "pour-over living trust" that will leave its assets directly to the testamentary trust. It appears from a close reading of the Medicaid statute that a pour-over living trust technique would work. Under this planning method, the living trust assets would not go through probate.

This technique can be analogized to a life insurance policy

naming a testamentary trust as its beneficiary. Just like life insurance proceeds, the living trust property is not subject to probate.

We do not recommend this technique in every estate plan. Under current Medicaid rules, a spouse's testamentary trust can own a large amount of assets. Only trust principal or income that is paid or used for the benefit of the spouse will be considered for purposes of determining eligibility. The problem is that the trustee must severely limit the trust income available to the spouse in order to qualify for Medicaid. When eligibility is desired, the trustee must restrict total monthly income so that *total* income from all sources does not exceed eligibility levels, which are from $900 to $2,000 depending on the state. To remain qualified, the spouse can receive few benefits from the trust and must rely almost totally on the state for his or her care. In a nursing home, any income received must be applied to the nursing home bill. The spouse is only allowed to keep a personal needs allowance that runs from $30 to $70 monthly, and certain other small allowances. Any payments by the trustee on the spouse's behalf, such as payments to outside physicians, would be counted as income and could disqualify the person from receiving benefits.

The primary advantage of such a trust is that the spouse would have the option to leave state care and return to private care if that should be desired. Whether a testamentary trust should be created depends on many factors, including age, health, and individual priorities. The possibility of using a living trust–funded testamentary trust to take advantage of Medicaid is something that should be considered in the estate plan but not necessarily implemented. A more efficient use of assets might well be purchase of long-term care health insurance policies. Even when using this technique or when using a will with a testamentary trust, few real benefits can be provided to a spouse without disqualifying the spouse for Medicaid.

Our Conclusion

A testamentary trust can potentially qualify a surviving spouse for Medicaid payments. A revocable living trust cannot.

· 11 ·

General Lifetime Consequences of Funding a Living Trust

Questions for Discussion

- Do people have to change the way they transact their affairs if they have a living trust?
- Does a living trust create income tax difficulties during the life of the trust maker?
- Is it difficult to fund a living trust?

A revocable living trust has no adverse income tax ramifications during its maker's life. Transferring property into a living trust is not a difficult task. The so-called difficulty in funding a living trust is considered to be one of its primary disadvantages. This criticism is not warranted. In fact, fully funding a living trust is one of its greatest advantages!

The Federal Income Tax Ramifications of Creating and Funding a Living Trust

The rules governing the income tax ramifications of revocable living trusts are found in the grantor trust rules of the Internal Revenue Code.[1] Generally, a *grantor trust* is any trust whose income is taxed to its maker because he or she is considered to have control over the trust or certain rights in it.

The maker of a living trust has so much control over the trust and the property in it that the trust is not a separate taxable entity. Trust makers are responsible for all the income, deductions, and credits which trust property generates.[2] In essence, a revocable living trust and its maker are one and the same for the purposes of federal income tax.

If the trust maker is the sole trustee or a co-trustee of the trust, all of the income, deductions, and credits generated by the trust property are reported on the maker's personal income tax return.[3] The maker's social security number is used as the federal taxpayer identification number of the trust.[4]

If the trust maker is not a trustee, a separate taxpayer identification number must be obtained for the trust, but the maker still reports all income, deductions, and credits on his or her personal income tax return. In this case, the trust is required to file an information return. A revocable living trust does not become a separate taxable entity until the death of its maker.[5]

Living trusts do not change the financial lives of their makers, nor do they appreciably affect their bookkeeping and accounting responsibilities.

The Real and Perceived Difficulties of Funding a Living Trust

Funding a living trust is necessary for avoiding financial guardianship proceedings and probate. An unfunded trust, while still having many advantages over will-planning/probate, does not guarantee that a financial guardianship and probate will be avoided.[6]

A living trust can own virtually any type of property. One of the most noted experts in trust law states, "While the most common types of property held in trust are bonds, stocks, mortgages, titles to land, and bank accounts, any transferable interest, vested or contingent, legal or equitable, real or personal, tangible or intangible, may be held in trust."[7] Except for specific legal or tax restrictions to the contrary, all property interests can be held in a trust.

Despite the fact that a trust can hold any type of property interest, living trust critics have focused on the process of funding the trust as a significant drawback to using a living trust. The reasons for this criticism include expense, the complications that occur in the operation of a trust, and the failure of trust makers to continue to fund their trusts on an ongoing basis.

General Funding Principles

Every type of property has distinct rules for transferring its title. As a rule of thumb, the same form of document by which the property was received by the trust maker should be used to transfer the property to the living trust.

Deeds are used to transfer real property into living trusts. Bills of sale are used for transferring personal effects. Assignments are commonly used to transfer intangible personal property, such as partnership interests and non–publicly traded stocks into living trusts. Publicly traded stocks and bonds are endorsed to trusts, and new certificates are generated in the name of the trust. Change of beneficiary forms are used to name trusts as beneficiaries of life insurance and employee benefits. For vehicles, boats, brands for livestock, and other property interests that have special types of ownership, the title is changed by complying with local statutes.

Because a revocable living trust is not a separate income tax entity, and because it is the alter ego of its maker, most state and local governments exempt the transfer of the maker's property into his or her trust from sales and use taxes. The same is true of documentary stamps required for the transfer of real estate. However, it is not unusual for filing and administrative fees to be required, but these are usually minimal. For example, the fee to record a deed may be a few dollars per page. The cost to change title to a car may be a $10.00 title fee. Generally, the fees that are required do not exceed a few dollars.

Sometimes, questions arise as to what should be done with the maker's indebtedness on the assets that are transferred to a living trust. There is no need to transfer a trust maker's debt, or debt instruments, into a living trust. During the maker's life, he or she will remain liable for the debt. A living trust does not relieve the trust maker from his or her debt while he or she is living.[8]

While it is possible for a living trust to cut off the claims of unsecured creditors after the death of the maker, it is both usual and ordinary for the trustee to pay these creditors from trust property.[9] Because unsecured creditors are paid even when assets do not pass through probate, they do not object to the transferring of their debtors' assets into fully funded living trusts. There is no requirement that a trust maker notify his or her unsecured creditors of the transfers.

The transfer of encumbered property to a living trust may present some initial practical problems. However, these problems are usually unfounded and arise from a creditor's lack of understanding of the transaction and living trusts in general. Many secured creditors confuse revocable living trusts with irrevocable living trusts. These trusts are as different as cars and boats. Secured creditors sometimes initially object to the transferring process until they understand that their rights are not weakened by the transfers in any way.

The law is clear that the debt on secured property follows the property, no matter to whom or where the property is transferred. A secured creditor cannot lose rights in the property when it is titled in the name of a living trust. The existence and funding of a living trust do not, in any way, adversely affect the rights of secured or unsecured creditors.

Many mortgages contain "due-on-sale" clauses that accelerate payment if the property subject to the mortgage is sold or otherwise transferred. Whether or not the transfer of mortgaged property to a living trust will trigger a due-on-sale clause is generally governed by the terms of the mortgage. If the mortgage is not clear one way or another, since the transfer of property to a living trust is not a transfer to an independent entity, it is likely that the mortgage's due-on-sale clause will not be triggered.[10] In any event, knowledgeable lenders usually waive their rights under a due-on-sale clause when the real estate is transferred into a revocable living trust if they are properly notified and briefed.[11] We believe that it is important that trust makers obtain lender approval prior to making these transfers.

The rules for conveying property to revocable living trusts vary from jurisdiction to jurisdiction. These jurisdictional variations apply because of differences in statutes and local customs.

Living trusts are amazingly resilient and flexible documents that are designed to expedite the transfer of property, not to hinder it. The reluctance that third parties occasionally have in dealing with living trust transfers is due almost exclusively to a lack of trust knowledge, rather than any specific legal prohibitions. A lack of familiarity with living trusts can cause people to be cautious and provoke concern in commercial matters.

Once a business community is familiar with the living trust concept, there is usually little or no problem in dealings between trust makers and the various enterprises involved in trust transfers. This is aptly demonstrated by the fact that bank trust departments and trust companies have for centuries successfully operated trusts for their customers. There is an overwhelming amount of legal and commercial precedent for living trust transactions.

Holding Title in a Trust

The traditional method for funding a living trust is to title assets directly in the trust's name. In most jurisdictions, titling assets directly in the name of the trust means that the title of the property is transferred into the names of the trustees as the legal title holders of the property: this concept is known as *bare legal title*. Even though the trustees have bare legal title, the property in the trust can only be used for the benefit of the trust's beneficiaries: they have *equitable title* to the trust property. Equitable title is superior to bare legal title because the equitable title holders have all of the rights to the income from and use of the property.

Local title standards for real estate and statutes dealing with the requirements for transferring ownership of real property may affect how title is held by trusts in different jurisdictions. Some jurisdictions require the recording of a portion or all of the trust document. Because of these variations, several acceptable methods of titling trust property have been developed over the years.

Perhaps the most universal method of titling trust property is to name each of the trustees, or their successors, as the title holders and then reference the trust document itself. For example:

> *Charles T. Davidson and June C. Davidson, Trustees, or their successors in trust, under the Charles T. Davidson Living Trust, dated March 11, 1985, and any amendments thereto.*

Such a lengthy designation of ownership can be inconvenient. However, the burden of writing a few more words in order to convey title to a trust can hardly be considered as onerous. Often, trust makers shorten this designation:

> *The Charles T. Davidson Living Trust dated March 11, 1985.*

In practice, the hardest part of transferring property into the name of the trustees is that there may not be enough space on the document of transfer; this necessitates very small writing or precise printing by a very good hand.

Third parties dealing with a trust at times request to see a copy of the trust. They almost never need to see the full trust document. Their concern is that the trustee has the power and authority to deal with the trust property. A knowledgeable third party will want assurances that the trustee has the legal power and ability to transfer or deal with the trust property.

An affidavit of trust is usually acceptable in lieu of the trust document. It discloses only that information that is relevant to the concerns of third parties. It includes the names of the trustees, their powers, and evidence that the trust has been properly signed. The trust provisions appointing successor trustees are usually included as well.

The Nominee Partnership

Another method that is used to avoid disclosing the trust is the *nominee partnership*. A nominee arrangement is an agreement that one party will act on behalf of another. A nominee partnership is created solely to act as agent for the trustees of a living trust.

Creating and using a nominee partnership eliminates the need for the trustees to disclose either the existence or the terms of a living trust. It provides that its partners, who are almost always the trustees and trust makers, are to deal with the trust property in the name of the partnership rather than the name of the living trust.

A nominee partnership does not have capital of its own and is not a venture that is entered into for profit. The importance of the nominee approach to funding rests in the ease by which it facilitates commerce, because most third parties are more accustomed to dealing with partnerships than they are with living trusts.

The nominee partnership is not a new device in keeping individual living trusts confidential. It was established as an acceptable estate planning tool in the 1960s with the publication of a law review article.[12]

The banking industry has long used the nominee concept to facilitate the administration of its trust accounts. When a bank's trust department invests for purposes of its many trust accounts, it does not do so in the name of each account. It transacts its trust business in the name of a nominee. Dealing in the nominee name simplifies the transactions, because the nominee name is used in lieu of a number of specific trust account names.

Nominee corporations, which can be used instead of a nominee partnership, are not nearly as effective as nominee partnerships. The Supreme Court has set out guidelines establishing the standards required for the successful use of a nominee corporation, but because creating and operating a nominee corporation are complex, usually it is not worthwhile to do and entails unnecessary risk.

Because a partnership is a readily acceptable form of doing business, there is little trepidation among third parties in dealing with it or its partners. A partnership agreement can also encompass an orderly succession of partners if one or more of the partners become incapacitated or die. There is no separate income tax levied at the partnership level, so there are no double-taxation issues with which the trust maker and his or her advisers must contend. If a title company or other third party requires recording of the instrument, a trade name affidavit or a fictitious name certificate can satisfy this requirement. A trade name affidavit and a fictitious name certificate are usually one-page declarations setting out the name of the partnership, its partners, and general information about the partnership agreement. With a nominee partnership, there is no need to record the trust agreement.

A nominee partnership must have its own federal identification number. If income is reported as having been paid to a nominee partnership, the partners must file a federal income tax information return, but the nominee will not have to pay any tax. The tax is paid by the trust maker as if the living trust and nominee arrangement did not exist. Married couples can each have a nominee for their respective trusts, or they can use a single nominee to service their joint trust.[13]

A potential disadvantage of the nominee partnership is

that it requires at least two partners. In the case of a trust maker who is acting as a sole trustee, the creation of the nominee partnership means that a nontrustee must act as a partner. We do not recommend that there be a sole trustee because of the difficulties we discussed earlier with respect to the Doctrine of Merger and other practical reasons.

By using the nominee partnership as an agent for the trust, most of the title problems encountered with titling property directly in the name of a living trust are circumvented.

"The Magic Wand of Estate Planning"

For married couples with joint tenancy property, Frederick Keydel's "Magic Wand" is a convenient and effective method for making transfers of property into a revocable living trust while retaining the convenience of joint ownership.[14]

Under this innovative concept, a husband and wife who are trustees of each of their respective living trusts sign a recordable instrument stating that all of the property held in their joint names belongs to their respective living trusts equally.

This method of titling property takes the place of a nominee partnership and eliminates most of the problems of dealing directly in the name of a living trust. No special income tax reporting is required under this arrangement. We commend Mr. Keydel for this innovation and believe that this method of trust ownership will become more and more popular as the number of married couples who use living trust planning increases.

Unrecorded Deeds and
After-Death Assignments

Two additional methods for funding a revocable living trust are available in some states. These are the unrecorded deed and after-death assignments.

Under the *unrecorded deed* method for funding a living trust, the trust maker signs deeds transferring real estate to his or her trust, but the deeds are not recorded until the trust maker's incapacity or death. Should the trust maker dispose of the real estate during his or her lifetime, the unrecorded deeds are destroyed. Because the deeds are not recorded until needed, there is no immediate reason either to disclose the living trust's existence or to record it.[15]

Another way to transfer some types of property into a living trust is found in the Uniform Probate Code. The UPC provides that certain financial accounts such as bank savings accounts can be assigned at death without passing through probate.[16] This form of assignment is called a *payable-on-death* assignment or "POD" designation. A POD designation can be used to fund a living trust on the death of its maker without probate and administration.

The drawback to assigning property under a POD is that if the maker becomes disabled, the property is held outside the trust. Thus, it is always wise to create a limited durable power of attorney that specifically allows the agent to transfer POD property to the trust.[17]

Combining Funding Methods

Many professionals and clients believe that a single funding method must be selected and then utilized. This is a rigid viewpoint that is not accurate. Living trusts can be funded in a number of ways. Mixing funding options is totally acceptable and is often a practical necessity.

The Benefits of Forward Planning

Fully funding a living trust forces title issues into the open, where they can be dealt with before it is too late to take action to correct problems that might be unsolvable and unduly expensive after disability or death. During the funding process, a person not only finds out precisely *what* he or she owns but, more importantly, *how* he or she actually owns it. At that time, each asset can be reviewed in light of a person's estate and financial planning goals.

Taking the time to title property properly on the front end eliminates much of the uncertainty and confusion when the plan is ultimately put to the test on the maker's death or incapacity. Estate planning means exactly that: instituting a plan for the preservation and disposition of an estate.

Typical Examples of Trust Funding

Funding can be accomplished in many ways, depending on the nature of the assets, how they are owned, and the specific motives and desires of the trust makers. The following is a list of assets that are representative of what a typical married couple might own and how they might own it.[18] The value of their property is not relevant because we will assume that their attorney will choose a plan that will take into account federal estate tax planning. The funding choices the example assumes are not necessarily those that every married couple would make.

The Smith Family Finances

Asset	Title to Asset
Residence	Joint Tenancy
Checking Account	Joint Tenancy
Money Market Account	Joint Tenancy
Investments—Public Securities	Joint Tenancy
Investments—Privately Held stock	Mr. Smith
Investment Property—Out of State	Joint Tenancy
Qualified Retirement Plan	Spouse as Primary Beneficiary
Life Insurance	Spouse as Primary Beneficiary
Personal Effects	Joint Tenancy
Automobiles	Joint Tenancy

Liabilities
Mortgage on Home
Home Equity Line
Credit Card Debts
Loan on Cash Value of
   Life Insurance

For ease of illustration, we will assume that the Smiths have one trust for both of them, which is called a *joint living trust*.

Residence

Their residence will be transferred directly to the name of their living trust by a deed prepared by their attorney. The mortgage holder should be notified prior to making the transfer. They should also talk to their property and casualty insurance agent to make sure that no changes are needed on the policy to reflect the new ownership. Except for having a new deed in the name of the trust, the Smiths' rights to their residence will not change.

Checking Account

Their checking account will be retitled directly in the name of their trust by filling in a new signature card at the bank. This can be done by the Smiths. Retitling this account does not affect how the checking account may be used by the Smiths.

Money Market Account

Their money market account will be retitled in the same manner as their checking account, although an account agreement must be changed instead of a signature card. Retitling the money market account will not affect the Smiths' ability to use the money in it.

Investments—Public Securities

Their public securities will be retitled through the stock transfer agent. The Smiths will sign a "Stock Power" form provided by their broker or financial adviser that will accomplish the name change. If they have a street name account, their broker will have them sign a new account agreement in the name of their trust.

By naming the trust the owner of their securities or of their street name account, the Smiths will have as much control over their securities as they did before retitling the securities.

Investment Property—Privately Held Stock

Mr. Smith will have either the attorney or the secretary of the corporation issue a new stock certificate in the trust name. Mr. Smith's rights in the stock will not be affected by retitling it in the name of the trust.

Out-of-State Investment Property

The title to the land will be deeded to their trust by an attorney in the state in which their property is located. Retitling the land does not adversely affect the way the property can be used by the Smiths.

Qualified Retirement Plan

Mr. Smith's retirement plan beneficiary designation will be changed to their trust by his company. Since there are potential income and estate tax ramifications, the Smiths' attorney and other advisers should be consulted.

Life Insurance

The beneficiary designation will be changed by the Smiths' life insurance adviser. If there is cash value, ownership of the policy can be changed to the trust as well. By naming the trust as the beneficiary, the Smiths will have more ability to control the life insurance proceeds. Changing the beneficiary or changing the ownership of the policy will not affect their ability to use the policy.

Personal Effects

The Smiths' personal effects will be transferred to their trust by a bill of sale prepared by their attorney. Retitling personal property does not restrict its use or change the Smiths' real ownership of it.

Automobiles

When the Smiths pay their annual registration fee, they will retitle their cars in the name of their trust. At the same time, they should notify their casualty insurance agent of the transfer. Titling their automobiles in the trust will not affect the Smiths' use of their automobiles.

Most of the title changes in the typical living trust–centered estate plan can be made by the trust makers and their nonattorney advisers, such as their accountants, financial advisers, and insurance agents. The process should be supervised by their attorney so that he or she can review the changes and coordinate the overall funding effort.

The funding of the Smiths' trust will take a little time and will be accomplished without a great deal of effort. If managed on an organized basis and with well-prepared instructions given to them by their attorney, their funding should be accomplished in a matter of days or weeks.

Because the Smiths have chosen to use a joint trust, they will be required to keep records of which one of them originally owned the assets. This record-keeping requirement assures that there will be no question as to which of them owns the property for purposes of paying federal estate tax and other issues. Keeping track of which one originally owned the asset is simple to do and does not require a lot of time and effort.

The cost of funding the Smiths' living trust will not be high. It will likely cost no more than one-quarter of their attorney's charge for drafting their trust documents. Once the Smiths understand how to fund their living trust, it will be easy for them to title their future acquisitions directly in their trust's name.

Problems that arise in the funding process should not be viewed as an indictment of the living trust process, but rather as benefits that result from the process. Because the trust funding process immediately uncovers titling problems and mistakes of ownership, it allows the trust makers and their advisers to solve these problems currently. Without the funding process, errors in title would likely remain undiscovered, only to surface during an adjudication of mental incompetency or probate. The cost and complications of correcting mistakes at that time would most likely be significantly greater.

Retitling assets in the name of a trust does not affect a trust maker's access to his or her property. It does not impair the trust maker's freedom to deal with the property in any significant manner.

Any attack on the use of the fully funded living trust that is based on the argument that funding the trust is an inconvenience simply misrepresents the ultimate purpose of estate planning. There is no question that prudent people want to have their affairs in order and generally do not mind making the commitment to plan correctly.

Our Conclusion

Funding a living trust is the essence of proper planning. It produces far better planning results than does will-planning/probate.

Assets That Require Special Tax Attention

Questions for Discussion

- What types of assets require special funding attention in terms of federal taxation?
- What techniques are used to preserve the income tax status of these assets while still avoiding guardianship and probate proceedings?

Some assets are given particular tax advantages by the Internal Revenue Code or are associated with special taxation rules. When these assets are transferred into a living trust, it is important that the transfer not adversely affect federal tax benefits.

Deferred Payment of Federal Estate Tax for Business Interests

If the value of an interest in a farm or other closely held business is more than 35 percent of the value of the adjusted gross estate of a decedent, an election can be made to defer payments of federal estate tax arising from the business interest.[1]

Under this election, the federal estate tax can be paid in ten equal installments beginning five years after the tax would otherwise have been due. Annual payments of interest only calculated on the federal estate tax applied to the first $1 million in value of the business interest are due for the first five years and a special 4 percent interest rate is used.

The transfer of a business interest to a living trust does not adversely affect this election to defer payments of federal estate tax.[2]

Flower Bonds

Certain Treasury notes issued prior to March 4, 1971, known as "Flower Bonds," are redeemable at their face value, plus accrued interest, if they are used to pay federal estate tax.[3] The face value of these bonds is included in the gross estate of the decedent, even though purchased at a discount. In instances where an individual is terminally ill, it may be advantageous to purchase these bonds for purposes of paying federal estate tax.

To be eligible for redemption, the bonds must be owned by the decedent at the time of his or her death and be included in the decedent's gross estate. Bonds held in a living trust will qualify for redemption if the trustee is required to pay the decedent's federal estate taxes pursuant to the terms of the trust.[4]

A properly drafted living trust can take full advantage of Flower Bonds.

Holding Period of Assets

How long a taxpayer has owned an asset is important in determining its income tax effect when it is sold. For example, if a capital asset such as a building is sold after it has been "held" (owned) by a taxpayer for more than one year, any gain on the sale will be taxed at a maximum rate of 28 percent. This is called a *long-term capital gain.* If that building is sold in less than a year, then the maximum income tax rate is 31 percent. This is called a *short-term capital gain.*

These same holding period rules apply if there is a loss on the sale of a capital asset. They also are used to determine how much capital gain and capital loss a taxpayer has to report in a year.

Since a living trust has no tax existence independent of its trust maker, the holding period of any assets transferred to it by the maker is the same as if the maker owned the property.[5] Thus, if the property is sold from the trust, the determination of capital gains and losses will be the same as if the maker of the trust sold the property. All capital gains and losses of trust property would be reported on the maker's income tax return.

Upon a person's death, all of his or her assets, whether owned in the decedent's living trust or held by him or her individually, are considered to be held for more than one year, producing either long-term capital gain or long-term capital loss on later disposition.[6] For purposes of determining the holding period of assets, trust property and nontrust property are treated in exactly the same manner.

Installment Obligations

Under special rules of the Internal Revenue Code, when casual sales of personal property and sales of real property are made over a period of time, payment of any taxable gain attributable to each payment can be deferred until the payment is actually received.[7] When these installment sales are made, the seller receives some sort of promissory note or contract from the buyer. A "disposition" of one of these installment obligations accelerates the tax on any deferred gain.[8]

The transfer of an installment obligation to a revocable living trust is not considered to be a disposition that accelerates gain.[9] The trust maker continues to report the gain as if the trust did not exist.[10]

When a husband and wife as joint tenants sell property and receive an installment obligation and then transfer it into a revocable living trust, there are no adverse income tax results as long as both have the power to revoke the trust. If only one can revoke the trust, then the joint tenant who cannot do so may have disposed of his or her share, causing acceleration of the tax on his or her share of any deferred gain.[11]

An installment obligation can be transferred to the maker from a living trust without accelerating the gain, so taking the obligation out of a living trust also does not present a problem.[12] The death of the maker does not accelerate the gain.[13]

Oil and Gas Interests

Proven oil and gas reserves can be transferred to a revocable living trust without affecting the trust maker's right to percentage depletion. Similarly, a transfer back to the maker from the trust does not affect the maker's right to percentage depletion. After the death of the maker, the trust can take percentage depletion and so can beneficiaries to whom the proven oil and gas reserves are transferred.[14]

Partnership Interests

A revocable living trust can be a general or limited partner, except if prohibited by state statute or case law. The maker of a living trust is treated for federal income tax purposes as a partner of any partnership interest transferred to the trust. At the trust maker's death, partnership interests held by the living trust are allowed a step-up in basis adjustment.[15]

Some states allow partnership agreements to provide that a partner may designate a successor in interest on the partner's death or incapacity.[16] Such a provision may even allow the conversion of the partnership interest from a general to a limited interest. These provisions can be used to automatically fund a living trust on the death of its maker.[17]

Buy-Sell Agreements

It is common practice for small business owners to enter into buy-sell agreements. Buy-sell agreements do not usually pose funding problems.

Buy-sell agreements should be reviewed before transferring a business interest into a living trust. At times, there are prohibitions against such transfers in the agreement. When this occurs, written permission from the other owners may have to be obtained in order to make the transfer. In our experience, this permission is always given.

A buy-sell agreement may have to be modified to provide for ownership by a living trust. Although it is almost certain that a trustee will be bound by the terms of the buy-sell agreement even though not a signatory to it, fewer problems will be created at the death or disability of a party if the documentation recognizes and sanctions the living trust.

Principal Residence

When a taxpayer sells his or her principal residence and reinvests the proceeds in a new residence within two years of the date of sale, no gain has to be recognized.[18] This allows a person or a married couple to move into a more expensive home without having to pay income tax on any gain.

If the owner of a principal residence transfers it to a revocable living trust, gain can still be deferred under these provisions. If the residence passes to a trust for the benefit of the surviving spouse, deferral is also available as long as the spouse is treated as the maker of the trust.[19]

A taxpayer who is fifty-five years of age or older has the right to a one-time $125,000 exclusion of gain upon the sale of a principal residence.[20] The IRS has held that this treatment is also available to a living trust.[21] In fact, the IRS has ruled that a surviving spouse who receives the residence in a trust that qualifies for the unlimited marital deduction can take advantage of the $125,000 exclusion.[22]

Savings Bonds

A purchaser of a U.S. Series E or EE savings bond can defer taking the accrued interest into income until the bond matures or until it is redeemed. These bonds can readily be transferred to a revocable living trust without causing any of the accrued interest to be currently taxable to the owner.[23] Series H bonds are subject to these same rules.[24]

S Corporation Stock

S corporation stock is easily transferred into a revocable living trust without causing the termination of the S corporation election. A revocable living trust is specifically allowed to be an S corporation stockholder.[25] If a husband and a wife, neither of whom is a nonresident alien, own stock in an S corporation and transfer it into a joint trust where they have the joint right to revoke the trust, the trust is an eligible S corporation stockholder. The husband and wife will be treated as one individual for purposes of qualifying the revocable living trust as an eligible stockholder as long as they file a joint income tax return.[26]

The ramifications of holding S corporation stock in a trust

after the death of the maker are discussed fully in Appendix A, "S Corporation Stock."

Special Use Property

A decedent's property that was used in farming, ranching, or other qualified businesses does not have to be valued at its highest and best use. It can be valued on the basis of methods that determine its value in the business itself rather than its speculation or development value.[27] The fair market value of the property can be reduced by up to $750,000.[28] This special use valuation is important to farmers, ranchers, and small business owners.

Ownership of special use property by a living trust does not adversely affect special use valuation. Property acquired by a beneficiary from a living trust is eligible for special use valuation to the extent that the property is includable in the decedent's gross estate.[29] An heir who receives special use property from a decedent may also transfer the property to his or her own revocable living trust as long as the heir retains full control over the trustee and maintains his or her right to revoke the trust.[30]

Sole Proprietorship Property

Living trusts can be easily funded with sole proprietorship property.[31] Since sole proprietorships generally consist of tangible personal property, an assignment or bill of sale can be used to transfer most of the assets into the name of the trust.

After-acquired assets can be titled in the name of the trust by assignment or bill of sale, or the sole proprietorship can do business in the trust's name. However, doing business in the name of a trust can be somewhat awkward, especially in areas of the country that are not familiar with the concept of the living trust. If this is the case, a nominee partnership can be created to hold title to the sole proprietorship assets. Nominee partnerships are discussed in Chapter 11, "General Lifetime Consequences of Funding a Living Trust."

It is also possible for a sole proprietorship to do business under a fictitious name. In most states, an individual and a living trust can carry on a business in a trade or fictitious name by filing the appropriate documentation in the county where the business is located.

A living trust which carries on a trade or business could be classified as an "association" taxable as a corporation for federal income tax purposes.[32] This characterization can be avoided if the primary purpose of the living trust is to protect or conserve property for estate planning purposes.[33]

Waiver of Attribution
Under Stock Redemptions

When a family-owned corporation purchases the stock of a stockholder, the proceeds received by the stockholder can be taxed as a dividend rather than as a capital gain. The Internal Revenue Code provides that certain redemptions of stock of a corporation owned by family members will not be treated as dividends if stringent requirements are met.[34] One of the methods for qualifying under these requirements requires a complete redemption of all of the stock of the corporation owned by the redeemed stockholder.[35]

A factor that makes a complete redemption of a family member difficult is that the Internal Revenue Code attributes the ownership of stock to related persons.[36] If there are other stockholders who are related to the redeemed stockholder, their stock ownership is attributed to the redeemed stockholder. For example:

> *Bill and Peggy Thatcher own 80 percent of a family-owned corporation. Their daughter, Linda, owns the other 20 percent. Their son, Mike, owns no stock.*
>
> *Under the attribution rules of the Internal Revenue Code, Bill owns 100 percent, Peggy owns 100 percent, Linda owns 100 percent, and Mike owns 80 percent.[37] If the corporation buys back all of Linda's stock, she is still considered to own 100 percent of the corporation.*

As is evident from the example, application of the attribution rules means that a family-owned corporation may not be able to redeem a family member's stock completely, creating potentially adverse income tax consequences.

The attribution rules can be waived if an agreement is entered into by all related persons.[38] Entities, including a living trust, can waive the family attribution rules.[39]

Qualified Retirement Plans

Qualified retirement plans generally include company pension and profit sharing plans, employee stock ownership plans (ESOPs), individual retirement plans (IRAs), and simplified employee pension plans (SEPs).

A revocable living trust can be named as the beneficiary of a qualified retirement plan as long as provisions of the Internal Revenue Code and its regulations are met. A trustee of a living trust may elect the form of the benefit to be received by the plan. By naming the trust as the beneficiary of a plan, the tax benefits that are chosen will inure to the benefit of the beneficiaries of the trust. The benefits selected are not impaired by naming a revocable living trust as a beneficiary.[40]

Naming the beneficiary for a qualified retirement plan can be, and often is, a complex process. Unfortunately, since the Employee Retirement Income Security Act of 1974 (ERISA) was passed, Congress has turned a once-comprehensible body of law into a convoluted labyrinth of constantly changing rules and regulations in order to correct perceived abuses in the use of qualified plans.[41] Thus, before any beneficiary is named, a trust maker must always consider the many income tax, estate tax, and practical factors that may affect the choice of a beneficiary.

The general rule is that in most situations a revocable living trust is effective as a beneficiary of qualified plan proceeds.

Why a Revocable Living Trust Should Be the Beneficiary of Qualified Retirement Plan Proceeds

There are many advantages to naming a living trust as the beneficiary of a qualified plan. The greatest advantage is that a maker's trust instructions will control plan death benefits. Upon the disability or death of a plan participant, his or her living trust agreement can determine how the proceeds are used and who will benefit from them. This offers control that a standard beneficiary designation cannot possibly offer. Control can be especially important for purposes of estate liquidity. If the liquid funds are paid to a named beneficiary, that beneficiary may not be willing to lend cash to the estate for its liquidity needs.

In the case of a spouse who needs investment assistance or one who may be a spendthrift, a living trust can be used to protect that spouse. The same is true for adult children. For minor children, the trust can avoid the publicity, time, and expense of a court-controlled financial guardianship. If an adult beneficiary is incapacitated for any reason, the trust can also avoid a financial guardianship.

A living trust is invaluable for naming contingent beneficiaries. A traditional beneficiary designation often does not provide sufficiently for contingent beneficiaries. Rather than relying on a beneficiary designation that states something like "to my children, *per stirpes*" or "to my issue, share and share alike," a trust can properly pass the benefits in exactly the manner the maker chooses.

In the event of the simultaneous deaths of a husband and a wife, a living trust can determine the order of death for planning purposes. This important planning consideration cannot be accomplished by the usual and ordinary beneficiary designation.

A living trust can also be used to accomplish proper federal estate tax planning. If, for example, a beneficiary designation names a spouse as the primary beneficiary of qualified plan proceeds, it may overfund the marital deduction. This overfunding can cause the loss or reduction of a person's $600,000 exemption equivalent amount and engender $235,000 of unnecessary federal estate tax.

In some cases, the payment options provided in a qualified plan may be structured in a manner that will not qualify them for the unlimited marital deduction. A living trust can be written so that the marital deduction is preserved in circumstances where it would otherwise be lost.

Since the beneficiary of qualified plan proceeds must pay income tax on them as *income with respect to a decedent*— income that was due the decedent but which was not paid during his or her life—naming a living trust as beneficiary can also allocate this income in such a manner as to reduce federal estate tax upon the death of the surviving spouse.

This is an important planning consideration in many estates.

While it is true that qualified plan proceeds paid directly to a beneficiary, including a living trust, avoid probate on the death of the plan participant, it is not uncommon for the beneficiary designation to name the participant's probate estate as the beneficiary. While this procedure is legal, it is bad planning. The proceeds will be subject to probate and may also be subject to the claims of creditors! This would not happen if a living trust were the recipient of the proceeds. In addition, proceeds payable to a probate estate may be subject to state inheritance taxes that can be eliminated by the use of a living trust.

A complete discussion of all the ramifications and considerations necessary for determining how proceeds should be paid from a qualified plan is outside the scope of this book. However, the discussion of a few fundamental rules is critical to an understanding of why a living trust should be named as the beneficiary of a qualified plan.

Spousal Annuity Rules

Qualified plans, except for IRAs, SEPs, and profit sharing plans, are subject to the spousal annuity rules.[42] Under these rules, if a plan participant is married, his or her spouse will automatically receive the plan benefits at the participant's death in the form of an annuity. A participant must waive these rules in order to name another beneficiary of the plan and the participant's spouse must consent to the waiver.

We call this rule to your attention because many people want to name their revocable living trusts as the beneficiary of their plans. It is extremely important that this waiver be obtained when naming a living trust as the beneficiary of a qualified plan. If the waiver is not properly signed, the living trust will not control the proceeds and they will pass directly to the spouse under the spousal annuity rules.

Income Tax Considerations

The recipient of the proceeds of a qualified plan pays income tax on the proceeds as they are paid out. A beneficiary who receives qualified retirement plan proceeds as the result of the death of a participant must receive them under a method that satisfies the "minimum distribution rules." The application of these rules depends on whether or not the participant dies before or after plan payments begin.

If a participant dies before payments from the qualified plan begin, the beneficiary has a choice of how to take the proceeds. The beneficiary can take the proceeds in a lump sum and pay income tax under the five-year averaging method,[43] take the proceeds within a period not to exceed five years after the participant's death,[44] or have the proceeds paid over his or her life expectancy.[45]

The participant's spouse can defer receipt of the benefits of a qualified plan by taking the proceeds in a lump sum, rolling them over into an IRA, and deferring their receipt, and the income tax on them, until age 70½.[46] At age 70½, the spouse can begin to take the proceeds out over his or her own life expectancy and pay the taxes as the proceeds are received.

If the participant dies while receiving plan payments, the remaining proceeds must be paid out to the beneficiary at least as quickly as under the distribution method in effect on the participant's death.[47] They may also be taken over the life of a "designated beneficiary."[48]

"Designated Beneficiary"

A *designated beneficiary* is a special IRS concept that is used to determine the length of time over which the benefits of a qualified plan must be paid after the death of a participant.

A designated beneficiary is generally defined as an individual who is named as a beneficiary under the terms of a qualified plan or who is named as the beneficiary in a participant's beneficiary designation.[49] Not every beneficiary who receives plan benefits meets the requirements of a designated beneficiary. For example, a designated beneficiary cannot be a probate estate but can be a trust under certain circumstances.[50]

The period over which payments from the plan can be taken after the death of the participant can be longer in cases where there is a designated beneficiary. This period of time varies, depending on whether the participant began taking payments from the plan prior to his or her death.

Without a designated beneficiary, the ability to take the proceeds into income over the life expectancy of a spouse or a beneficiary is lost, which means the benefit of deferring income tax may be lost.[51] If there is not a designated beneficiary and the participant received payments under the plan, only the participant's life expectancy can be used for determining the period over which his or her benefits must be paid.[52] If there is not a designated beneficiary and the participant dies before taking payments from the plan, then the entire proceeds from the qualified plan must be paid out within five years of the date of the participant's death.[53]

A living trust must meet the following requirements to be a designated beneficiary:

1. The trust must be valid under state law or valid but for the fact the trust has no assets in it (corpus).
2. The trust must be irrevocable.
3. The beneficiaries of the trust must be identifiable from the trust instrument.
4. A copy of the trust instrument must be provided to the plan administrator.

Where a participant has not begun taking payments from the plan, a properly funded revocable living trust can easily meet these criteria. The only criterion a revocable living trust apparently cannot meet is that it must be irrevocable. But a living trust becomes irrevocable on the death of its maker, or, if a joint trust, on the death of one of its makers. It therefore meets this requirement.

While the participant is living, his or her trust is revocable. A living trust will receive plan benefits when the participant dies. It is then that the revocable living trust becomes irrevocable, allowing it to meet the second requirement. Thus, when the participant dies prior to receiving payments and a living trust is named as a beneficiary, it is a designated beneficiary, and the payments can be taken over the life expectancy of the oldest identifiable beneficiary of the trust.[54]

If payments from a qualified plan began prior to a participant's death, a living trust cannot meet the second requirement, because a revocable living trust only becomes irrevocable upon the death of its maker. It cannot receive benefits while the participant is living and at the same time be a designated beneficiary.

Losing the tax deferral on qualified plan proceeds by extending the length of time over which they can be taken may or may not be a detriment. It will depend on the circumstances at the time distributions are to be made. In many circumstances, the proceeds will be paid out in a lump sum, so that having a designated beneficiary will be of no importance. In other circumstances, payment over a five-year period may constitute adequate tax planning.

Federal Estate Tax Considerations

With a few rare exceptions,[55] qualified retirement plan proceeds are subject to federal estate tax.[56]

One of the most important elements of proper federal estate tax planning for married couples is the proper use of the unlimited marital deduction. The unlimited marital deduction prevents property that passes to a surviving spouse from being subject to federal estate tax on the death of the first spouse. To qualify for the unlimited marital deduction, the surviving spouse must receive, as a minimum, all of the income payable at least annually for the life of the surviving spouse from property left by the deceased spouse.[57]

Death benefits from a qualified plan can qualify for the marital deduction. Qualification often depends on how the benefits are paid out to the spouse. Lump sum payments clearly qualify for the marital deduction.[58] Some annuity and installment benefits can be structured to qualify for the marital deduction, but there are some annuities and installment payments that cannot.[59]

Annuities and installment payments that do not qualify for the unlimited marital deduction are those that end on the occurrence of an event or after a specified interval.[60] For example, allowing a spouse to receive only part of the income from a qualified plan for his or her life, with all of the remaining income and principal passing to the participant's descendants on the spouse's death, does not qualify for the marital deduction. Or allowing the spouse income from property for only a certain amount of years does not qualify for the marital deduction.

If a spouse is named as the beneficiary of a plan that does not pay out all of its income, then the proceeds are not sheltered by the marital deduction. They are subject to federal estate tax on the death of the participant; the federal estate tax is not deferred until the death of the surviving spouse.

By naming a living trust as the beneficiary of a plan that does not pay all of the income out annually, it is possible to qualify the plan proceeds for the unlimited marital deduction.[61] The ability of a living trust to qualify otherwise non-eligible plan payments as marital deduction property is a definite advantage.

A testamentary trust can also have this advantage. However, naming a testamentary trust as the beneficiary of plan proceeds can generate unnecessary federal estate taxes because a testamentary trust is created after the death of the will maker. This leads to a severe lack of flexibility in properly controlling the proceeds for purposes of federal estate tax planning.[62] The trustee of a living trust has the flexibility to determine how qualified plan proceeds can be best allocated for maximum federal estate tax benefits.

The Excess Retirement Accumulation Excise Tax

The Tax Reform Act of 1986 added an excise tax of 15 percent on excess accumulations in retirement plans.[63] An excess accumulation is when a person's benefits in all his retirement plans at the time of his death are greater than the amount allowed by law.[64] The law penalizes excess accumulations to encourage people to withdraw their benefits when they reach retirement age instead of leaving the benefits in a retirement plan to continue to grow income tax free. This tax cannot be offset by any deductions, including the marital deduction, or any credits, including the unified credit, and is not deductible for income tax purposes when the benefits are received.[65] The tax on excess accumulations is deductible from the estate.[66] Generally, this excise tax is due when the federal estate tax return is filed. However, a surviving spouse can elect to add any qualified plan amounts to his or her own retirement plan and defer the excise tax.[67]

When a revocable living trust or a testamentary trust is named as the beneficiary of a qualified plan instead of the spouse, the excise tax is due immediately. The surviving spouse cannot defer the tax by electing to treat the plan proceeds as if they were his or her own. This is an important consideration when determining who should be the beneficiary of a qualified plan if it appears that there may be an excess accumulation problem.

Income in Respect of a Decedent

Qualified plan payments received after the death of a participant are called *income in respect of a decedent*. This term, which comes from the Internal Revenue Code, means that the value of the plan proceeds are included in the estate of the participant and they are included in the taxable income of a beneficiary as they are received. This is a kind of double tax on qualified plan proceeds. However, the beneficiary who receives the proceeds can take a deduction on his or her federal income tax return for the federal estate tax that the proceeds generated in the decedent's estate.[68] The federal estate tax and income tax consequences of income in respect of a decedent are unaffected by the use of a living trust as the beneficiary of those proceeds.

There is a potential problem in naming a trust as the beneficiary of qualified plan payments because of some special rules surrounding the income tax treatment of income in respect of a decedent. These rules are especially relevant in an estate plan for a married couple that is designed to save federal estate tax.

The Internal Revenue Code gives every taxpayer a $600,000 exemption equivalent amount that he or she can pass to anyone free of federal estate tax. It is a very valuable tool in estate planning.

In addition to the exemption equivalent, the Internal Revenue Code allows married couples another method to defer federal estate tax: the unlimited marital deduction. The unlimited marital deduction shelters all property left to a surviving spouse from federal estate tax when the first spouse dies.

By properly combining the use of the exemption equivalent and the unlimited marital deduction, a married couple can, with proper planning, pass a total of $1,200,000 to their children or others totally free from federal estate tax. For example, in most federal estate tax planning for married couples, the marital deduction and the $600,000 exemption equivalent are maximized by a formula clause in the estate plan of the deceased spouse that creates two separate and distinct shares for the surviving spouse and children. Usually, the formula clause allocates some of the decedent's property to a marital trust for the benefit of the surviving spouse and the remainder of the property to a family trust for the benefit of the surviving spouse and the decedent's children and grandchildren. The property that goes into the marital trust qualifies for the unlimited marital deduction and is free from federal estate tax. The property that goes into the family trust is sheltered by the $600,000 exemption equivalent and is also free from federal estate tax.

If the death proceeds of a qualified plan are allocated to a marital trust, any income taxes paid by the surviving spouse because of the income from the marital trust reduce the size of the surviving spouse's estate. If the death proceeds are paid to a family trust, the income taxes paid reduce the amount available for estate-tax-free growth. Since the value of the family trust, regardless of its size, will not be subject to federal estate tax when the surviving spouse dies, it may not be wise to pay the income tax out of the family trust.

A trustee of a living trust, to a great degree, can control the payment of income taxes on income in respect of a decedent by allocating the proceeds either to the marital trust or to the family trust. A testamentary trustee does not have this luxury because the maker must name the specific testamentary trust to which the proceeds are to be paid. The testamentary trustee has no discretion over how the proceeds are allocated and cannot perform any meaningful after-death income tax planning for qualified plan proceeds.

Because the trustee of a living trust has the discretion to allocate qualified plan proceeds to either the marital or the family trust, another potential income tax problem can arise, depending on how the living trust document is actually written. Without proper legal drafting, allocation of qualified plan payments to the family trust can cause all of the proceeds to be subject to immediate income taxation.[69] Under these circumstances, a special formula clause is used to alleviate any potential income tax problem.[70]

There are two types of formula clauses that are typically used in federal estate tax planning for married couples. One type is called a *pecuniary* clause and the other is called a *fractional share of the residue* clause. Sometimes, when qualified plan proceeds are allocated to a marital trust or a family trust by a pecuniary bequest in a will or a trust, the allocation accelerates all of the income tax due on the proceeds. This acceleration can occur because of the special rules relating to the transfer of income in respect of a decedent. The effect of this income tax acceleration can be devastating. If the qualified plan states that the death proceeds are to be paid over several years, but the income tax on all of the proceeds is due immediately because of the improper use of a pecuniary clause, the beneficiary will owe all of the income tax without having any of the plan proceeds to pay the tax. A fractional share formula will not cause the acceleration of the income tax. Pecuniary and fractional share formulas are discussed later in Appendix A, "The Nonrecognition of Losses Between a Trust and Its Beneficiaries."

A properly drafted living trust–centered plan can be very effective in planning for income in respect of a decedent because a living trust trustee can be given discretion in how qualified plan proceeds can be allocated for the best income tax result. Will-planning/probate is less flexible, in that important decisions as to whether the marital trust or the family trust is the recipient of the plan proceeds must be made by the will maker while he or she is living. Since circumstances may change drastically between the time when the will maker comes to a decision and the time of his or her death, there may be harmful consequences. The testamentary trustee must then implement these decisions even though they may not be particularly wise after the maker's death.

Disclaimer Planning

Because there are so many variables that must be considered when determining the beneficiary of qualified plan proceeds, the utmost flexibility is required. An effective method for gaining flexibility is the use of living trust disclaimer planning.

The trustee of a living trust can be given the right to disclaim any qualified plan benefits made payable to the trust.[71] The trust should provide that the trustee may decline to accept plan proceeds so that they will be paid directly to the surviving spouse. This technique will qualify the proceeds for a spousal rollover to an IRA.

A living trust expert has created an innovative method for using a disclaimer hierarchy as part of the beneficiary designation of a qualified plan.[72] Under this method, the beneficiary designation is structured so that a living trust is the primary beneficiary, the family trust is the second beneficiary, the surviving spouse is the third beneficiary, the trust maker's descendants are the fourth beneficiary, and the estate is the final beneficiary. Disclaimers are then used to reach the beneficiary who is best suited to take the proceeds.

It makes good sense to name a properly written living trust as the beneficiary of a qualified plan in most situations. However, a thorough analysis of all of the income and estate tax effects of making a decision as to the beneficiaries of a qualified plan must be made regardless of the beneficiaries ultimately named.

Our Conclusion

A living trust can own tax-sensitive property without adversely affecting the tax status of that property.

· 13 ·

Assets That May Not Be Readily Transferred to a Living Trust

Questions for Discussion

- What types of assets present funding difficulties?
- What are the funding difficulties associated with professional corporations?
- How may homestead exemption laws be affected by a living trust?
- What is Section 1244 stock, and why does it present funding problems?
- What are stock option and purchase plans, and what are their funding problems?

There are four types of assets that for one reason or another may present difficulties if they are held in the name of a living trust:

- Professional corporation stock
- Homestead property
- Section 1244 stock
- Stock options

Trust critics sometimes cite the problems of funding a living trust with these assets as proof that living trusts do not work well. Each of these assets is unique and can present funding difficulties. However, these difficulties can often be overcome with proper living trust–centered planning.

Professional Corporation Stock

Stockholders of professional corporations are required by state law to be licensed members of their profession.[1] Because of this requirement, it may not be possible for professionals to transfer their stock into their living trusts without violating the technical provisions of governing state statutes.

The purpose of the laws restricting the transfer of professional corporation stock to people who are not members of the profession is to assure the public that laypersons are not involved in making decisions that should be made only by licensed professionals. States do not prohibit professionals from putting their professional stock into living trusts, but, with one exception,[2] they do not specifically authorize this practice either.

There is no meaningful reason why a state could object to a professional's putting his or her stock into a living trust as long as the professional retained total control over the trust. Such a transfer would in no way be injurious to the public and would simply allow a professional to do proper estate planning like everyone else. If a professional decided to place professional corporation stock in a living trust, this transfer would in no way change the professional's conduct or practice.[3]

Whether professional corporation stock may be held in a revocable trust either while the professional is living or during the winding up of his or her affairs after death depends upon state law. There is no policy reason why the maker of a revocable trust who has complete control over trust assets cannot place professional corporation stock in his or her trust.

We can only conclude that the absence of law dealing with this issue means that it is effectively a nonissue, and, if the choice were ours, we would recommend funding a living trust with professional corporation stock.

Homestead Property

Many states have a homestead exemption for purposes of exempting residences from property taxes and the claims of creditors. For example, in Florida, the first $25,000 of value of a homestead is not subject to real estate taxes.[4] In addition, there is an unlimited homestead exemption from creditors other than a mortgage holder on the residence itself.[5]

Herb and Diane live in a $150,000 home in Miami. Herb entered into a disastrous business deal that resulted in a judgment against both Diane and him in the amount of $300,000.

Herb's and Diane's creditor seeks to enforce the judgment by taking their home.

Under the homestead law of Florida, their home is immune from the creditor's claim. Since the creditor does not have a mortgage on the house, it is not subject to the creditor's claim.

Homestead exemptions are personal in nature and are subject to statutory restrictions as to their use. As a result, there is a question as to whether or not a residence that is transferred into a living trust will continue to qualify under a state's homestead law.

Most states have no law on whether or not a homestead exemption is preserved or lost if the homestead is transferred to a living trust. At least one state has taken a position on this issue. In Oklahoma there is an attorney general opinion that allows a transfer of a homestead into the name of a living trust without the loss of the homestead exemption benefit.[6]

In states that allow unrecorded deeds, the homestead property can be conveyed to a living trust without recording the deed until after the owner has died. This technique will effectively allow the trust maker to avoid probate without putting creditors on notice that any conveyance has been made.

The loss of homestead status that might result from transferring a homestead to a living trust has no logical basis. It does not appear to be against public policy and in no way changes the relationship between a creditor and a debtor.

The lack of state law on conveyances of homesteads to a living trust is a good example of the lack of awareness among state legislatures of how living trusts can be used in the estate planning process. However, before transfer of homestead property into a living trust, the homestead law should be examined in detail to determine the effect of such a transfer.

Section 1244 Stock

Section 1244 of the Internal Revenue Code provides that a loss on the sale or exchange of the common stock of a small business corporation which would otherwise be treated as a capital loss will be treated as an ordinary loss if certain conditions are met. The amount of the loss in any one year can be as high as $50,000 for an individual or $100,000 for a married couple filing a joint income tax return.[7]

Even though the favorable capital gains income tax rate was eliminated by the Tax Reform Act of 1986, the restrictions on taking capital losses were retained. A capital loss may be offset against capital gains.[8] Any excess can only be deducted at the rate of $3,000 per year.[9] An ordinary loss can be offset against all income in a year and may be either carried forward or carried back.[10] Because an ordinary loss can offset ordinary income on a dollar to dollar basis, an ordinary loss is much more beneficial than a capital loss in most planning circumstances.

Section 1244 stock is routinely issued to business owners who incorporate their new or existing business ventures:

Sam and Jennifer are starting a new dry-cleaning business, and because they wish to limit their liability they seek out the services of their lawyer, Ted Gilbert, to incorporate their venture.

Ted cautions them that a high percentage of new business ventures do not succeed, and that if theirs should be among them, they will want to be able to write off their business losses against their ordinary income. He explains to them that if the business is incorporated under Section 1244 of the Internal Revenue Code, that is precisely what they will be able to do.

The ordinary loss treatment of stock under Section 1244 is allowed only to individuals and to partnerships who have continuously held the stock from the date of its issuance.[11]

A trust or an estate is specifically prohibited from qualifying for ordinary loss treatment under Section 1244.[12]

> *Two years after launching the business, Sam and Jennifer again seek out the services of Ted Gilbert for estate planning. Ted recommends that they use a living trust as the core document in their estate plan.*
>
> *After Sam and Jennifer have signed their trust documents, Ted advises them that they should fund their trusts. However, he explains that they will lose the benefits of their Section 1244 stock if they transfer it to their living trusts.*

Because a transfer of stock to a living trust will disqualify it for Section 1244 treatment, the determination as to the importance of Section 1244 as compared to the benefits provided by placing ownership of the stock in a living trust is a question that must be resolved.

In many instances, there may be no reason to be concerned about Section 1244 treatment because a corporation is highly profitable and there is little chance that a loss will ever occur. In other situations, the corporate owners may have capital gains that can offset a capital loss of stock so that ordinary income tax losses are not necessary.

Section 1244 Stock and S Corporations

Section 1244 is of less importance to many corporate stockholders than it was in the past. Beginning in the late 1970s and culminating in the Tax Reform Act of 1986, Congress eliminated most of the reasons to use a regular corporation for the small business owner. Many companies that were incorporated as regular corporations have been converted to S corporations. A significant number of new corporations are being incorporated under the Subchapter

S law. By doing so, their owners eliminate many of the disadvantages of regular corporations.

The original purpose of Section 1244 was to put a regular corporation's stockholders on par with sole proprietors or members of a partnership.[13] A sole proprietor or a partner can deduct the operating losses sustained in a business. These ordinary losses offset their other income. A stockholder of a regular corporation cannot deduct corporate losses; they are only deductible against the corporation's income.

A stockholder of a regular corporation can only recognize a personal loss when the corporation is sold or liquidated or becomes worthless. When any of these events occurs, the resulting personal loss is a capital loss, not an ordinary loss. Section 1244 stock allows a small business owner to take an ordinary loss rather than a capital loss.

An S corporation can reach the same result without Section 1244. S corporation losses can be taken against the income of their stockholders. As a practical matter, the losses taken under an S corporation will be the same as those under Section 1244. Here is an example of the comparability of Section 1244 corporations and S corporations:

> *Sam incorporates his business, in which he has invested $100,000. The corporation is a regular corporation and qualifies under Section 1244. The corporation loses $20,000 a year for five years. Sam's corporation declares bankruptcy in the fifth year. Sam can take, as an ordinary loss, $100,000 on his personal income tax return.*

> *Sara incorporates her business, in which she has invested $100,000. She elects S corporation status, so losses are passed through to her. Her corporation loses $20,000 a year for five years. In each year, Sara writes off the*

*$20,000 loss on her personal income tax return. At the
end of five years, her corporation goes out of business.*

Each of our unfortunate entrepreneurs lost $100,000 and
could deduct it as an ordinary loss. Sara had the advantage
of being able to write off her losses earlier than Sam. This
is an advantage which S corporation shareholders have over
shareholders of regular 1244 stock corporations. This example is extremely simplified. It does, however, demonstrate that S corporations work as well as, or better than,
Section 1244 corporations in passing ordinary losses
through to shareholders.

It is difficult to understand why Congress does not allow
Section 1244 treatment for stock held in a living trust. The
purpose of Section 1244 is not thwarted by allowing a living
trust to hold Section 1244 stock for estate planning purposes. Therefore, there is no reason why Section 1244
should not be amended to allow such transfers. With the
growing proliferation of living trust–centered plans, it is
likely that Section 1244 will be amended to allow living trusts
to hold Section 1244 stock without loss of its benefits.[14]

Stock Options

The Internal Revenue Code provides special income tax
advantages for certain qualified stock option and purchase
plans.[15] Under the Code, a person who receives stock from
a qualified stock option plan does not have to take the value
of stock received into income when he or she receives it.[16]
Gain is only recognized during the later disposition of the
stock.[17]

These plans require certain holding periods. If an individual fails to meet any of the holding period requirements, then the favorable income tax benefits are lost.[18]

The regulations governing these special stock provisions are not clear as to whether the transfer of either the option or the stock to a living trust violates the holding period rules. Because a living trust is not a separate entity for tax purposes, the transfer of either stock or options to a living trust should not violate the holding period provisions. Unfortunately, another Code provision defines *disposition* as a sale, exchange, gift, or transfer of legal title. A transfer from a trust maker to a living trust is a transfer of legal title.[19] The Internal Revenue Service regulations that explain the law state only the following with regard to transfers to a trustee:

> If an individual exercises a statutory option and a share of stock is transferred to such individual in his name as trustee for another, the individual has made a disposition of such share.[20]

The language of this regulation is not clear, but it does not appear that it applies to a transfer to a revocable living trust. However, because the law is unclear, caution should be exercised in transferring these options to living trusts.

There is another potential problem with these options. Another regulation seems to state that a qualified stock option can only pass by will or by the laws of intestacy.[21] Since a living trust is a will-substitute, it should qualify under this regulation, but there is no law on the subject. Even if a transfer to a living trust does not qualify, there is no penalty in the Code or regulations for making this transfer.

This same regulation states that a qualified option can be exercised after the death of the employee by his or her probate estate, by an heir, or "by reason of the death of the decedent."[22] This implies that a trustee of a living trust who holds the option at the death of the option holder could exercise it. But, once again, there is no specific law on the point.

As with other provisions of the Internal Revenue Code, there seems to be no policy reason for favoring wills or intestacy over revocable living trusts. It appears that the stock option rules were written by legislators who were unfamiliar with living trusts.[23]

Stock options that are held in a revocable living trust will avoid probate on the owner's death and financial guardianship if the owner becomes disabled. Because of the uncertainties in the tax law about stock options, it is important to balance the need for living trust–centered planning with the potential pitfalls of will-planning/probate. For many people, the decision is not difficult: they prefer the certainty of living trust–centered planning to the uncertainty of the tax laws. Others may feel differently. In any event, it is important to appreciate some of the issues that surround stock options and their ramifications.

Our Conclusion

The law does not prohibit placing professional corporation stock, homestead property, and qualified stock option and purchase plans into a living trust. However, these interests should not be transferred to a living trust without the advice of an attorney. Section 1244 stock loses its benefits if held in a living trust.

· 14 ·

Gifts Made from Living Trusts

Questions for Discussion

- Are there adverse estate tax consequences in making gifts directly from a living trust?
- What is the IRS's position on gifts made from living trusts?
- Can a gift program be continued after the giver's incapacity?

It is not uncommon for a trust maker to instruct the trustee to make a gift of trust property directly to third parties. This apparently harmless act may have adverse federal estate tax consequences for people who have federal estate tax liability. If a trust maker should die within three years of the time that a gift has been made directly from his or her living trust, the value of the gift could be included in the maker's estate for federal estate tax purposes.

Will-planning/probate and trust advocates have voiced concern over this apparent problem. This concern is warranted but should not be overemphasized, because this potential estate tax problem can be easily overcome with proper trust drafting.

A gift program can be continued after a person becomes incapacitated. Although will-planning/probate advocates believe that a durable power of attorney should be used to continue a gift program, living trust planning can continue a gift program more effectively.

IRS Recommendations on How to Make Gifts from a Trust

The value of a gift is not, as a general rule, included in a person's estate on death. "Gifts in contemplation of death" are an exception to this rule.

Prior to 1976, the Internal Revenue Code provided that gifts made within three years of a person's death were *presumed* to be in contemplation of death and were included in a decedent's estate unless this presumption could be overcome.[1] The rationale for this rule was understandable. At that time, the federal gift tax rates were less than the federal estate tax rates, making it more likely that people would use deathbed gifts for estate tax avoidance. The result was extensive litigation with the government over whether these gifts were made in contemplation of death.

In 1976, Congress changed the law so that all gifts made within three years of the date of death were includable in decedents' estates, and the presumption was eliminated.[2] In 1981, Congress repealed virtually all of the gift in contemplation of death statute but kept a few of its provisions.[3] Now, the gift within three years of death rules apply only to certain types of transfers.[4]

According to the IRS, a gift of trust principal made directly from a living trust to a person other than the trust maker is one of the few types of gifts to which the gift within three years of death rules apply.[5] The IRS's position sent shock waves throughout the estate planning professional community as an unfortunate and unfair reading of the Code.

In 1990, the IRS responded to this professional concern and took a more liberal posture that literally ignored their previous position.[6] The IRS suggested that living trusts be drafted so that trustees are prohibited from making gifts to third parties from living trusts. The IRS concluded that if a living trust is drafted in this manner, even if the trustee violates the terms of the trust by making a direct gift to a third party, there will not be a gift within three years of death problem.[7] By offering this solution, the IRS seemed willing to look the other way even if the trustee knowingly violated the provisions of the trust.

Another solution recommended by the IRS is that living trust language should contain a provision that states that any gifts made to third persons are considered to be transfers that are first made to the trust maker and then to the person receiving the gift. According to the Internal Revenue Service, this language will eliminate the application of the three-year rule.

The IRS's final suggested solution is for the trust maker to take property out of the trust, title it in his or her own name, and then make the gift to the third party.

The IRS also made it clear that living trusts which allow the trustee to make distributions for the legal support obligations of the trust maker and distributions for the direct benefit of the maker do not fall within the three-year rules. The IRS also stated that distributions made by a trustee to a trust maker's agent under a durable power of attorney that allows the agent to carry on a gift program are acceptable.[8]

The gift within three years of death rules are not a factor in making gifts of trust property directly to third parties as long as one of the suggested IRS solutions is used.[9]

Continuing Gift Programs After Incapacity

Sometimes an individual will enter into a gift program that may last for many years. This is particularly true when a person has a relatively large estate and would like to reduce it by making periodic lifetime gifts. A gift program can be continued after the incapacity of a trust maker as long as the proper estate planning documentation has been put into place.

Will-planning/probate advocates recommend that a durable power of attorney be used to continue a gift program after a will maker becomes incapacitated. While a durable power of attorney can be used for these purposes, it must specifically authorize the gifts.[10] In addition, the agent's power to make gifts must be limited so that gifts cannot be made for his or her own benefit. Without such a limitation, if the agent dies prior to the principal, all of the principal's property will be included in the agent's estate for federal estate tax purposes![11]

Some lawyers draft durable powers of attorney that allow the agent to initiate gift programs even though the principal is not presently making gifts and has no intention of doing so in the future. Other lawyers limit these powers of attorney to situations where there are existing gift programs. In either event, the agent is given broad powers to dispose of the principal's property with few, if any, restrictions. Allowing an agent under a power of attorney the unfettered discretion to make gifts, especially after one is incapacitated, opens the possibility of significant abuse and the danger that the assets will be incorrectly given away. A properly written living trust–centered plan can effectively carry on a gift program. A durable power of attorney is not the best legal instrument for purposes of continuing a gift program.[12]

Living Trusts

A trustee is in a much better position to evaluate the trust maker's overall estate planning desires than a mere agent under a power of attorney. In addition, a trustee's fiduciary responsibilities are better defined than those of an agent. A trustee can carry on an existing gift program or initiate one with great assurance that he or she is following the precise instructions and intent of the trust maker.[13]

If a gift program is required to be continued after the giver's disability, a revocable living trust will offer significantly more control, direction, and fiduciary responsibility than a power of attorney.

A living trust is the most effective method for carrying on a gift program after the trust maker's incapacity. It is far more effective than the power of attorney alternative, in spite of the claim of probate advocates to the contrary. The gift within three years of death issue is not important if IRS guidelines are followed.

Our Conclusion

Gifts can be made from a living trust to third parties without adverse estate tax consequences. A living trust–centered plan is better than will-planning/probate for continuing the gift programs of incapacitated people.

· 15 ·

Federal Estate
Tax Planning

Questions for Discussion

- How does federal estate tax generally apply?
- Why does typical will planning fail to plan adequately for federal estate tax?
- Why is will-oriented disclaimer planning ineffective?

Federal estate tax planning becomes an important issue when an individual's estate is in excess of $600,000 and when a couple's combined estate exceeds $600,000. Because federal estate tax rates begin at 37 percent and quickly reach a maximum of 55 percent,[1] estate planning professionals view it as of primary concern in the estate planning process.

Some living trust advocates make the claim that a revocable living trust is superior to a will in terms of accomplishing federal estate tax planning. Will-planning/probate advocates take exception to this claim. They emphatically deny that the living trust can accomplish more effective estate planning than will planning.

There is no doubt that the provisions of a properly drafted

will can create exactly the same federal estate tax planning benefits that a living trust can. But that is hardly the point. Will advocates neglect to acknowledge the realities of the way most will planning is done. While many wills have the *capability* to carry out federal estate tax planning, in reality they do not actually fulfill that capability.

The Federal Estate Tax

The federal estate tax is an excise tax imposed on the right to transfer property at death. As such, it taxes literally everything that a person owns at his or her death, including joint tenancy property, life insurance death proceeds, ownership in a business, and almost anything else that one can think of. Only a handful of property interests are not subject to the federal estate tax, but they are rare.[2]

Property that avoids probate does not necessarily avoid the federal estate tax. Probate has nothing to do with the federal estate tax.

Every taxpayer is granted a credit of $192,800 against the federal estate tax.[3] The dollar value of this credit is $600,000, which is commonly referred to as the exemption equivalent. This exemption equivalent means that $600,000 of a decedent's taxable estate is sheltered by this credit. The exemption equivalent can be used to shelter taxable lifetime gifts as well as federal estate tax.

For married couples, the Internal Revenue Code offers a method to defer federal estate tax called the *unlimited marital deduction*.[4] The unlimited marital deduction shelters all property left to a surviving spouse from federal estate tax when his or her spouse dies.

Because of the exemption equivalent and the unlimited marital deduction, a married couple can, with proper planning, pass a total of $1,200,000 to their children or others totally free of federal estate tax. Unmarried persons do not have the luxury of using the unlimited marital deduction. They can only pass $600,000 at death federal-estate-tax-free.

When trust and will-planning/probate advocates speak of federal estate tax planning, they are generally referring to the planning that can be accomplished for a married couple. Little or no federal estate tax planning is available with either will-planning/probate or living trust planning for unmarried people, because they cannot take advantage of the unlimited marital deduction.[5]

Will Planning and
Federal Estate Tax Planning

A married couple generally wants the surviving spouse to receive all of their marital property upon the death of the other spouse. At the death of the surviving spouse, a married couple usually wants any property that is left to pass to their children or grandchildren. To memorialize this desire, many couples dutifully fulfill what they perceive as their estate planning responsibility by having their attorney draft simple wills.

The Simple Will

Simple wills include no federal estate tax planning. They are designed to pass a spouse's property to the surviving spouse, if living, and, if not, to their surviving children. Because all of the deceased spouse's property is left outright to the surviving spouse, the unlimited marital deduction applies when the first spouse dies. There is no federal estate tax, and this is true even though property passes directly to a spouse as a result of joint tenancy property or through a beneficiary designation.

To the extent this method is used, and the couple's combined assets exceed $600,000, there will be up to $235,000 of unnecessary federal estate tax on the death of the surviving spouse. This unnecessary tax is generated because a simple will does not allow the use of the $600,000 exemption equivalent amount on the death of the first spouse. It is relatively common for estates to reach this $600,000 floor when life insurance and employee benefit proceeds are taken into account.

An often-touted advantage of a will is that the cost of its preparation is usually much lower than that of a trust. From a practical perspective, this means that a lawyer will spend far less time investigating client needs than if a more substantial fee is charged. When a low fee is charged, the attorney does not usually take the time needed to evaluate the estate tax ramifications of the plan.

The American Bar Association (ABA) has recognized this problem. The ABA Committee on Significant New Developments in Probate and Trust Law Practice found that law firms use wills as loss leaders and that this practice may lower the quality of the planning work done.[6]

Many estates that were originally planned with a simple will currently have outgrown this planning and desperately need federal estate tax planning. However, it would appear that their makers do not realize this and die without doing adequate financial planning.

Wills That Address Estate Planning

Wills that purport to address federal estate tax planning are not often effective in doing so. These wills generally create two testamentary trusts, a marital deduction trust and a credit shelter trust.[7] They contain a *formula clause* that is designed to allow the full utilization of the marital deduction and the unified credit amount when the first spouse dies. If the formula clause is successful, it will take into account the value of the deceased spouse's probate property at his or her death so that $600,000 worth of property will pass to a credit shelter trust and the remainder will pass to a marital deduction trust. The goal of this planning is to shelter $1,200,000 of the couple's property from federal estate tax.

Having a will for federal estate tax planning purposes does not guarantee the will maker that federal estate tax will, in fact, be avoided. A will does not control joint property, nor does it control property that passes by beneficiary designations. Nonprobate property constitutes a significant percentage of most couples' estates. Married couples own most, if not all, of their property in joint tenancy. Their retirement plan benefits, IRAs, and employee benefits pass by beneficiary designation. As a consequence, their wills control little or none of their property. Statistics bear this out.

In 1989, the American Association of Retired Persons released a booklet entitled *A Report on Probate: Consumer Perspectives and Concerns.*[8] It reported that, in a survey of three states, more than three-quarters of all the probate cases sampled were for people who were single at the time of their deaths. The report reached the conclusion that the reason for such a large number of probate proceedings for single people was that probate was avoided by joint tenancy property and beneficiary designations on the death of the first spouse.

If a substantial amount of property bypasses the will, little or no estate tax planning can be accomplished. Joint tenancy property between spouses and beneficiary designations naming spouses qualify for the unlimited marital deduction, thereby avoiding all federal estate tax on the death of the first spouse, but do not take advantage of the $600,000 exemption equivalent. This can result in $235,000 of unnecessary tax when property is left to the next generation.

A number of married couples have gone to the time, trouble, and expense of having wills prepared that allegedly address federal estate tax issues. But, because their wills do not control their nonprobate property, little, if any, federal estate tax planning is accomplished.

Disclaimer Planning—Escape or Trap?

Probate lawyers respond to this problem by asserting that it can be "fixed" after the death of the will maker by "qualified disclaimer" planning.[9] A qualified disclaimer is an irrevocable and unqualified refusal to accept an interest in property.

There are four requirements for a valid qualified disclaimer[10]:

1. The disclaimer must be written.
2. The disclaimer must be made no later than nine months after the day on which the transfer is made.
3. A disclaimer is valid only if the person disclaiming the property has not accepted it or any of its benefits prior to making the disclaimer.

4. The disclaimed property must pass to someone other than the person making the disclaimer.

Disclaimed property passes under state laws of descent and distribution or intestate succession unless there is a provision in a will or trust to the contrary. Passing property to heirs who are determined by state law is not prudent planning. Bar associations have spent decades convincing people that they should prepare wills so that their property will not be distributed under state descent and distribution statutes. If the disclaimer advocates' arguments are to be accepted, the disclaimed property will be distributed to statutory heirs, a result which is the exact opposite of the bars' recommendations.

A disclaimer is supposed to be used to rectify a planning oversight. It usually works like this:

> *John died with a will that included federal estate tax planning. Unfortunately, John and his wife, Debra, owned all of their property in joint tenancy. John also had a substantial amount of life insurance and some retirement benefits that named Debra as their beneficiary.*
>
> *Because the property passed to Debra outside John's will, his $600,000 exemption equivalent was lost. This planning error could cost John and Debra's children an additional $235,000 of federal estate tax on Debra's death.*
>
> *The attorney for John's estate recommended that Debra disclaim $600,000 worth of the property. Under state law, this disclaimed property will pass equally to John's children.*

As a practical matter, it is difficult to convince a surviving spouse that a disclaimer is in his or her best interest. It is not likely that a surviving spouse will give up $600,000 of his or her inheritance for a future intangible tax benefit for the children. Disclaimer planning is hardly the model for definitive estate planning. Leaving such an important decision to a grieving spouse is not prudent professional planning.

In our example, John's children were also Debra's children. If John had children from a prior marriage, they would have received the disclaimed property. Would Debra be willing to disclaim the property so that John's children would get the property and save tax dollars?

What if John and Debra's children are minors when John dies? If Debra disclaims, the disclaimed property will pass to the probate court for the benefit of the children and will stay there until each child takes his or her share on reaching adulthood. Since minor children cannot own property, a guardian will have to be appointed for them. In some instances, even though the surviving spouse is the natural guardian of the children, he or she still may have to go to court to be appointed as the formal legal guardian for purposes of transfers of some property, such as real estate.

And, worse yet, that same property will be subject to the claims of John's creditors. With disclaimer planning, creditor-free assets suddenly become assets subject to the claims of creditors. In this instance, disclaimer planning might save federal estate tax but it could totally annihilate John's other planning desires.

Disclaimers and Joint Tenancy Property

Qualified disclaimers are not simple estate planning devices. They are subject to precise rules, have certain practical problems in terms of application, and have been the subject of major litigation, especially when applied to joint tenancy.

Disclaimer planning may not work well, or at all, for joint

tenancy property. The IRS takes the position that a surviving joint tenant cannot disclaim any part of an interest in property, including a survivorship interest, if more than nine months has passed since the transfer creating the joint tenancy.[11] The federal courts are divided on how disclaimers of joint tenancy property work.[12] The result of this disagreement between the IRS and the courts is that in some jurisdictions a qualified disclaimer may be effective for joint tenancy property, and in others it may not. It is almost certain that the IRS will continue challenging disclaimers of joint tenancy property until the issue is finally resolved by the Supreme Court. Under such uncertain and potentially costly circumstances, relying on a qualified disclaimer for joint tenancy property is not a wise planning alternative.

Living Trusts and Federal Estate Tax Planning

Funding a living trust does not make it exempt from the federal estate tax, nor does it magically make the tax, or any part of it, disappear.[13] The retention of the right to revoke, alter, or amend a trust causes the trust property to be included in the maker's gross estate if the power is held by the maker at his or her death or if that power has been relinquished by the maker within three years of death.[14] While the revocable living trust does not offer any special advantages in minimizing federal estate tax, it can effectively maximize use of the unlimited marital deduction and the unified credit, as well as offering myriad other planning advantages.

For trust estates that are subject to the federal estate tax, the appropriate formula clause can be chosen to maximize tax planning in terms of planning motives, type of property, and other factors. Properly funding a living trust eliminates the planning pitfalls of joint tenancy and beneficiary designations that are so destructive to will-centered estate plans. Living trust planning also does not rely on disclaimer planning; it relies on the trust maker's instructions.

An estate planning expert makes the powerful argument that even an unfunded revocable living trust that has the proper formula clause in it is superior to a will.[15] He states that a formula clause in a will does not operate on all of the maker's probate and nonprobate assets. Because of this failing, too much property may be sheltered by the marital deduction and not enough may be sheltered by the $600,000 exemption equivalent. The result is that a married couple cannot pass a full $1,200,000 federal-estate-tax-free to beneficiaries. An unfunded living trust's formula operates on all of a trust maker's property and avoids the problem of overqualifying the marital deduction and underutilizing the exemption equivalent. The only time that an unfunded trust may not maximize federal estate tax savings is when a married couple owns a substantial amount of joint tenancy property. In Chapter 24, "Comparing Living Trusts with Joint Tenancy Planning," we explain why joint tenancy is not a wise way to own property for estate planning purposes.

Our Conclusion

Living trust–centered planning is superior to will-planning/probate for purposes of federal estate tax planning.

· 16 ·

Continuity in Business Affairs

Questions for Discussion

- How do financial guardianship and probate proceedings disrupt a person's business affairs?
- How can a fully funded living trust prevent these disruptions?

A common problem of financial guardianship and probate proceedings is that they are both subject to court supervision and statutory constraints and invariably cause disruptions in the continuity of a ward's or decedent's ongoing business affairs.

Because a living trust continues to function on the disability or death of its maker, it does not have this disadvantage.

Lack of Continuity in
Financial Guardianships and Probate

A number of people own closely held business interests that require constant management and supervision in order to retain their value. Upon the adjudication of mental incompetency of the owner, the probate court takes immediate jurisdiction over all business interests. In effect, the financial guardian, which in some jurisdictions is called a *conservator*, becomes the manager of the business interests, and the owner becomes a ward of the court. In a probate, the probate court takes immediate jurisdiction over all business interests and the executor becomes the manager of the business interests.[1] Executors and financial guardians are agents for the court, acting for the court but always subject to its regulation.

Professor James A. Casner, writing in the *Columbia Law Review* about the benefits of probate avoidance, pointed out that the probate process requires the assets of a decedent to go through two distinct "managerial shifts" after the death of the owner.[2] On the owner's death, management shifts to the estate's executor. When the assets of the estate are distributed, management again shifts from the executor to the appropriate heir.[3] He says that a revocable living trust may prevent the expense, delay, and lack of management continuity that each of these shifts produces.

Because of the inherent complexity and red tape of financial guardianship and probate proceedings, all court-controlled business activities are usually impaired and often come to a halt. While the financial guardian or the executor begins the process of gathering assets and paying creditors, there can be no business activity that would compromise the claims of its creditors. This legal hiatus plays havoc with assets that require active and continuous management.

A court order may be required in order for the business to continue. This means that a petition must be filed with the court requesting that the financial guardian or executor be granted formal authority to operate the business. A hearing is often held to present evidence on the merits of the request. The judge will decide the initial fate of the enterprise, and the financial guardian's or executor's skill will determine, in large part, whether or not it survives.

Vendors, customers, and creditors are given notice of the proceeding and will be fully cognizant of the situation. The proceeding will give them the opportunity to review business records and the financial affairs of the disabled or deceased business owner. This review process can impair an executor's or financial guardian's ability to continue existing credit relationships, which are often critical to maintaining the enterprise's ability to buy urgently needed goods and services.

Other problems of a similar nature can arise. For example, it is not uncommon for some forms of debt and performance bonds to contain provisions that provide for the acceleration of payment on the adjudicated incapacity of the debtor. Once the adjudication is formally made by the court, the acceleration is triggered. Creditors can then use the court as a convenient forum to collect debt. Since financial guardianship, like probate, requires an accounting and an inventory of all of a ward's assets and liabilities, creditors can use this information to their benefit, and to the detriment of the ward's business.

If a ward or a decedent owns stock in a corporation, the continuity of the corporation may not be affected to the same extent as a sole proprietorship or partnership. Because the management of a corporation is separate from its own-

ership, the business of the corporation can continue unin-
terrupted. The executor or the financial guardian controls
the stock of the corporation, but existing management runs
the business. In reality, the intervention of the legal system,
even in the form of stock ownership, makes customers and
suppliers uncomfortable, potentially interfering with the
corporation's business.

Because of the difficulty in operating and maintaining
business interests after the disability or death of the business
owner, it is often necessary for the financial guardian or
executor to sell the business or its underlying assets. This
may not be what the ward or decedent would want and may
not necessarily be in the interests of the remaining family
members. However, in most cases, the heirs do not have to
be consulted as to the executor's or financial guardian's decision to sell.

Selling a closely held business is often difficult. Any sale
initiated by a financial guardianship or estate is considered
by many people as a "fire" sale, where bargains are expected.
The public nature of the sale, the access to confidential
information by third parties, and the circumstances of the
sale can make a sale burdensome and costly.

Using a Fully Funded Living Trust to Reduce Continuity Problems

Continuity problems are not as likely to arise when a
business owner has a fully funded living trust. This is because property held in the name of a living trust is not
affected by the death or incapacity of the trust maker, a
trustee, or a beneficiary.

If the trust maker becomes incapacitated, the trust does
not stop, nor are there intervening court proceedings. The

trust continues. Its trustees follow the trust maker's instructions placed in the trust for precisely that event. Every properly written living trust has instructions to its trustees about what they are to accomplish on the incapacity or death of the maker.

When a properly drafted living trust is in place, there is no incentive for a family to petition a court to initiate a financial guardianship proceeding. This is because a properly written trust document will always contain

- The names of the trustees who are to continue the trust maker's business affairs
- The instructions for the care and economic benefit of the trust maker and other specified family members
- The instructions for the care and nurturing of the trust maker's business and other financial interests

The trust maker's business will continue and will not be impeded by the procedural rules that are so much a part of the adjudication process.

A properly written living trust will not be affected if a guardianship proceeding is initiated. A court-appointed personal guardian has no control over the finances of the ward. He or she will not be a factor in the ward's business. A financial guardian will not have control over a ward's living trust assets as long as the trust is properly drafted.

When a trust maker dies, his or her living trust will continue without disruption in its activities. The trust assets will not be subject to probate. The trustees will continue to administer the trust without court interference for the benefit of the beneficiaries.

A well-written living trust contains instructions that name successor trustees on the disability or death of the trust maker and the subsequent death or disability of any trustee. If a trustee, including the maker, is no longer able to serve because of death, incapacity, or any other reason, a successor trustee immediately takes his or her place. There is no court intervention, nor is it necessary to stop any financial, business, or economic activity. The trust will continue pursuant to the instructions of the trust maker, just as a household continues when it is left in the management of a trusted caretaker.

It is important that the terms of the trust address special financial situations with special instructions. If a closely held business interest is held by the trust, the trust maker may want the trustees to appoint experts as advisers to the trustees. If the trust maker has special instructions as to how the business should be operated after his or her disability or death, then those instructions can easily be written into the trust instrument.

Our Conclusion

A fully funded living trust is superior to will-planning/ probate for business continuity planning because it enables business to proceed in the usual manner.

· 17 ·

The Rights of a Spouse

Questions for Discussion

- Does a surviving spouse have rights to a deceased spouse's property?
- What are the ramifications of state statutes that provide spousal rights to a deceased spouse's property?
- Can a living trust be used to circumvent these state statutes?

State statutes allowing a surviving spouse the right to share in a deceased spouse's property are called *spousal election statutes*. They generally allow spouses to take a portion of a deceased spouse's property even if the deceased spouse attempted to leave it to someone else.

In approximately half the states, the spousal election does not apply to property held in a deceased spouse's living trust.[1] A living trust can prevent the application of spousal election statutes in those states.

A Spouse's Statutory
Right to Take Property

Spousal election statutes are modern versions of ancient English laws of dower and curtesy. *Dower* was "[t]he provision which the law made for a widow out of the land or tenements of her husband, for her support and the nurture of her children."[2] *Curtesy* was the similar right of a husband.[3] Most states have abolished these common law provisions in favor of statutes that give a surviving spouse a right to some portion of the property of the deceased spouse. Every state but Georgia has its own spousal election statute.[4]

The Ramifications of a Spousal Election

Some states allow a spousal election only against probate assets.[5] Others allow the surviving spouse access to all assets, including those that do not pass through the probate process.[6]

Janet and Bill did not have a good marriage. On Bill's death, his will left all of his property directly to his adult children by a prior marriage.

Janet's attorney informed her that in their state she was entitled to 50 percent of all of Bill's property and that she could select the precise 50 percent that she wanted.

Some state statutes specify that only property that is controlled by a spouse's last will and testament can be taken by a surviving spouse and that property that avoids probate cannot be taken.

On Jack's death, his living trust left all of his trust property to his sister.

Sherry, Jack's wife, was informed by her attorney that in their state she is entitled to only 50 percent of Jack's will-planning/probate property and that, since he left everything in a living trust, she was entitled to nothing!

The distinctions that different state statutes make between probate and nonprobate property are critically important to a surviving spouse's statutory rights.[7]

There are eight community property states and one quasi–community property state.[8] Community property states do not have spousal election statutes per se. Community property laws protect a surviving spouse in a different way. All property acquired in a marriage, with few exceptions, is considered to be owned equally by each spouse. A spousal election is not necessary because the surviving spouse already owns one-half of the community property on the death of his or her spouse. A spouse can leave his or her community share to anyone.

In the approximately forty states that allow a spousal election, a surviving spouse ordinarily has the choice of either accepting what is left to him or her under the deceased spouse's estate plan or electing to take the statutory share. From a public policy perspective, these statutes can be beneficial:

Ben and Dottie were married for forty-five years. During all that time, Ben insisted on titling their property in his name alone. Dottie owned nothing in her name.

When Ben died, he left all of the property to his three brothers. Dottie was left penniless. Fortunately, her state's law allowed her the right to take 50 percent of Ben's estate.

This type of situation is what the spousal election statutes are designed to address. As in Dottie's case, spousal election laws emphasize the protection of the surviving spouse, rather than providing the surviving spouse with a windfall. But these laws can also cause unfair results and sometimes far exceed the purposes for which they were designed.

Spousal election statutes give the surviving spouse the right to pick and choose among the estate's assets. Under the typical spousal election statute, a spouse can decide on precisely what property he or she can take. This gives the spouse the advantage of being able to take that property which has the greatest potential for appreciation or income production. Unfair results can occur.

Planning to avoid spousal election statutes is a sensitive subject. Some practitioners take the view that a client's property is his or her own and that its ultimate disposition is personal to that client. Others believe that public policy dictates that a spouse should have the absolute right to a share of that property. This is a decision that only a property owner can make.

Using a Living Trust to Circumvent Spousal Election Statutes

A living trust may be used to circumvent a spousal right statute by adopting the more favorable laws of another state, as fully developed in Chapter 9, "Conflicts of Law." Planning to disinherit a spouse takes extraordinary skill and research and should be accomplished only by knowledgeable attorneys.

Our Conclusion

Living trust–centered planning can circumvent spousal election statutes in many states; will-planning/probate cannot.

· 18 ·

Trustee Liability Under the Comprehensive Environmental Response, Compensation and Liability Act (CERCLA)

Questions for Discussion

- How does CERCLA apply to will-planning/ probate?
- How does CERCLA apply to a revocable living trust?

The Comprehensive Environmental Response, Compensation and Liability Act of 1980 (CERCLA) is federal legislation that determines liability for the cleanup of toxic waste.[1] Rather than making federal or state government responsible for the costs of such cleanup, this federal statute imposes strict retroactive joint and several liability for the costs of cleanup on "potentially responsible parties." Potentially responsible parties include past and current owners and operators of contaminated property. Articles reviewing CERCLA litigation have sounded the alarm regarding this statute's impact on estate planning.

Trust critics claim that a trustee of a living trust may have more liability than an executor or a testamentary trustee under CERCLA. It has also been suggested that living trust beneficiaries may have greater potential CERCLA liability than heirs under a will.

Under CERCLA, it appears that both a trust and a probate estate are considered to be owners of the contaminated property and are therefore liable for cleanup costs.[2] In addition, it is possible that a fiduciary, whether an executor, administrator, or a trustee, can be personally liable for cleanup costs if the decedent's property is insufficient to cover those costs.[3]

Here is how CERCLA liability *might* be imposed:

> *Frank Ledor owned a corner gas station for many years. On Frank's death, his cousin, Mac, was named the executor of the estate, which was composed almost entirely of the value of the gas station.*
>
> *During the course of the probate, it was discovered that gasoline had leaked out of the underground tanks for years and that Frank had buried oil and chemicals used at the station in a corner of the property.*
>
> *The cost of the cleanup was $350,000. Frank's estate was worth only $150,000. Mac may have personal CERCLA liability of $200,000.*

A fiduciary can assert limited defenses to avoid CERCLA liability. One defense is that the contaminated property was acquired by inheritance or bequest.[4] This provision might protect an executor, a testamentary trustee, or even a successor trustee under a living trust because their status with respect to the ownership of the tainted property arises only after the death of the owner.

A potential problem with this defense is that fiduciaries do not acquire property by inheritance or bequest. Fiduciaries manage property for the benefit of the heirs or beneficiaries who will eventually receive it.

It is clear that persons who acquire property as heirs are free of liability if they meet certain other statutory requirements.[5] In this respect, they may not have personal liability for a CERCLA claim even though all of the decedent's property may have to be sold to satisfy the CERCLA liability.

Another defense to a CERCLA claim is that "the defendant did not know and had no reason to know that any hazardous substance . . . was disposed of on, in, or at the facility."[6] Because of the nature of this defense, it is incumbent on fiduciaries to exercise due diligence before accepting their appointment.

How CERCLA May Apply to a Living Trust

While assets of a trust or an estate may be subject to CERCLA liability, it is not yet clear whether a trustee of a revocable living trust, an executor of a probate estate, or the trustee of a testamentary trust is a responsible party under CERCLA.[7] The precise extent of their potential liability is unknown, because the law is still relatively untested.

While an executor and a testamentary trustee may be able to assert the defense that they have acquired the property by inheritance or bequest, there may not be a similar defense for property acquired from a revocable living trust even though the situation is exactly the same as for a testamentary trust. It seems reasonable that a living trust successor trustee who takes over on the death of the trust maker could argue that a successor trustee performs the same function as an executor or testamentary trustee under a will. Like much of the information concerning the application of CERCLA, the extent of a trustee's liability, whether arising out of a testamentary or a living trust, is simply not known because the law is embryonic.

Another strategy that might be used in living trust planning is for a maker to create a living trust for all of his or her property except the tainted CERCLA property. The CERCLA property would pass under the maker's will. This strategy would keep the tainted property separate from the untainted trust property and allow the maker's heirs to inherit the property without personal liability.

Still another approach to eliminate the personal liability of beneficiaries might be to leave the tainted property in a conditional testamentary or living trust worded as follows:

> *I leave any property that is subject to CERCLA liability to my spouse as long as the property is not subject to any liability under CERCLA that is equal to or greater than the value of that property.*

> *If the CERCLA liability is equal to or greater than the value of the property, I instead leave it to the United States of America as an absolute and unrestricted charitable gift.*

Unfortunately, the law under CERCLA is uncertain. There is a ray of hope, however. There is congressional legislation pending that would limit or eliminate the liability of an executor or a trustee. The bill would exclude from the definition of "owner or operator," for purposes of CERCLA, any corporate or individual fiduciary who takes title to property for purposes of administering an estate or trust. This type of legislation is desperately needed to clear up the confusion of the application of CERCLA to fiduciaries.[8]

Our Conclusion

The trustees and beneficiaries of a living trust may have greater personal exposure to CERCLA liability than fiduciaries and heirs under will-planning/probate.

· 19 ·

The Ability of Nonresident Fiduciaries to Serve

Questions for Discussion

- What is a nonresident fiduciary?
- Does will-planning/probate create nonresident fiduciary problems?
- Does a living trust eliminate nonresident fiduciary problems?

People often name family members or close friends who live in other states as executors or trustees. Naming an out-of-state fiduciary in a will may not work if state law restricts or prohibits nonresident fiduciaries from serving. Living trusts do not suffer from these restrictions.

Nonresident Fiduciaries
Under Will-Planning/Probate

Some states, as a matter of policy, are very concerned about having their citizens name out-of-state executors and testamentary trustees. There are several reasons for this concern, not the least of which is the difficulty for nonresident fiduciaries of doing the job. It can be very time consuming and difficult to act as an executor and a testamentary trustee. The difficulties of acting as a fiduciary under a will or testamentary trust are magnified when the fiduciary is out of state. In addition, it may be harder for the heirs to collect from a nonresident fiduciary who makes mistakes than from an in-state fiduciary. States, by regulating nonresident fiduciaries, are attempting to protect their interests and those of their citizens.

According to a digest of state laws published by the American Bar Association, in approximately eighteen states there are restrictions on the use of nonresident executors.[1] Some states require that a nonresident executor post a significant bond. The purpose of a bond is to protect the estate from the mistakes or negligence of the nonresident executor. A bond allows the heirs of an estate to collect any losses caused by a nonresident executor without many of the risks of having to proceed directly against the executor. Georgia, for example, requires a nonresident executor to post a bond that is double the amount of the estate. Virginia permits appointment of a nonresident executor, but only if the executor is a close relative or sole beneficiary, and the executor must post bond in addition to meeting other requirements.

Many states have statutes dealing with the appointment of nonresident corporations and nonresident individuals as trustees of testamentary trusts. Some state statutes prohibit or significantly restrict nonresident testamentary trustees.[2] These restrictions sometimes make it difficult for those who use will-planning/probate to name the trustees they want in the trusts that they create in their wills.

The Ability of Living Trust Trustees to Avoid Restrictions on Nonresident Fiduciaries

One of the most effective ways to prevent the problems sometimes encountered in naming nonresident executors and nonresident testamentary trustees is to use a revocable living trust.[3] State laws place few restrictions on the trustees of living trusts. The general rule is that the trustee of a living trust can act without confirmation or application to a court.[4]

Our Conclusion

Living trust–centered estate planning is better than will-planning/probate for preventing nonresident fiduciary problems.

· 20 ·

Family Considerations

Questions for Discussion

- What effect does the divorce of a trust maker have on a living trust?
- Does a living trust adequately protect after-born and adopted children and grandchildren?

Divorced couples sometimes forget to change their wills after they are divorced. State statutes provide that divorced persons cannot receive distributions from their ex-spouses' wills if they were signed prior to the divorce. Living trust critics claim that these statutes do not apply to living trusts.

Parents sometimes forget to change their wills to include children who are adopted or born after their wills were signed. State statutes provide that adopted and after-born children can nevertheless receive their inheritance. State statutes also make the assumption that if a child is not mentioned in a will, the omission was inadvertent and the omitted child can nevertheless take his or her inheritance. These statutes are called *pretermitted heir statutes*. Living trust critics claim that these statutes generally do not apply to living trusts.

The Divorce of a Trust Maker

States' laws governing will-planning/probate generally provide that if the maker is divorced, and absent any provision in the will to the contrary, his or her divorced spouse will be treated as having predeceased the will maker. These statutes prevent an ex-spouse from inheriting under a will that has not been changed or canceled after a divorce. These statutes almost always do not apply to living trusts.[1] This automatic statutory protection for wills has been cited by will-planning/probate advocates as an advantage that a will has over a living trust.

The argument of will-planning/probate advocates that a will gives better protection on divorce than a trust is not well founded. A trust's terms can provide exactly the same divorce protection for its maker that a will statute provides for will makers. The divorce protection language in a trust gives trust makers the added protection of knowing that, regardless of what state they are subsequently domiciled in, they will be protected in the case of divorce.

Pretermitted Heirs and Adopted Children

Almost all states have laws called *pretermitted heir statutes* that provide that a share of a decedent's estate must pass to children who are born after a will is drafted and who are not named in the will.[2] The share given to these children is usually the part a child would receive by law if the parent had died intestate.[3]

Agatha Smith died leaving a will that left everything to her children, Darla and Ignatius. Two years after signing her will, she gave birth to Samantha. Agatha never bothered to change her will and it did not contain any instructions as to after-born children.

Under the pretermitted heir statutes of Agatha's state, Samantha will receive an equal share of her mother's property.

The pretermitted heir statutes of most states do not apply to revocable living trusts.[4] In some states, living trusts are covered by case law applying those statutes to living trusts.[5] Will-planning/probate advocates argue that wills offer more protection for after-born or inadvertently omitted children than do trusts. Their argument is not meaningful.

Pretermitted heir statutes generally only give a child the share he or she would have received if there was no will or will-substitute. This share only applies to probate assets. If a decedent owned a substantial amount of nonprobate property, the share would be insignificant.

Let's assume that in our example Agatha left life insurance to her two older children, that she owned her home and savings accounts in joint tenancy with her sister, and that she owned an investment account worth $10,000 in her own name. Under these facts, Samantha would only take one-third of the $10,000 brokerage account under the pretermitted heir statute. She would have no right to any of the other property.

Pretermitted heir statutes assume the intent of a decedent and attempt to correct assumed errors in drafting. They are weak substitutes for proper planning and drafting.

A properly drawn living trust always contains language that protects children who are born after the trust has been signed. A trust maker will not have to rely on state pretermitted heir statutes that apply only to probate assets.

Most state statutes grant adopted children equal rights of inheritance. Trust critics correctly point out that these statutes may not apply to living trusts. In the states where they do not, the adopted children will be protected because a properly drawn living trust will contain language that treats adopted children and grandchildren exactly the same as natural descendants. This language will be omitted only in those cases where a client's desires dictate the contrary.

Antilapse Statutes

An issue that is closely related to pretermitted heir and adopted children statutes is the application of *antilapse statutes*. These are state laws that automatically provide for the inheritance of what state statutes assume is a forgotten heir. A very strong argument can be made that a child born before a will was signed and not mentioned in that will is a child whom the will maker intended to disinherit:

> *Gordon was a widower who had three adult children, Thomas, Lilly, and Alice. Gordon and his son, Thomas, fought continually.*

> *Gordon went to his lawyer and specified that he wanted his property to go equally in his will to Lilly and Alice; he did not tell his lawyer about Thomas. The lawyer did not ask questions that would have brought out Thomas's existence. Gordon's will did not mention Thomas.*

On Gordon's death, Thomas, Lilly, and Alice each took one-third of their father's estate because of their state's antilapse heir statute.

Even though Gordon wanted his daughters to receive one-half of his estate each, they only received one-third. Thomas received a statutory windfall because of the state's antilapse statute.

Under the common law rule, absent any provision in the will to the contrary, the gift to a predeceased heir lapses or cancels itself out, and that person's heirs take nothing:

Harry left all of his property to his two children, Shirley and Jennifer, equally. That's all his will said. Shirley predeceased Harry and left a son, Sammy, Harry's grandson, who wants the share that would have gone to his mother.

Under the common law Sammy would not receive anything from his grandfather; his aunt Jennifer would receive it all.

Modern antilapse statutes generally modify the common law rule and allow such gifts to pass to the heirs of the primary heir unless the will provides otherwise:

If Harry were domiciled in a state with an antilapse statute, his grandson Sammy would receive Shirley's inheritance; Sammy's aunt Jennifer would get her half and Sammy would get the half-share left to his mother.

The common law rule for a lapse under a trust is the same as the common law rule for a will: the gift lapses and the heirs of the beneficiary do not take any of the gift.[6] Whether an antilapse statute will apply to trusts depends on the terms of the statute and the terms that are contained in the trust.[7]

No matter whether the common law rule applies or whether the state antilapse statute applies, the attorney managing the estate planning should do everything possible to cover these simple contingencies and not rely upon these catchall antilapse statutes, which may, or may not, accomplish the desires of the client. It is important to understand that the trust document itself can contain lapse provisions. The lapse provisions included in a trust will preempt state antilapse laws and will control how trust property is distributed when there is a lapse. With proper drafting, an individual can determine how lapsed property passes rather than allowing the state or common law to make that decision.

Our Conclusion

Living trust–centered estate planning and will-planning/probate can accomplish the same results with respect to divorce and pretermitted heirs.

· 21 ·

After-Death
Income Tax Issues

Questions for Discussion

- Are living trusts and probate estates subject to the same after-death income tax rules?
- How significant are these after-death income tax issues?

Upon a trust maker's death, his or her living trust becomes a separate taxpaying entity. Similarly, when a person dies with will-planning/probate, the probate estate is a separate taxpaying entity. Even though it would seem logical that living trusts and probate estates would be treated in exactly the same manner for income tax purposes, Congress has chosen to treat them differently. Because of this disparate after-death income tax treatment of living trusts and probate estates, will-planning/probate advocates say that probate has an advantage.

It is true that in some areas of after-death income taxation, probate estates have been granted certain advantages over living trusts. However, four factors significantly diminish the importance of these after-death income tax advantages:

1. With the compression of income tax brackets under the Tax Reform Act of 1986, the benefits of both living trusts and probate estates as separate taxpayers have become far less meaningful.
2. The number of individuals who qualify for the advantages of the after-death income taxation of estates is minimal.
3. Any after-death income tax advantages that a probate estate may have last only as long as the probate estate is kept open.
4. A proper living trust–centered estate plan can use a nominal probate estate to take advantage of any necessary after-death income tax advantages.

After-death income tax planning is not of great importance for most estates. Where it may be of some consequence, living trust–centered planning is still the better estate planning solution, even if a probate estate must be opened to use the after-death income tax advantages that a probate estate does have.

A major point that will-planning/probate advocates often do not address is that testamentary trusts and living trusts are taxed in exactly the same way after the death of the maker and are subject to the same technical income tax rules. The few after-death income tax advantages that a probate estate receives can only be utilized during the period that the probate estate is open.

Because of the growing popularity of revocable living trusts, in March 1991, the chair of the Section of Taxation of the American Bar Association wrote a letter to the chief counsel and staff director of the House Ways and Means Committee, accompanied by a proposal for tax simplification, advocating that the after-death taxation of probate estates and living trusts be the same.[1] This proposal summarizes the problem it seeks to redress as follows:

Summary of Problem: Under current law, individuals who take advantage of a funded revocable living trust are taxed differently in a number of circumstances from those who do not. These differences in tax treatment have no justifiable basis, other than an historical one.

Discussion: In recent years, there has been an increasing estate planning use of revocable trusts holding assets during the settlor's lifetime. Use of a funded revocable trust offers significant non-tax advantages over a traditional estate plan, in that it provides (1) a convenient vehicle for managing the property of the settlor, particularly in the event of illness or incapacity, and (2) a means of reducing or eliminating the delay, expense and potential lack of privacy associated with probate at death.[2]

In June 1991, the Tax Simplification Bill of 1991 was introduced into the House and the Senate.[3] In response to this letter and as a result of a growing awareness by Congress of the trend toward revocable living trust planning, a section of the Bill treated living trusts as probate estates in certain areas of after-death income tax planning.[4] The reason given for these proposed changes in the federal income tax law was that because estate planners use revocable living trusts to avoid probate, making the after-death income tax rules the same for trusts and estates will simplify planning and reduce the role of tax considerations in decisions about whether to use revocable living trusts.

This bill did not adopt all of the changes recommended by the chair of the Section of Taxation of the American Bar Association. It did, however, take a step forward in eliminating the arbitrary and unnecessary differences in the after-death income tax treatment accorded living trusts and probate estates.

In early 1992, the Tax Simplification Bill of 1991 became a casualty of budget and tax disagreements between the president and Congress. Although the act's provisions relating to living trusts were not controversial, they were not enacted, becoming lost in the struggles over more visible issues. Nevertheless, the provisions of the bill equalizing tax treatment of living trusts in after-death planning are proof that the growing popularity of living trusts among consumers has finally been recognized by Congress. Because of this recognition and because the loss in tax revenue caused by allowing living trusts and probate estates the same after-death income tax benefits would not likely be significant, we believe these provisions will be introduced again.

Because the after-death income tax issues are not particularly significant, we have given the technical explanation of each of these issues in Appendix A, for those readers who are interested.

Our Conclusion

Probate estates have some advantages over living trust–centered estate planning for purposes of after-death income tax planning, but these advantages are not significant.

° 22 °

The Pour-Over Will

Questions for Discussion

- Is a will a necessary part of a living trust–centered estate plan?
- What purposes do a pour-over will serve?

A living trust–centered plan should always include a "pour-over" will. The primary function of a pour-over will is to act as a fail-safe device to make sure that any property not held in a living trust prior to the death of its maker will pass to the trust after the maker's death. The ability of the pour-over will to leave property to a living trust gave the pour-over will its name: it pours over any probate assets into a living trust.

All states and the District of Columbia have adopted the Uniform Testamentary Additions to Trusts Act or some other type of statute authorizing a will to pour over property into a preexisting living trust.[1] However, certain formalities must be observed in using a pour-over will. For example, the Uniform Testamentary Additions to Trusts Act, which has been adopted in forty-five states and the District of Columbia, requires that the trust be executed before or concurrently with the will.[2] The pour-over statutes in the other states have similar requirements.

The Purposes of the Pour-Over Will

Although the primary purpose of the pour-over will is to make sure that any property not owned by the trust on the death of its maker will pass to the trust, there are other reasons to use a pour-over will.

Control of Property if the Trust Is Invalid or Inoperable

A living trust can be invalid under some circumstances. Examples of events that may cause the invalidity of a trust are improper drafting or execution of the trust, apparent revocation of the trust with no document to replace it, and successful challenge to the trust's validity.

If a living trust is found to be invalid, the pour-over will determines where and how the maker's property will pass. If the pour-over will reaffirms the terms of the living trust, the maker can be assured that, no matter what occurs, the terms of the trust will be preserved. This planning technique eliminates the ability of and incentive for disgruntled heirs to attack the living trust in the hope of gaining a greater inheritance. The only way the disgruntled heirs could have a chance of prevailing would be by invalidating both the trust and the will.

Naming of the Guardian of Minor Children

Most people think that by naming a guardian for their children in their will, they control who actually will be named. This is not true in most jurisdictions. A probate judge will most often determine the appropriate personal guardian for minor children after the deaths of their parents. The parents' choice of guardian will, of course, be given great weight, but a judge will make the final determination.

Because of this judicial power, it does not matter whether or not a will or a living trust is used to name the guardian. The only difference in using a will or a living trust to name a guardian is that all documents that are relevant to the appointment of the guardian are filed with the court and are a matter of public record. If the guardian is named in a living trust, the living trust will have to be made public. If the guardian is named in the pour-over will, the living trust will not have to be made public. For reasons of privacy, we recommend that the guardian be named in the pour-over will.

Availability to Commence a Wrongful Death Action

If a decedent dies because of the negligence or wrongdoing of a third party, a lawsuit for the decedent's wrongful death may be instituted. In a number of states, a wrongful death action may be brought only by the executor of a probate estate. A pour-over will used in conjunction with living trust planning can name an executor and allow such a wrongful death action to be brought.

"Pour-Ups" for After-Death Income Tax Planning

While it is clear that a probate estate has relatively few substantive after-death income tax advantages over a trust, it may be advisable or necessary to create a probate estate for purposes of after-death income tax planning. This can be accomplished by *pouring-up* certain assets from a living trust to a probate estate.[3] This technique is sometimes called *reverse funding*. It allows the probate estate to have the appropriate assets and income so that after-death income tax benefits can be used.

Pour-ups are discretionary distributions from a maker's revocable living trust to the maker's probate estate. The trust is used "as a vehicle for funneling funds to the executor when [the executor is] in need. In reality, a pour-up distribution is one where the trustee is authorized or directed to pay to the executor such sums as the executor requires for debts, expenses of administration, taxes and legacies."[4] In order for this technique to succeed, both the living trust and the pour-over will must have specific language authorizing the distributions.

There should be significant after-death income tax advantages to justify the expense of creating a probate estate. The pour-up technique may have disadvantages other than this expense. For example, some authorities feel that this technique has not been legally supported because the IRS and the courts have not, in a reported ruling, definitively approved its use.[5] Another potential disadvantage is that by creating a probate estate and actually making distributions to it, assets that are creditor-free when held in a living trust may be subject to the probate estate's creditors, even if only for the cut-off period.

Cutting Off of the Claims of Creditors

In a few states, the creation of a probate estate is the only method that can take advantage of the statutes that cut off the claims of creditors within a short period. It appears that a pour-over will can be used to open a nominal probate to cut off the claims even though the decedent's property is held by his or her living trust.

Apportionment of Expenses, Claims, and Taxes

How expenses, claims, and taxes are apportioned after a death is a major issue in estate planning. For example, should the heirs who receive property pay their pro rata share of expenses, claims, and taxes, or should one heir pay more than another? States generally have statutes that control the apportionment of taxes and other expenses, but in many instances, planning may dictate that the state's law should not be followed. By using other apportionment language in a will or a trust, state law can be overridden.

The general rule is that in order to apportion expenses, claims, and taxes in a manner that differs from state statute, the apportionment language must be contained in a will. If it is not, state law controls. To be absolutely sure that the desired apportionment takes place, it is important that identical apportionment language be placed in a pour-over will and a living trust. If this is done, the correct apportionment language will be followed for expenses, claims, and taxes that are paid out of the trust.

Coordination of Activities of the Executor and the Trustee

When it is necessary to have both a living trust and a probate estate, it is important that the pour-over will and the living trust be written in a consistent manner. All of their terms must be coordinated to assure that the utmost flexibility is granted to the trustee and the executor so that the best practical, legal, and tax results can be provided to the maker's beneficiaries.

Our Conclusion

Pour-over wills are concise documents that embellish a living trust–centered estate plan by adding to its flexibility.

PART TWO

Living Trust–Centered Planning Compared to Testamentary Trusts and Joint Tenancy

Comparing Testamentary and Living Trusts

Questions for Discussion

- Is it valid to compare a simple will to a living trust-centered estate plan?
- What are the similarities between living trust-centered planning and testamentary trust planning?
- What are the differences between living trust-centered planning and testamentary trust planning?
- Is living trust-centered planning preferable to testamentary trust planning?

In most instances, trust critics compare revocable living trusts to simple wills. Comparing a people-oriented living trust–centered estate plan to a simple will is like comparing an automobile to a tricycle and then saying the latter is less complex and therefore better. It is a comparison that is not relevant.

A simple will distributes property outright only to heirs. The thousands of simple wills that we have reviewed over the years almost always contain language that says, "To my spouse if living, and if my spouse is not living, then to my descendants *per stirpes*." Simple wills do not provide for tax planning or include instructions for loved ones.

If a simple will is compared to a revocable living trust, the living trust is better for virtually all planning purposes. An argument can be made that a simple will has a few minor advantages, but even these advantages quickly disappear when testamentary trust planning and revocable living trust planning are compared. To level the playing field, it is critical that the debate ultimately be focused on the testamentary trust versus the living trust. When this comparison is made, the distinctions and similarities between them become readily apparent.

A *testamentary trust* is a trust that is created by a will. A testamentary trust does not have an independent existence until after the death of a will maker and receives property only at the death of the will maker. Once it is created by a will, a testamentary trust functions exactly as a living trust functions after the death of its maker, except for one important feature: A testamentary trust can be subject to probate court jurisdiction for part or all of its existence. A living trust is not subject to court supervision either during the life of its maker or after his or her death.

In our experience, most practitioners prepare wills as loss leaders that become a probate cache which, like an annuity, will generate future probate fees. There are a number of probate practitioners who routinely prepare wills that create testamentary trusts for minor children and for affluent couples with taxable estates. The more sophisticated will-planning/probate practitioners create trusts for children and descendants that contain extensive instructions. A smaller number of specialist probate lawyers also routinely prepare special living trusts such as irrevocable life insurance trusts, grantor-retained income trusts, and irrevocable trusts for minor children. However, when it comes to everyday estate planning, most diehard will-planning/probate attorneys are pro–testamentary trust.

A major difference between living trust lawyers and will-planning/probate lawyers is in their opinion about when trust planning should begin. Should it come into effect immediately or only upon death? Will-planning/probate advocates would argue that death is soon enough for a trust to come into existence. Advocates of living trust–centered planning would argue that a trust cannot be instituted soon enough.

Living and Testamentary Trust Planning for a Client

Regardless of whether a practitioner uses living or testamentary planning, there is little or no difference in the time he or she will spend with a client or in the preparation of the appropriate documentation. If two identical clients respectively sought the services of a probate lawyer and trust lawyer, they would theoretically be billed the same amounts for their consultations and the resulting documents.

Each attorney would have to analyze each client's situation carefully by gathering complete personal and financial information. Each attorney would enter into a dialogue with the client in order to exchange information and would familiarize the client with the law as it pertains to the client's situation. Each client would familiarize his or her attorney with personal goals, objectives, beliefs, and biases.

Both attorneys would draft documentation to meet the client's planning needs and desires. Identical planning would take place but for the choice of legal delivery vehicles. The probate lawyer would use a will, and the trust practitioner would use a living trust plan. Each would draft ancillary documentation, such as durable powers of attorney, living wills, and property agreements. The living trust lawyer would also create a simple pour-over will as a legal fail-safe mechanism.

Each attorney would explain the documents so that the client could judge whether they met all of the agreed upon objectives and would supervise the signing and witnessing of the documents.

Both attorneys would then have to make title changes to their clients' affairs so that their respective planning would control the appropriate assets. The will-planning/probate practitioner would want the title in the client's name; the living trust practitioner would want it in the name of the client's trust. This might entail new deeds to property, changes to the title of securities, or title changes to other property. Both practitioners would be sure that all beneficiary designations were changed so that the testamentary or living trust was the named beneficiary.

In either case, the client would generally participate in the title changing process. It is likely that the client's other advisers, including life insurance agents, financial advisers, and accountants, would offer their assistance to the attorney in rearranging the client assets. As the client, the attorney, and the client's other professional advisers worked together, the client's assets would be arranged so that the operative planning document would control them.

What real difference is there in the practices involved in establishing a testamentary trust plan and a living trust plan? The answer is, *very little*. The living trust plan requires that the property be titled in its name; a testamentary trust requires that it be titled in the will maker's name.

The differences in the costs of initiating and preparing the respective plans should not be significant. However, funding a living trust is almost always more time consuming and expensive than rearranging the title to a will maker's property. If the client chose not to fund his or her living trust immediately, the costs of living and testamentary trust planning would be theoretically identical.

But why wait to fund the trust? In essence, funding a living trust is probating one's estate now instead of waiting until death or disability. We firmly believe that there is no reason—or excuse—to delay funding a living trust. Some of the reasons we have heard over the years for not funding a trust are that the clients are just not old enough to justify the cost of funding, that funding now would be too much trouble, or that funding should be done only when the client has more assets. Obviously, each of these is an excuse rather than a reason. Since none of us know when we may become disabled or when we are going to die, there is no reason to delay proper planning. This is especially true in light of funding; we have shown that funding a trust is not as difficult as some will-planning/probate critics would argue. It is also not expensive.

Although we believe that creating a revocable living trust without funding is not the best and most responsible estate planning method, unfunded trusts often exist. At least nine primary reasons have been suggested as to why even an unfunded living trust plan is superior to a testamentary trust plan:

1. The marital deduction formula operates on more assets, thereby maximizing federal estate tax planning for married couples. See Chapter 15, "Federal Estate Tax Planning," and Appendix A, "The Nonrecognition of Losses Between a Trust and Its Beneficiaries."
2. Probate court supervision of the postdeath trust administration is avoided because the court would not have continuing jurisdiction over the trust: privacy and cost savings are achieved. See Chapter 1, "A Pro-

bate Perspective," and Chapter 4, "Delays in Administration."

3. Nonresident trustees may act. See Chapter 19, "The
Ability of Nonresident Fiduciaries to Serve."

4. The trust may be easily moved to another state. See
Chapter 9, "Conflicts of Law."

5. One may choose which state law governs the trust as
long as there is some legitimate reason to choose a
given state. See Chapter 9, "Conflicts of Law."

6. A bypass trust is available if the "trustless" spouse dies
first to maximize federal estate tax savings. See Chapter 15, "Federal Estate Tax Planning," and Appendix
A, "The Nonrecognition of Losses Between a Trust
and Its Beneficiaries."

7. Everything is pooled together under one document,
giving the maker much more control. See Chapter 11,
"General Lifetime Consequences of Funding a Living
Trust."

8. Liquidity is placed in the proper hands so that expenses, claims, and taxes can be paid with less complication and disruption.[1] See Chapter 11, "General
Lifetime Consequences of Funding a Living Trust,"
and Chapter 12, "Assets That Require Special Tax
Attention."

9. If the maker becomes incapacitated, the trust is available to be used without the need for a financial guardianship.[2] See Chapter 3, "Disability Planning."

In our experience, the rearrangement of title to assets is
commonly neglected in will-planning/probate. This reality
goes to the heart of the debate. Most will-planning/probate
advocates assume that a will is less expensive because there
is less to do on the front end. This assumption is untrue.
The real reason that wills are initially less expensive is that
will-planning/probate practitioners know that probate will

eventually rearrange the title to the assets, and, like cleaning the family garage, they postpone the task to a later date.

The Relevant Differences Between Living Trust and Testamentary Trust Planning

To this point we have seen a remarkable similarity between testamentary and living trust procedures that does not satisfactorily account for the differences between the two camps. But, there are differences!

Probate

Before a testamentary trust can become operative, it must go through probate. A living trust avoids probate.

Continuing Probate Court Supervision of a Testamentary Trust

Many states require that a testamentary trust be supervised by the probate court throughout the period of its existence; this period can last for decades. Only when the trust terminates by its own terms or by law does that supervision end.

Each state has its own requirements as to the amount of the local court's supervision, but even in limited supervision jurisdictions additional fees, paperwork, and administrative headaches are present. At a minimum, periodic reporting will be required with all of the requisite formality.[3] The reason for this supervision is that it allegedly ensures that the trustee is acting in a prudent manner. This is a redundancy since the trustee is required to report to the beneficiaries in any event and is subject to extensive legal rules with regard to fiduciary duties.

There is no required court supervision for a revocable living trust. Some revocable trust critics have made the point that judicial supervision of a testamentary trust is a meaningful requirement because it will ensure that the beneficiaries have a forum to challenge the acts of the trustee. Beneficiaries of a revocable living trust have the right to challenge the actions of a trustee at any time. Living trust planning does not deprive beneficiaries of their right to a fair hearing in a court of law. It does eliminate the necessity for continuing judicial supervision.

Probate Fees

The evidence clearly demonstrates that attorney probate fees are substantial. When executor fees are added to these attorneys' fees, the difference in the costs of living trusts and testamentary trusts is even greater. A married couple who relies upon testamentary trust planning will generate two probates—one on the death of each spouse—with respect to the same assets. The facts are clear: testamentary trusts are far more expensive than living trusts because living trusts do not go through probate.

Trustees' Fees

Both testamentary and living trusts generate continuing trustees' fees after the death of the decedent if paid trustees are named. In a testamentary trust, the trustees' fees begin after death. Even though a living trust is created during the lifetime of the maker, it rarely generates current trustees' fees because trust makers typically assume this function. Like testamentary trustees' trust fees, living trust trustees' fees, if any, generally begin after death.

There are no relevant differences in trustees' fees between testamentary and living trusts.

Disability Planning

A testamentary trust is not a lifetime planning instrument and cannot be used to protect the maker from the problems associated with disability. Attorneys who prepare powers of attorney in conjunction with testamentary planning do not provide the same degree of disability protection that can be achieved by combining them with living trust–centered estate plans.

Disability planning can be accomplished with living trust planning; no disability planning can be accomplished with a testamentary trust.

Delays in Administration

Testamentary trusts go through probate and probate creates delay. A testamentary trust does not automatically spring into full operational existence upon a person's death. The assets of the decedent's estate must be "probated" into the trust. Because of probate's many requirements, the executor will seldom make timely distributions immediately after death. Lengthy probate can prevent a testamentary trust from being fully funded for several years after the death of the will maker.[4] Delay will be exacerbated if there are disputes with creditors or if a disgruntled heir contests the will. It can also take several years before testamentary trusts can be properly funded if federal estate tax issues are involved. These events are apart from the fact that the estate's executor must take the time to locate and value the decedent's property and notify and pay creditors, tasks which can be formidable in even small estates.

During the probate hiatus the beneficiaries are not entitled to distributions of the estate's assets. Family needs will have to be satisfied by assets such as joint tenancy or life insurance that were kept outside the probate estate or by miserly statutory allowances.

A living trust comes into existence the day it is signed. Its terms and conditions continue for the benefit of its beneficiaries on the incapacity or death of its maker. There is absolutely no delay when either of these events occurs.

Multiple Probates and the Problems with Ancillary Administration

If a person plans with a testamentary trust and owns real property in more than one state, another probate—ancillary administration—will be necessary in the state where the real property is located. This entails the intervention of another executor, another lawyer, and another probate court in every state where real property is located. Ancillary administration causes excessive fees and delay.

Numerous states have statutes that set forth requirements as to the qualification of "foreign" testamentary trustees, and it is often difficult for a testamentary trustee to qualify in a state other than the "home" state of the decedent.[5]

A revocable living trust completely eliminates this multiple-probate problem. In addition, state statutes dealing with the qualification of foreign trustees generally apply only to testamentary trustees and not to living trust trustees.[6]

Privacy and Confidentiality

The terms of a testamentary trust are a matter of public record and are open to the inspection and scrutiny of anyone. Every transaction that is required to be filed with the court is also a matter of that estate's public record. This is not the case with a living trust.

Will and Trust Contests

If a will containing testamentary trusts is found to be invalid, the trusts created within it are also invalid. Wills are not difficult to attack, which means that the testamentary trust planning within them is equally vulnerable.

A will contest can delay the creation of a testamentary trust for long periods because the very existence of the trust is expressly contingent on the will's validity. Because testamentary trusts are subject to continuing court supervision, they are also susceptible to continuing litigation.

A living trust is not under the jurisdiction and supervision of a probate court and is unlikely to be challenged. Living trust litigation is far more difficult to initiate.

Protection from Creditors

Testamentary trust property is subject to the claims of the decedent's creditors. The typical probate creditor statutes effectively limit the time span in which most creditors can submit their claims; however, because the law now requires that known creditors be given actual notice of a decedent's death, the benefit of these statutes is significantly reduced.

Both testamentary and living trusts offer after-death creditor protection to their beneficiaries through state laws called *spendthrift statutes*. However, testamentary trust planning may have an adverse effect on the creditor-free status of life insurance proceeds, retirement benefits, and other property passing by beneficiary designation to the estate of a decedent.

It is not uncommon for a testamentary trust to be named as the beneficiary of a life insurance policy on the life of the will maker. Life insurance proceeds are typically paid quickly. Yet a testamentary trust may not come into existence for some time. In this case the proceeds might have to be paid directly to the estate, destroying the creditor-free nature of the assets.[7] In many states, proceeds paid to a named beneficiary are exempt from state death taxes. Proceeds paid directly to the estate may be subject to unnecessary state death taxes.[8]

A revocable living trust does not suffer from these problems. After a trust maker's death, a living trust totally cuts off the claims of all of the maker's unsecured creditors in most states. Since the revocable living trust is in existence at its maker's death, third-party beneficiary contract proceeds can be paid directly to the trust free of the claims of creditors. If necessary, a nominal probate can be created with a living trust plan so that the shorter cut-off statutes can be effectively utilized.

Conflicts of Law

The result of having the laws of different jurisdictions determine not only the validity of a will but also the way its terms will be interpreted can be devastating. If a dispute arises out of a testamentary trust and property is owned in more than one state, the resulting litigation will involve conflicts of law that will likely be complex.

A testamentary trust is also subject to questions with respect to its separate validity.[9] These questions may be determined under the laws of the state designated in the testamentary trust but only if the state has a substantial relation to the trust. Otherwise, the validity of the trust, at least for purposes of personal property, will generally be determined under the laws of the state where the trust is administered, and this is true even if the trust is invalid under the laws of the state in which the decedent was domiciled at death.[10]

Conflicts of laws can be more easily anticipated and resolved by using revocable living trusts. Revocable living trusts can be used to "borrow" the more favorable laws of other jurisdictions in which property is owned because trust law allows a maker to choose, in the main, the state law to be used.

Medicaid Planning

Medicaid rules require indigence in order for the government to help pay for the costs of skilled nursing care and other Medicaid benefits. Most people do not want to lose virtually all of their assets and income before they can qualify for Medicaid. They attempt to give their property away "with strings attached" to close family members in order to qualify. Giving property away either outright or in trust often doesn't work.

Under federal law, when a deceased spouse creates a testamentary trust for his or her surviving spouse, the property in the testamentary trust does not count toward the surviving spouse's eligibility for Medicaid. This is a distinct advantage a testamentary trust has over a living trust.

However, a revocable living trust can both eliminate probate and take advantage of this Medicaid testamentary trust loophole if it is used in conjunction with a pour-over will that creates a testamentary trust for the benefit of a surviving spouse. The property in the living trust can then "pour over" into the testamentary trust, avoiding probate, but funding a testamentary trust designed to allow the surviving spouse to qualify for Medicaid benefits.

Lifetime Income Tax Issues of Funding a Revocable Trust

A testamentary trust does not come into existence until the death of its maker and therefore has no lifetime income tax issues. It is funded after the death of the will maker as part of the probate and administration process. Until then, no real funding issues arise. However, the after-death funding of a testamentary trust can be a complex, time consuming, and difficult process.

A revocable living trust should be fully funded. Funding a living trust is exactly like "probating" assets while the maker is alive and well. It is far less expensive and time consuming to face funding issues while a person is alive and well than to wait until he or she is disabled or dead. The ability to fund a trust while the maker is alive is a great advantage of revocable living trust planning.

A living trust is not a separate taxable entity and does not become one until the death of its maker; there are no adverse income tax ramifications in establishing a trust. Living trust makers do not have to change the way they live or do business to enjoy the benefits of a trust. With minor exceptions, a living trust can own virtually any type of property, and transferring property into it is an easily accomplished task. Funding a trust is not a planning obstacle; it is a planning benefit.

Gift Tax Issues

No gift tax problems are associated with testamentary trusts because they do not come into effect until after the death of their makers. Trust makers can make gifts from living trusts without problems if appropriate IRS guidelines are followed. A gift program that survives the giver's incapacity can be appropriately structured; this is best accomplished through the use of a revocable living trust.

Federal Estate Tax Planning

A testamentary trust and a revocable living trust can accomplish identical estate planning results. But testamentary planning often does not constitute good federal estate tax planning. It can only achieve maximum federal estate tax planning for married couples if it controls the property of the first spouse to die.

It is common practice for married couples with testamentary planning to retain the ownership of their property in joint tenancy. In addition, married couples often name each other as the primary beneficiary of their life insurance and other third-party beneficiary contracts. Under these circumstances, testamentary planning generally will not accomplish optimum federal estate tax planning. The only hope of salvaging federal estate tax planning in these situations is with after-death disclaimer planning, a technique which yields uncertain results. The problems with disclaimer planning are explained Chapter 15, "Federal Estate Tax Planning."

Funded living trusts assure that many federal estate tax problems will be prevented. A living trust's federal estate tax formula clause will control more property than the typical formula clause in a will.[11] This characteristic is especially important if the client and the attorney have not spent the time and energy to examine and retitle assets correctly.

Continuity in Business Affairs

When property must be administered as part of the probate process, the continuity of the decedent's affairs will be disrupted. As the custodian or executor gathers assets, pays creditors, and administers the ward's or decedent's property, most financial activities will come to a grinding halt. This is true even in states with simplified probate procedures because testamentary trusts do not prevent financial guardianships or probates.

Disability and death do not have to be disruptive in terms of bringing all of the decedent's business and financial activities to a halt. Because living trust trustees and their successors are the legal title holders of the trust assets, the death or incapacity of the maker, the beneficiaries, or the trustees will not affect the continuity of the trust.

The Rights of a Spouse

A will, and the testamentary trusts within it, cannot be used to avoid spousal election statutes. However, in many jurisdictions, a revocable living trust can be used to effectively avoid the application of the spousal election statutes.

Trustee Liability Under the Comprehensive Environmental Response, Compensation and Liability Act (CERCLA)

CERCLA may hold heirs, executors, and trustees liable for the costs of toxic cleanup. A defense may be available for property owners who acquire the property through inheritance or bequest. Any trustee may be accountable for cleanup because the government may contend that the property was not acquired directly by inheritance or bequest. Therefore, trustees of either a living trust or a testamentary trust will likely be equally responsible under CERCLA.

The Ability of Nonresidents to Serve as Trustees

A testamentary trustee often has difficulty attempting to act in another state. Often a will maker would like to name an out-of-state fiduciary to serve as a testamentary trustee but is prevented from doing so by state laws that prohibit naming nonresidents to serve in a fiduciary capacity. Through the use of a revocable living trust, the trust maker has the complete flexibility to name fiduciaries without regard to their geographic location.

Divorce and Children

Every state has laws that provide that a will with testamentary trust planning is automatically terminated with respect to a divorced spouse upon the dissolution of the will maker's marriage. Living trusts can be drawn with a clause which terminates the rights of an ex-spouse in precisely the same manner as these statutes.

Almost all states have laws that provide that a share of a will maker's estate must pass to children who are born or adopted after a will is signed and who are not named in the will. These statutes also protect children who are unintentionally left out of a will. An identical clause can easily be added to a living trust in order to accomplish the same objectives.

After-Death Income Tax Issues

Testamentary and living trusts are taxed in exactly the same manner after the death of the maker and are subject to the same technical income tax rules.[12] The few after-death income tax advantages which an estate receives are only operative during the period the estate is in the probate process.

A noted legal expert, addressing the differences between living trust planning and testamentary trust planning, states:

One assumes that there must be some rationale for the use of a testamentary trust over a revocable living trust, but no one has yet provided a plausible argument which can withstand serious scrutiny.[13]

Our Conclusion

The facts speak for themselves. Living trust–centered estate planning is far preferable to testamentary trust planning. And yet a majority of the nation's lawyers continue to avoid the living trust. They appear to be following the old German proverb, "An old error is always more popular than a new truth."[14]

· 24 ·

Comparing
Living Trusts to
Joint Tenancy Planning

Questions for Discussion

- What is joint tenancy ownership?
- What are the consequences of using joint tenancy as an estate planning substitute?
- Is joint tenancy planning less expensive than other methods of estate planning?

Living trust critics make the argument that joint tenancy planning is an inexpensive alternative to living trust–centered estate planning for some people. The purpose of this chapter is to compare living trust–centered planning to joint tenancy planning to see whether this criticism is warranted.

Joint tenancy is the most common "will-substitute" used by married couples.[1] It is also used from time to time by single people. Joint tenancy ownership is not particularly well understood and is condemned by living trust planners and most will-planning/probate planners as well.[2] Much has been written about joint tenancy's problems. Yet because of the ignorance about its negative planning ramifications on the one hand, and the fact that it avoids probate on the other, many people rely on it as a substitute for proper planning.

The General Characteristics
of Joint Tenancy Ownership

Joint tenancy is a self-contained estate plan that is a partial will-substitute because it avoids probate as long as one tenant is still living. The full name of joint tenancy is really *joint tenancy with right of survivorship*. If two people own property in joint tenancy, when the first joint tenant dies, the other joint tenant automatically receives ownership of the property. There is no need for probate because ownership passes by operation of law. Joint tenancy is a "winner take all" planning strategy because a joint tenant cannot control where the property will pass at his or her death by will or by trust; it will pass to the surviving joint tenant. Only the last surviving tenant can control the disposition of the property at death.

Contrast this with tenancy in common ownership. When two people own property equally in tenancy in common, they each own 50 percent of the property. When one of the tenants in common dies, he or she can leave his or her 50 percent ownership in the property by will or by trust. Since there is no "right of survivorship" feature in tenancy in common, a tenant can control his or her share of the property at death with a will or a trust.

Because joint tenancy property passes to the surviving tenants by operation of law, it is impossible to integrate it into a properly drafted estate plan without changing the joint tenancy ownership to tenancy in common or by having only one of the joint tenants own all of the property. In our experience, title to joint tenancy property is rarely reviewed or changed in will-planning/probate, so the will does not control any of the joint tenancy property.

A living trust–centered estate plan controls all of its maker's property and contains all of the maker's estate planning instructions. When a living trust–centered plan is prepared, joint tenancy property is almost always changed into tenancy in common property as part of the funding process. This allows the living trust to control the property. For example, if a husband and a wife own real estate in joint tenancy, one-half of the real estate would be put into the wife's trust and one-half would be put into the husband's trust. This would eliminate joint tenancy with right of survivorship, and the trusts would each own one-half of the property as a tenant in common.

The same principle would apply to a joint trust. When joint tenancy property is properly transferred into a joint trust, the property loses its survivorship feature. Each trust maker is considered to own one-half of the property, thereby allowing the trust to control each maker's half of the property.

Estate Tax Issues

One-half of the value of joint tenancy property is included in the estate of the first spouse to die, regardless of which spouse furnished the funds to purchase the property.[3] For nonspouses, the full value of jointly owned property is included in the estate of the first joint tenant to die unless the survivor can prove that he or she contributed funds for the property's acquisition or unless the property was acquired by gift or inheritance.[4] An example of this follows:

Betty purchased a valuable painting for $50,000 in 1982. She titled it in joint tenancy with her cousin, Ted, because Betty was concerned about her health. She felt that if Ted owned the painting in joint tenancy with her, then if it needed to be sold at a later time when Betty was ill, Ted could sign the papers. Even though Betty really didn't intend to make a gift, by titling the painting in joint tenancy, she inadvertently made a gift. This "mistake" resulted in a taxable gift of $25,000. Part of the gift was sheltered by Betty's $10,000 annual exclusion. The remaining $15,000 was sheltered by using part of Betty's $600,000 exemption equivalent, so no gift taxes were due.

Betty died ten years later, when the painting was worth $150,000. The painting automatically passed to Ted by operation of law. The full value of the painting was included in Betty's estate for federal estate tax purposes.

If Betty's estate is subject to federal estate tax, it is possible that Betty's estate will have to pay the estate taxes due on the painting even though it did not pass to her estate. That means that not only will Betty's heirs not receive the painting, they will receive even less of Betty's estate because it was reduced by the tax.

Joint tenancy property owned by spouses often has adverse federal estate tax consequences. Because joint tenancy property automatically passes to the surviving spouse, the ability to use marital deduction and exemption equivalent planning to minimize federal estate taxes is often lost. Two contrasting examples illustrate this point:

A married couple, Stan and Connie, owned all of their property in joint tenancy. When Stan died, the total value of their joint property for federal estate taxes was

$1,500,000—$750,000 of which was included in Stan's estate. Because the property was owned jointly, it passed to Connie free of federal estate tax because of the unlimited marital deduction.

Connie died shortly thereafter. The value of her federal taxable estate was $1,500,000. The federal estate tax due was $363,000.

Contrast this result to a slightly different set of facts:

Stan and Connie owned all of their property in tenancy in common. When Stan died, the total value of his interest in the property for federal estate tax purposes was $750,000.

Stan's property was held in a revocable living trust that allocated $600,000 of the property to a family trust and the remainder to a marital trust for Connie. The property in the family trust was free of federal estate tax because of Stan's $600,000 exemption equivalent; the unlimited marital deduction sheltered the amount in Connie's marital trust.

Connie died shortly thereafter. The value of her taxable estate was $900,000: her $750,000 interest in the property plus the $150,000 in the marital deduction trust.

The federal estate tax due was $128,000—$235,000 less than if the property was held in joint tenancy.

Because joint tenancy property cannot preserve the exemption equivalent amount of the first spouse to die, it is totally inadequate for federal estate tax planning.

Living trust–centered planning does not create federal estate tax problems but rather saves federal estate taxes.

The After-Death Income Taxation of Joint Tenancy Property

Joint tenancy property owned by spouses passes to the survivor free of federal estate tax but robs the surviving spouse of the ability to receive a 100 percent step-up in basis. "Step-up in basis" means that when a person dies, property that is included in his or her estate for federal estate tax purposes gets a new cost basis that is equivalent to its fair market value at the date of death. For example, if a person bought stock for $1000 during his or her life and sold it for $5,000, there would be a $4,000 taxable gain. However, if the person died owning the stock and the stock was worth $5,000 when he or she died, the decedent's heirs would receive a new cost basis of $5,000. If the stock was subsequently sold by the heirs for $5,000, there would be no taxable gain.

For joint tenancy property, the general rule is that the surviving tenant receives a stepped-up basis in the property to the extent that the property was included in the deceased tenant's estate for federal estate tax purposes.[5] For married couples, only one-half of joint tenancy property is included in the estate of the first spouse to die. The surviving spouse receives only a step-up in basis for one-half of the jointly held property:

> *Joe and Martha bought a commercial lot as an investment. They paid $20,000 for it and titled it in joint tenancy. Joe subsequently died. For federal estate tax purposes, the property was valued at $50,000.*

The cost basis for Martha's half of the property (which was not included in Joe's estate) is $10,000, representing one-half of the original cost of the lot.[6] The stepped-up basis for the half that was included in Joe's estate is $25,000, one-half of its federal estate tax value. By adding the original cost basis of Martha's half of the property—$10,000—and the stepped-up basis of Joe's half of the lot—$25,000—we see that Martha's new cost basis in the property is $35,000.

If Martha sells the property for $50,000, her taxable gain is $15,000 ($50,000 minus her $35,000 basis).

What if Joe and Martha titled their property differently?

Joe and Martha bought the commercial lot but titled it in Joe's name. On Joe's death, the entire value of the property was included in his estate. Joe left the property to Martha. No federal estate tax was due because of the unlimited marital deduction.

The property's cost basis is $50,000 after Joe's death, because it received a stepped-up basis equal to 100 percent of its federal estate tax value of $50,000.

If Martha sells the property for $50,000, there will be no taxable gain.

A step-up in basis is an even more important issue in community property states.[7] Upon the death of the first spouse, all community property receives a 100 percent step-up in basis.[8] This benefit is extremely important in terms of estate planning in community property states. The benefit can be lost, however, if property is held in joint tenancy.

Joint tenancy property is *not* community property. Married couples in a community property state who hold property in joint tenancy with right of survivorship lose the complete step-up in basis: only one-half of joint tenancy property owned by community property couples receives a step-up in basis.

Joint tenancy in property is not conducive to planning for the step-up in basis rules. A living trust–centered estate plan offers the greatest opportunity to maximize these benefits, because step-up in basis planning is addressed during the funding process.

Probate Avoidance

Probate avoidance is foremost among the perceived advantages of joint tenancy. Recent studies by the American Association of Retired Persons (AARP) conclude that joint tenancy is commonly used by married couples as an inexpensive method of avoiding probate.[9] However, one AARP study found that 75 percent of the estates that went through probate belonged to people who were *single* at death.[10] This study appears to confirm that married couples are delaying probate rather than totally avoiding it. After a spouse dies, joint tenancy property is owned in the name of the surviving spouse. It will go through probate on that spouse's death unless other planning is implemented.

The most efficient means of avoiding probate is a fully funded living trust,[11] which has the advantage of avoiding probate on the death of each spouse.

Immediate Access to Funds

Joint tenancy gives a survivor immediate access to the joint property without the delay of probate. A living trust–centered estate plan also gives its beneficiaries immediate access to the trust property without the interference or delay of probate.

Planning for Disability

The incapacity of a joint tenant can present problems. Should one joint tenant become incapacitated without other planning the property cannot be sold or otherwise disposed of without a court-imposed financial guardianship.

People often use joint tenancy as a substitute for proper disability planning. It is not uncommon for elderly or infirm persons to title their property jointly with relatives or friends so that they can be cared for in the event of disability. When this is done, unanticipated problems occur:

Mary is in her late seventies and is concerned about her health. Mary has two sons and a daughter, June. Her sons live in other states, but June lives close to Mary. Because June lives close to her mother, Mary titled all of her property in joint tenancy with June. Mary felt that if she could no longer manage her financial affairs, adding June as a joint tenant would allow June to act on her behalf.

On Mary's death, June presented Mary's will to a local attorney for probate. The will named June as the executor

*and left all of Mary's property equally to her three chil-
dren. Even though Mary intended that her property be
divided equally among her three children, June got all
of the property by virtue of her joint tenancy ownership.
June's brothers received nothing.*

Gift Tax Problems

Gift tax problems do not generally arise when property
is placed in joint tenancy between spouses.[12] The gift tax
results are entirely different for joint tenancy between nonspouses. With the exception of U.S. savings bonds, bank
accounts, and brokerage accounts, when an individual titles
property in joint tenancy with anyone other than a spouse,
that person makes a gift to the extent that the other joint
tenants have not contributed equally to the purchase of the
property.[13]

In our prior example, the instant that Mary put her property into joint tenancy with June, she made a gift to June
of 50 percent of the value of her property for purposes of
federal gift tax law. Whether or not Mary intended to make
a gift to June is irrelevant for purposes of federal gift tax.[14]
However, the gift will not be taxable to the extent that it
qualifies for Mary's $10,000 annual exclusion.[15] To the ex-
tent that it does not qualify for Mary's annual exclusion, it
can be sheltered by her $600,000 exemption equivalent.[16]
If the value of Mary's gift exceeds her exemption equivalent,
federal gift tax will be due.[17]

If Mary does not file a gift tax return, her oversight will
not be unusual. Since a gift is not usually intended when
property is put in joint tenancy between nonspouses, a gift
tax return is usually not filed. When the IRS later discovers
the gift, it will attempt to collect penalties and interest on
any gift tax that should have been paid. The penalties and
interest will often far exceed the original tax. And, to the

extent that Mary's state's gift tax laws apply there may be additional taxes, interest, and penalties.

Liability Problems

There are also liability problems associated with using joint tenancy as a substitute for disability planning. If a person places his or her property in joint tenancy with a relative or friend, that property may be subject to the claims of that relative's or friend's creditors. That relative or friend can also use the joint tenancy property as collateral for his or her debts.

Unintended Heirs

When joint tenancy property is placed in the name of a relative or friend, the property is not controlled by the original owner's will or trust. Even though Mary's will left all of her property equally to her children, it all passed to June on Mary's death. This presents a dilemma for June. If she keeps the property, her brothers will not receive their fair share. If June wants them to have their fair share, she must give it to them. This may create federal and state gift taxes.[18]

When living trust–centered planning is used to accomplish disability planning, none of these problems associated with joint tenancy planning arises.

Creating Liability

Joint tenancy ownership may create more liability than is necessary. For example, when a married person wants to borrow money to purchase an asset, an institutional lender may encourage that the asset be placed in joint tenancy.

Should the lender be successful in its suggestion, it can then require the signature of both spouses on the underlying mortgage. Making both spouses liable is always in a creditor's best interests.

Tenancy by the Entirety Creditor Protection

Some states have a special type of joint ownership between spouses called *tenancy by the entirety,* which often has protective provisions for spousal property. In states that provide for tenancy by the entirety between spouses, it is the general rule that a judgment creditor of one spouse cannot levy against the tenancy by the entirety property. As a result, some attorneys feel that, in order to retain this creditor protection, tenancy by the entirety property should not be titled directly in the name of a living trust. Of course, if it is not, it loses the many benefits of having it titled in the name of a living trust.

There is some corroboration that tenancy by the entirety property retains its creditor benefits even if transferred into the name of a living trust.[19] Since a living trust merely holds the legal title to property, a transfer of this property may not affect its continuing character as tenancy by the entirety property. However, the law is not clear in this area. Where tenancy by the entirety provides crucial creditor planning, it should be integrated into the living trust–centered estate plan.

It also makes sense to consider using the "magic wand of estate planning" technique for titling property that is explained in Chapter 11, "General Lifetime Consequences of Funding a Living Trust." Under this method of trust funding, property can be left in tenancy by the entirety ownership and still be considered to be part of the trust. Of course, this possibility should not be explored without top-notch legal advice, but it does appear to allow the retention of creditor protection while preserving trust ownership.

Loss of Control

Joint tenancy between spouses implies a partnership in ownership as well as love. Spouses take great comfort in knowing that their marriage property is owned "equally" by each of them and that their jointly owned property will pass to the survivor. They take additional comfort from the fact that their jointly owned property will avoid probate on the death of one of the spouses. Joint tenancy is popular, in large measure, because of these perceptions.

When they look at the idea of joint tenancy, most couples see only these so-called positive aspects. However, there are a number of significant problems with jointly held property:

- Should the surviving spouse remarry, all or part of the property will likely pass to the "new" marital partner rather than the children.
- If the surviving spouse is incapacitated, the property will be subject to a financial guardianship proceeding.
- All of the joint tenancy property passing to the surviving tenant is subject to the claims of the surviving spouse's creditors.
- The surviving spouse can leave the property to whomever he or she wishes without regard to the deceased spouse's wishes.
- The surviving spouse has the full burden of the preservation and administration of assets passing to him or her with no preplanned instructions or help.

- Absent any other planning, the property will be subject to probate on the death of the surviving spouse.
- The potential for optimum federal estate tax planning will be lost.
- Step-up in basis planning cannot be accomplished.

Each and every one of these deficiencies can be addressed by using living trust–centered planning.

The Cost of Joint Tenancy Versus the Cost of Living Trust–Centered Planning

Joint tenancy is viewed as "cost-free" estate planning by many people. It is a mistake for a person to fall into the trap of believing this fallacy. The real costs of joint tenancy result from its consequences.

Joint tenancy planning is often used by people who have modest estates as a planning substitute. Many times, they have been told by friends or advisers that "real" estate planning is too expensive for them and that joint tenancy is a viable alternative to estate planning. People who own modest estates do not care any less for their loved ones than do people of more affluent means. They cannot afford to lose any of what they have to the adverse effects of joint tenancy planning. Joint tenancy is not a poor person's estate plan. It is simply poor estate planning. As there are modest estates, there are living trust plans that can be implemented by professional advisers for modest fees.

Our Conclusion

Joint tenancy ownership has many disadvantages and should not be used as a substitute for proper living trust-centered estate planning.

PART THREE

Why America Is Abandoning Wills and Probate

25

Living Trust Planning
Is Superior to
Wills and Probate

To illustrate the overwhelming superiority of living trust–centered planning over will-planning/probate, in this chapter we summarize our conclusions for each of the issues that we have addressed into three categories, *Pro–Living Trust, Pro–Will-Planning/Probate,* and *No Significant Difference.*

Pro–Living Trust

- All of the evidence conclusively proves that fully funded revocable living trusts cost significantly less than will-planning/probate.
- Living trust–centered estate plans are far more effective for disability planning than will-planning/probate, which relies on guardianship proceedings and powers of attorney.
- Living trust–centered planning substantially reduces or avoids the short- and long-term delays that are implicit in will-planning/probate.

- Will-planning/probate necessitates ancillary administration when real property is owned in more than one state. Fully funded living trusts avoid it.
- Will-planning/probate is a public proceeding that often discloses personal and financial affairs to the public. Living trust–centered planning is far more successful in keeping sensitive financial and personal information confidential.
- Will-planning/probate encourages litigation. Living trust–centered planning gives more assurance that planning efforts will be free of litigation.
- Living trust–centered estate planning is more effective for after-death creditor planning than will-planning/probate planning.
- Fewer conflicts of law are associated with living trusts because the rules for determining their validity, interpretation, and construction are more liberal than those for wills.
- Funding a living trust is the essence of proper planning. It produces far better planning results than does will-planning/probate.
- Gifts can be made from a living trust to third parties without adverse estate tax consequences. A living trust–centered plan is better than will-planning/probate for continuing the gift programs of incapacitated people.
- Living trust–centered planning is superior to will-planning/probate for purposes of federal estate tax planning.
- A fully funded living trust is superior to will-planning/probate for business continuity planning because it enables business to proceed in the usual manner.
- Living trust–centered planning can circumvent spousal election statutes in many states; will-planning/probate cannot.
- Living trust–centered estate planning is better than will-

planning/probate for preventing nonresident fiduciary problems.
- The separate share rule gives a living trust–centered estate plan a planning advantage over will-planning/probate.
- The sixty-five-day rule is an after-death income tax advantage that a living trust has over a probate estate.

Pro–Will-Planning/Probate

- A testamentary trust can potentially qualify a surviving spouse for Medicaid payments. A living trust cannot.
- The law does not prohibit placing professional corporation stock, homestead property, and qualified stock option and purchase plans into a living trust. However, these interests should not be transferred to a living trust without the advice of an attorney. Section 1244 stock loses its benefits if held in a living trust.
- The trustees and beneficiaries of a living trust may have greater personal exposure to CERCLA liability than fiduciaries and heirs under will-planning/probate.
- A probate estate avoids income tax on capital gains generated from amounts permanently set aside for charity that are not paid to charity; a trust does not.
- Probate estates have preferential after-death income tax benefits that generate immediate capital losses. Living trust beneficiaries can only take these losses when the property is sold.
- Just like a probate estate, a trust does not have to recognize gain on a sale or exchange of depreciable property between it and its beneficiaries. If, however, the trustee chooses to recognize the gain, the trust will pay,

at most, 3 percent more tax than a probate estate will pay.
- A probate estate can recognize rental real estate activity losses for two years; a living trust cannot.

No Significant Difference

- A living trust can own tax-sensitive property without adversely affecting the tax status of that property.
- Living trust–centered estate planning and will-planning/probate can accomplish the same results with respect to divorce and pretermitted heirs.
- Federal tax legislation has significantly reduced the impact of income splitting. It is no longer a planning technique that gives will-planning/probate any advantage over living trust–centered planning.
- The perceived benefits of deferring income by choosing a fiscal rather than a calendar year in will-planning/probate are illusory.
- The difference between a probate estate's personal exemption and a living trust's exemption is insignificant.
- Probate estates and living trusts are treated the same for purposes of estimated income tax payments.
- A properly drafted living trust can hold Subchapter S stock, as can a probate estate.
- Administrative expenses incurred by a fully funded revocable living trust are generally subject to the same rules as those for a probate estate.
- Trustees of living trusts are treated as executors under the Internal Revenue Code for most purposes; where they are not, a pour-over will gives a living trust–centered plan the same after-death federal tax elections as a probate estate.

If we look to the substantive weight of the respective issues, there can be no doubt that living trust planning wins the debate in every single area except for a few which are controlled by federal legislation. These federal laws include an obscure passage within the Medicaid law, an arbitrary definitional distinction in the Comprehensive Environmental Response, Compensation and Liability Act, and an oversight in a few income tax sections of the Internal Revenue Code. In these areas, property that was acquired by will-planning/probate is given certain special treatment, as a consideration to heirs and estates. When these laws were enacted, Congress failed to remember that some "heirs" receive their inheritances through revocable living trusts. If Congress would act to make these few legislative changes to give equal treatment to assets that pass through living trust planning, there would be absolutely no reason to retain will-planning/probate as the estate planning method of choice. Given the growing popularity of living trusts, we predict that Congress will rectify these inequalities in the near future. It began this process with the introduction of the Tax Simplification Act of 1991.

Our Conclusion

The evidence shows clearly and convincingly that living trust–centered estate planning is vastly superior to will-planning/probate. We agree with Oliver Wendell Holmes: "Put not your trust in money, but put your money in trust."[1] But a difficult question remains. Why don't more lawyers use this planning approach?

26

Changing the Way America Plans

Why aren't all lawyers embracing living trust planning? In the larger sense, this question can be answered in terms of broad philosophical perspectives. Unfortunately, estate planning law as practiced today, in large part, is influenced by practical considerations that have little to do with philosophy. Both the philosophical and practical aspects need to be discussed to answer this question satisfactorily.

The Philosophical Perspective

Before the advent of specialized legal practice, virtually every lawyer wrote wills for clients. This tradition continues to be common in both rural and urban America because, even today, any lawyer can easily draw a simple will.

Writing simple wills does not involve significant time, energy, expertise, or fees. Property is routinely left to "my spouse if he or she survives me," and then to "my descendants, *per stirpes*," or "share and share alike." Even the most unskilled practitioners can prepare these wills—and often do.

Most wills are prepared by a secretary, paralegal, or associate using the firm's archives of forms. The finished products are reviewed by the lawyer, are stapled into their blue-backed binders with the law firm's or lawyer's name nicely printed on them, and are mailed to clients for their review.

The American Bar Association (ABA) has been instrumental in creating and perpetuating the long-held conventional view that signing a will is what responsible people do when they want to accomplish proper estate planning. The ABA has diligently attempted to educate the American public about the many reasons why each of us should seek out an attorney to have our will prepared. State and local bar associations and a number of law firms have participated in this public service effort. Their efforts have not been in vain. In 1974, 27 percent of the adult population had a will. In 1989, the percentage was up to 40 percent. This increase indicates that an aging population is hearing the will-planning message.[1]

There is also a growing trend among the public of seeking nonattorney solutions to fulfill their basic estate planning needs. As the average American family's demand for estate planning has increased, a new estate planning industry has developed to satisfy this demand. It consists of businesses aimed at a market of do-it-yourself consumers who are willing to buy fill-in-the-blank will and trust forms. These forms attempt to accomplish very basic planning without the need of an attorney.

Will kits can be purchased for under $10, and trust kits can often be purchased for as little as $30. Computer software stores stock software packages that allow their customers to prepare homemade estate plans. There are also a number of companies that prepare trust documents directly for the public, circumventing the traditional attorney-client relationship. It is clear that these businesses are basing their marketing strategy on the public's fear of lawyers and their fees.

The old-time cornerstones of credibility, confidence, and trust that buttressed the attorney-client relationship are seriously eroding. The public's confidence in and respect for the legal profession have been decreasing just as legal fees and litigation have been increasing. The lawyer joke has become socially acceptable and, if one believes there is truth in humor, the credibility of lawyers is at an all-time low. Increasing numbers of clients want proof of professional qualifications and skill levels and routinely interrogate lawyers as to the timeliness of their work product and the amount of their fees. The practice of shopping for second opinions is on the increase, as is fee shopping in general. Practitioners must often validate themselves through displaying their credentials and sincerity or by giving preliminary demonstrations of their professional skills before receiving the go-ahead on client engagements. Simply put, lawyerly professionalism is no longer assumed by a trusting public. Today's lawyers are subject to the same market demands as any business people and are feeling a growing pressure to furnish better client services.

Most people have experienced probate in one way or another. Stories abound of incompetent probate lawyers, red tape, court battles, outrageous fees, and delays. These stories gain momentum with each retelling and seem to create a reality of their own that encourages the public to distrust and avoid lawyers when it comes to conventional will-planning/probate.

When the public's demand for better prices and services is viewed in the context of the traditional will-planning/probate practice, there is an obvious clash. Probate lawyers, within certain broad parameters, are used to charging what they like for their time and services. They often resent clients and their surviving family members who believe that it is perfectly normal to question the fees.

There is often a gulf of misunderstanding between the estate's heirs and the estate's lawyer. The heirs want to talk about when they are going to receive their inheritance and about the size of the lawyer's fee, while the lawyer wants to talk about legal procedures. Probate lawyers want to be in charge of a family's affairs and view their services as indispensable in that regard. Heirs view them as unnecessary impediments Dad or Grandmother should have planned around.

There is also a gulf of misunderstanding between the perceptions, beliefs, and biases of will-planning/probate lawyers and those of living trust lawyers. Will-planning/probate lawyers and living trust lawyers face a clash of *paradigms*.

The Meaning of Paradigm

Richard Covey in his book *The Seven Habits of Highly Effective People* defines paradigm as follows:

> The word *paradigm* comes from the Greek. It was originally a scientific term, and is more commonly used today to mean a model, theory, perception, assumption, or frame of reference. In the more general sense, it's the way we "see" the world—not in terms of our visual sense of sight, but in terms of perceiving, understanding, interpreting.[2]

When probate lawyers embrace their will-planning/probate practices, they cling to an established pattern cut in the form of a prevailing logic box. Their paradigm is comfortable because there is historic consensus as to its validity. It gains impetus from its longevity and is believed to be accurate and reliable because it has always been so regarded.

When new paradigms compete with old ones, there is a transition period during which the old are replaced with the new. During this period, there are generally conflict and debate while the veracity of the new approach is being tested and weighed. We believe that estate planning is currently in the transition period from traditional will and probate planning to living trust planning.

The Importance of Culture

The probate bar's arguments have the force of tradition and longevity. However, probate lawyers are not coming to grips with the public's heightened knowledge and understanding of its planning options. Probate lawyers do not readily recognize that the public views wills and probate as outmoded.

The public is developing a rapidly expanding awareness that its affluence should not be shared by lawyers who merely provide a procedural conduit to pass wealth on to others. This is a perception that deeply influences the living trust controversy.

In past decades, estate planning information was not readily available to the public. It was carefully guarded by will-planning/probate lawyers as a professional secret through legal concepts and language that were foreign to the everyday experience of most clients. Today this same information is readily available through normal business and communication channels. Advertisements for estate planning products are commonplace, as are seminars and public forums for advancing general estate planning principles and strategies. The public expects more from estate planning lawyers quite simply because the public knows more about the law and how it applies to common planning situations.

This proliferation of estate planning information has also contributed to how the public views probate lawyers. Historically, American society put a premium on education and respected the professionals who achieved it. Society placed comparatively small numbers of well-trained professionals on a pedestal and then expected them to serve the public trust with dignity, compassion, and wisdom. There was little or no competition among these professionals and they flourished and prospered with comparative ease.

This historical view of lawyers explains, in part, why our grandparents and great-grandparents held them in such awe and took their advice so willingly without question or challenge. However, the passive client that meekly follows the advice and recommendations of his or her lawyer, doctor, or clergyman is quickly becoming the exception rather than the rule. The public now routinely questions all lawyers with regard to legal procedures and techniques.

This change in the public's perceptions and behavior reflects, in large measure, a cultural shift. The mere observation of these shifts in our society's culture creates an awareness that is key to explaining the intensity of the arguments on either side of the will-versus-trust debate. *It suggests a theory that the will-planning/probate tradition has not changed in the way it serves society; rather, society has changed dramatically in the way it wishes to be served!*

People do not want probate lawyers controlling their wealth and the lives of their surviving family members. They want to be in control of their affairs while they are alive, and they want their heirs to be in control thereafter. Wills and probate practice cannot possibly achieve this mandate. They represent the old legal view that puts lawyers in charge of clients rather than the other way around. Living trust lawyers leave their clients in control of their own affairs. We predict that it is only a matter of time before traditional probate lawyers will go the way of the carrier pigeon unless they change their practice perspectives.

Probate lawyers are holding tight to a practice with which

they feel comfortable. They only want to debate specifics within their practice paradigm. Living trust lawyers embrace a different practice perspective. They view probate specifics as irrelevant because they believe the system is ineffective and unnecessary. Living trust lawyers view the estate planning process as people-oriented planning that meets the hopes, fears, dreams, values, and aspirations of their clients. They view it as a system that places a family's affairs in the hands of trusted family members and advisers rather than in the exclusive grip of the probate lawyer.

The Shift from "Procedural Planning" to "People Planning"

For most practitioners, estate planning requires a modest set of will forms and a mature clientele concerned about their mortality. On the other hand, a relatively small number of estate planning specialists represent wealthy clients who need complicated strategies for saving federal and state income, gift, estate, and inheritance taxes. The law these specialists practice is, however, by far the exception to the usual practice rule.

Most lawyers practice estate planning law just as their great-grandfathers did at the turn of the century by writing "horse and buggy" simple wills with the expectation that they will be "probated" down the road. Probate lawyers are concerned with procedural technicalities, rules, and regulations that do not exist apart from the probate process.

The lawyer's fee for writing a will is often unbelievably low. Will-writing probate lawyers expect to make their profit later when the will maker dies.

In past years the public was not particularly concerned about spending time and money "today" to leave others an inheritance "tomorrow." Probate lawyers tell us that their clients have been comfortable underpaying on the front end in order to let their survivors settle the ledger down the road. This is a well-regarded theory which suggests that both probate lawyers and their clients traditionally viewed estate planning as death planning. Both parties do their very best to keep these "unpleasant conversations" as short and to the point as possible. Five-minute will conferences followed by a draft in the mail and a ten-minute execution ceremony are not at all unusual in the old view.

Today, spouses, parents, and grandparents care about their resources and are vitally concerned about planning for their golden years and for their families. More and more people want to become involved in planning for the disposition of their resources and for their own well-being as well as that of their loved ones. They want to minimize taxes and avoid probate. These concerns are inconsistent with will-planning/probate.

Regardless of their particular estate planning expertise, will-planning/probate attorneys view probate to be where the *real* law is practiced and hold to the traditionally defensible view that their knowledge of the rules, procedures, and systems is worthy of professional respect and dignity.

However, the main cause of the debate is not lawyers' fighting lawyers, but rather the public's demand for a new legal system that leaves the control and power over wealth and loved ones outside the nation's courts and law offices.

When a manager or coach of a professional sports team tells an old and grizzled star athlete that he can no longer play the game, the reaction is often unpleasant. This is precisely what is happening to the nation's probate lawyers. They are frightened that they will lose a portion of their livelihoods and are fighting to preserve a practice that has outlived its usefulness. However, unlike an over-the-hill athlete, they do not have to fall back on their pension plans, because they can easily convert their attitudes and skills into living trust practices that will both meet the demands of the public and provide these professionals with a comfortable living.

A Closer Look at the New-Paradigm Living Trust Lawyer

Today, more than ever, lawyers must take the time to listen to the hopes, fears, dreams, values, and ambitions of their clients. Modern practitioners must diagnose before prescribing. They must become extraordinarily good listeners who resist the temptation to impress the client with their knowledge and, instead, work diligently to become good communicators. *This means that verbal and written legalese must be avoided.* Modern practitioners must embrace language that is legally correct but can be understood and appreciated by clients.

Practitioners need to elicit client feedback so that planning can be fine-tuned to the client's satisfaction. In the modern view, the professional, with the input of the client's other advisers, should explain the law to the client as it applies to the client's situation. Clients must discuss their personal, financial, and family matters with the lawyer so that the resulting planning can meet their personal needs and objectives.

Planning that accomplishes these objectives emphasizes the needs and desires of the client, as opposed to the prejudices and biases of the client's professional advisers.

Contemporary lawyers should seek to extend their planning horizons well beyond mere legal technicalities. This is the kind of estate planning that we advocate in our book *Loving Trust* and through the National Network of Loving Trust® Attorneys.

If will-planning/probate practitioners concentrated on people-oriented legal documentation, their planning results would undoubtedly be enhanced. However, the resulting wills would still fall far short of gaining the public's unqualified endorsement because they would not avoid probate.

New-paradigm planning relies on lawyers who will work closely with other professional advisers in coordinating their clients' planning. It will foster living trust–centered documentation which contains carefully drawn instructions for disability planning and extensive instructions for beneficiaries. It will differentiate itself from will-planning/probate and unfunded boilerplate living trusts by

- Eliminating probate
- Providing extensive disability planning
- Keeping private affairs confidential
- Minimizing the likelihood of attack
- Working well on a multistate basis
- Providing for creditor protection

Contemporary Marketplace Demands

Most probate practitioners are proud legal technicians who have not, as a general rule, come to grips with the public's contemporary demands. We do not wish to suggest that these practitioners are impervious to the changing temperament of the estate planning marketplace. There is no question that they are trying to grasp the meaning of the shifting public mood. Most probate lawyers are aware of a changing marketplace but blame their woes on a public relations problem rather than their unwillingness or inability to meet the public's new and heightened demands for a people-oriented probate-free alternative.

A good example of this perceived public relations problem is the recent name change by the American College of Probate Counsel. This voluntary organization counts many of the nation's better estate planning attorneys as its members. It has recently dropped *Probate* from its name and is now called the American College of Trust and Estate Counsel. This change is both sensible and thoughtful.

New-paradigm trust practitioners attempt to convert client planning meetings from short and painful death-planning exercises into involved and meaningful planning sessions that will continue for more than a few minutes. These practitioners take responsibility for the client's understanding of the impact of legal issues and seek to serve rather than rule their clients and their families.

The Practical Considerations

Lawyers endure a legal education over which they have no control. Young practitioners join law firms with mores over which they have no control and associate with peers who experience this same lack of control. They follow precise legal procedures that they did not invent and are often chastised if they in any way buck the system. There are few instances that reward young lawyers for attempts at creativity.

These limitations on the practice perspectives of lawyers to a large degree have influenced their position on the great trust debate.

Why Are Trust Benefits and Mechanics a Mystery to Most Practitioners?

Living trust–centered law is not emphasized in law school. Law professors are committed to teaching their students how to think like lawyers rather than equipping them with specific practice skills. In addition, most professors are required to teach legal theory rather than practice specifics.

Law students are exposed to course loads that require stamina, memorization, and intellectual tenacity. Within a massive curriculum, students generally have a single course in wills and trusts, which emphasizes will-planning/probate case law. We do not know why this is the case but suspect that because law schools are so tradition-bound they find it convenient to follow will-planning/probate.

After graduation, students memorize unbelievable amounts of legal facts in preparation for their bar examination. Material is often learned for the first time because bar examinations and law school curricula are not necessarily the same. The material is ingested, regurgitated, and then discarded after the dreaded examination is completed. Thereafter, a vast majority of the novice practitioners either join a law firm or become associated with a mature practitioner. It is at this juncture that the novice's real education begins. The apprentice is immediately exposed to two new realities: the world of research and the world of forms.

Every law firm has filing cabinets full of its own practice forms, which are both reasonable and necessary since they represent the total of the firm's previous practice experience. The apprentice quickly learns that if it's been done before, there is no reason to reinvent the wheel when a similar matter occurs. A firm also has its own legal library full of forms books. When a novel legal question arises, these forms books are used. Both forms approaches save the firm and its clients time, energy, and money.

A law firm's dependence on its forms is legion. The expression "the tail wagging the dog" is an apt description of a lawyer's dependence on his or her forms file. Given the frenzy of the typical law practice, where the lawyer is constantly reacting to the needs and demands of others, there is little time to consider and create new practice alternatives. As a result, most practitioners start recommending—without even realizing what they are doing—only those solutions that fit the parameters of their forms files rather than seeking or inventing new solutions to meet specific client needs. This is a regrettable, but necessary, practice reality for most lawyers.

The firm's forms file becomes the associate's mentor. If the firm's practice has been centered on drafting wills and then probating them, it will most likely practice will-planning/probate estate planning law in the future simply because that is what the forms provide and that is what the young people learn.

Are Some Practitioners Ignoring Living Trust Planning Solely for Monetary Reasons?

We have taught hundreds of practicing attorneys over the years, and our experience has been that our students want to do what is right for their clients. In our introductory estate planning course, we expose attorneys to all of the problems and pitfalls associated with a will-planning/probate practice. We then contrast those problems with the solutions afforded through living trust–centered estate planning. The reaction of the typical class is no longer surprising to us. The behavior and reactions of most of our lawyer colleagues are predictable, and are something like this:

- They initially become angry and defensive with respect to our critiques of will-planning/probate.
- They readily participate in a spirited discussion of the pros and cons of the revocable living trust and of will drafting and probate.
- They come to understand what the public does not like about wills and probate.
- They become excited about what proper living trust–centered planning can do for their clients.

- They want to know more about how they can build a living trust–centered practice.
- They attend a number of advanced living trust–centered seminars.
- They start practicing anew with living trust–centered techniques.

This learning sequence is common to both general practitioners and will-planning/probate specialists. We are amazed at the uniformity of the responses we have observed from these disparate groups and continue to find an unaccountable homogeneity in the perceptions of our professional colleagues that belies their different practice expertise and experiences.

Over the years, it has become clear to us that most of our practitioner students are concerned less with generating probate income than with serving the needs of their clients in a professional and dignified manner.

Unfortunately, we have been exposed to a minority of practitioners who appear to be clinging to their will-planning/probate practice mores, in part, we suspect, because of the economic benefit of their probate files. The following stories put this in perspective:

The Sole Practitioner

We know of a sole practitioner who spent his early career doing probate administration for a large metropolitan bank. His training and skills were entirely in the administration of probate estates.

He left the bank many years ago and started his own will-planning/probate practice. He is a mature and bright attorney who knows estate planning literature well. He practices what he knows best, will-planning/probate law, and makes a decent living for his family. To ensure this result, he even names himself as the estate's attorney within each of his clients' wills.

We debated him on the will-planning/probate versus living trust issue in a professional symposium, and he readily agreed that living trust planning had its virtues but added that it wasn't for everybody. In the cordiality of the small talk that followed the debate, he could not resist bragging to us about the exact number of wills that he had in his will file.

He takes violent exception to any allegation that he is practicing solely for money and continually attacks living trust proponents and their literature as a way of defending his own practice. He has a methodical and plodding personality and is bewildered by what he views as unwarranted attacks on his practice procedures.

The Small-Firm Practitioner

We know of a small firm of specialist practitioners who have been doing responsible estate planning for decades. They have prepared numbers of testamentary trusts and simple wills and have prepared even greater numbers of living trust–centered estate plans.

As their practice has matured, they have been increasingly emphasizing their will-planning/probate practice and deemphasizing their living trust practice. They rationalize their position by maintaining that it is difficult to persuade their clients to fund their living trusts fully and that the process takes too much of their practice time.

They react aggressively to any suggestion that they are practicing will-planning/probate law simply for the additional probate fees it brings to their firm.

The Large-Firm Practitioner

We know of a practitioner who works for a large metropolitan law firm older than our friend is, and she is in her fifties. This firm has a wonderful clientele and a number of exceptionally talented attorneys who were hired from among the top ranks of the nation's best law schools.

Our friend's law firm occupies the very best office space and has the best of practice trappings, from the appointment of their offices to their excellent law library. The firm has enormous billings and equally enormous overhead.

It has a large and venerable probate department that has serviced the estates of its clients for decades. It's their policy that its lawyers do will-planning/probate and that they do living trust–centered planning only when it is specifically requested by a client, and then only when the client cannot be convinced otherwise.

Both the firm's partners and its associates react with hostility to any suggestion that their will-planning/probate practice is designed to enhance the firm's billings rather than serving the best interests of their clients.

Each of these examples discusses a mature practice that has a long-standing vested interest in its probate files. Each of these firms has prepared wills for years in the expectation of handling the probates that will inevitably follow. The decision they must make in the immediate future is a difficult one. Should they call the living trust alternative to the attention of their will and probate clients, or should they simply accommodate those clients who specifically request living trust planning? This is a dilemma of massive economic dimensions that must be answered by each firm within its collective conscience.

There are always exceptions to any rule, but we believe that in general most attorneys do not practice will-planning/probate law because of the proverbial pot of probate gold at the end of the will-planning rainbow. We believe that most attorneys practice will-planning/probate law because they are comfortable with this type of practice and because they are uncomfortable with living trust law and techniques.

Why Is Living Trust Planning Alien to Most General Practitioners?

The bulk of the will-planning/probate practice is accomplished by general practitioners rather than by estate planning specialists. The general practitioner handles an extraordinary variety of legal tasks and works hard attempting to keep current with ever-changing state and federal laws.

A major problem facing general practitioners is how they can find the time and tools to effectively convert their will-planning/probate practices to living trust practices.

The law is not as profitable as it used to be, and lawyers are working longer hours to generate necessary take-home income. Overhead has risen much faster than the ability of lawyers to raise their fees. There is not a lot of available time for a lawyer to learn new skills or master new material.

It is possible for the lawyer to learn new practice skills, but the task is formidable. It requires finding the right books, articles, courses, and colleagues, and it requires sacrificing significant billable time.

Law Books

Most law books assume a certain level of practice expertise that may simply not be there. They are designed to give lawyers the decisions of the courts (case books), or the decisions of the legislature (state and federal statutes), or an exhaustive background on any particular aspect of the law (the legal encyclopedias). They also provide forms (legal drafting sets) that enable a lawyer to view how a particular document should be written. They tell what the law is and not necessarily how the practitioner should apply it. In our experience, an attorney could not possibly hope to establish a living trust–centered estate planning practice solely by reading books.

Professional Journals

There are a number of excellent professional journals within the estate planning field; however, most of their articles are written by specialists or scholars for peers and colleagues who are essentially just like them in their knowledge and perceptions of the law. These authors are talented specialists who write about what interests them. The topics that pique their interests generally confuse, frustrate, or bore the average practitioner reader because, frankly, they are over his or her head.

Specialist authors are increasingly forced to write about technically detailed and myopic aspects within their estate planning specialty. There is immense pressure to find something new to write about, and, within an old and established field, this creates scholarly minutiae. This penchant for the scholarly is not what most general practitioners desire or need. They too often view these scholarly efforts as analyses of the fleas on the dog, rather than the dog they are trying to learn. In our experience, most general practitioners do not have the expertise that the journal articles assume they have.

Continuing Legal Education

Most lawyers routinely attend bar-sponsored continuing legal education seminars to keep their skills current. Estate planning seminar offerings closely follow the technical literature and are often taught by the authors of the journal articles or their colleagues.

Most general practitioners do not like these educational offerings for two reasons: They assume a level of knowledge and understanding that the average practitioner does not have, and they employ a theoretical rather than a practical approach to the material.

Other Attorneys

The old saying "Birds of a feather flock together" is an apt one. Will-planning/probate specialists routinely meet similarly minded colleagues at professional symposia and belong to mutual study groups. Their penchant to work with one another further enhances the status quo and excludes general practitioners who cannot hope to hold their own in the conversations.

Estate planning councils are associations of lawyers, accountants, trust officers, financial advisers, and life insurance agents. They have excellent continuing legal education programs throughout the year, but these are for professionals who specialize in the field and by definition exclude general practitioners from their membership.

It is possible for the general practitioner to learn a great deal about living trusts from books, articles, courses, and professional colleagues. However, given the logistics of time, expense, and effort required to accomplish this task, it is little wonder that most practitioners stay within the boundaries of their existing will-planning/probate practices.

Why Don't Estate Planning Specialists Use Living Trust–Centered Planning Exclusively?

The will-planning/probate tradition has been the educational foundation of most estate planning specialists. Professionals do what they know how to do and eschew what is unfamiliar to them. Unfortunately, this explanation cannot account for why many specialist practitioners continue to rely on will-planning/probate to service a significant percentage of their clientele.

Most estate planning specialists are conversant with living trusts and use them in their practices. A minority of them use living trusts exclusively. The balance use living trusts only for select clients. This difference in practice perspective can be explained.

Smaller Clients Don't Need Living Trusts

Most attorneys believe that living trusts are for the affluent client and not the smaller client because they do not feel that they can charge the smaller client enough money to justify the time and expense that go into preparing a complete living trust–centered estate plan. This is an incorrect perception. With modern practice aids, living trust–centered plans are not difficult to prepare. Furthermore, we have already proved that the smaller the estate, the larger the probate fee will be as a percentage of that estate. There can be no question that clients with smaller estates need living trust–centered estate planning every bit as much as affluent clients do.

Specialists are afraid that if they attempt to accomplish a complete and proper current estate planning job, they will lose either revenue or clients. In effect, specialists do not want to be accused of planning overkill and do not want to take the time that is necessary to educate the less wealthy client on why the living trust approach is better and will save significant future dollars.

Clients make it easy for the specialist to rationalize a will-planning/probate plan because they go to the attorney with the expectation that they will get a will. To change this expectation, the practitioner will have to devote time and energy and answer a number of questions and potential objections. Given the time constraints and frenzy of the typical successful specialist practice, it is often easier to give clients what they expect rather than what they need.

A Predisposition to Probate

Will-planning/probate specialists are in the business of probate. They have convinced themselves that it is the best practice for their clients and that the fees charged are more than justified by the efforts and results. Probate lawyers do work hard at the business of probate. They rationalize that if they try hard, work hard, and care about what they are doing, they have earned their fees.

They miss the point that the entire exercise is unnecessary if a fully funded revocable living trust plan is used. They look at probate from their point of view. They know and are comfortable with it and cannot understand why anyone would want to avoid it. It represents a comfortable and profitable environment for the probate lawyer. Why would anyone want to avoid or change this environment? The fact is that what is comfortable for probate lawyers is not comfortable for the families of their disabled or deceased clients.

We believe that probate lawyers believe that they are helping people. We also believe that they are looking at the issue from only their point of view and that this practice will likely continue as long as clients accept their will-planning/probate recommendations.

Specialist estate planners have significant will files that represent enormous potential revenue. They have staffs of trained probate associates, paralegals, and secretaries. They have computer programs, forms, and systems, all of which are geared to probating estates. Even if they wanted to convert their practices to living trust planning, the conversion would, in their minds, entail immense financial risk.

The Fear of Facing Their Clients

Many estate planning specialists who are probate lawyers acknowledge that the living trust is a better planning vehicle than will-planning/probate. However, they have a significant problem. How do they go back to hundreds or thousands of clients for whom they have done wills and say, "I need to change your estate plan"?

We have encountered this honest concern innumerable times in our careers. This is a real and sensitive issue. It involves pride, money, effort, and a certain amount of courage. When we talk with practitioners facing this dilemma, it becomes apparent that they feel that they have made a mistake in their earlier planning efforts and must somehow acknowledge that mistake to their clients.

We think that the lawyer's fear of client disapproval is incorrect. In our experience, clients appreciate it when their lawyers offer the living trust alternative. Also, if the will was inexpensive, the client has not yet suffered a major financial loss. It might be appropriate for the lawyer to apply the fee he or she charged for the will to the new living trust–centered plan.

The Funding Dilemma

Many specialists say that they do not recommend living trust planning because they do not want to put up with the "aggravation" of funding the trusts they prepare.

We find their position to be untenable. Wills are followed by probate. One of probate's main tasks is retitling property in the names of heirs. The living trust funding process is not different. It simply involves retitling assets in the trust. As we have repeatedly suggested, the retitling process is far easier, less time consuming, and remarkably less expensive if you do it while the client is alive and well.

Many specialist practitioners cite the inability of their clients to keep their living trust plans properly funded as a justification for will-planning/probate. And yet their offices are staffed with probate personnel who could easily take over the funding responsibility.

Does a Living Trust Have Hidden Drawbacks That Lead Lawyers to Advise Against Its Use?

The answer is no, yet many lawyers honestly believe otherwise. There are a number of articles written by probate lawyers in the law journals that frighten nonspecialist lawyers away from living trust planning. These articles fall into three categories:

*Technical Articles That Simultaneously Assault Trusts
and Defend Wills Within Precisely Delineated Perspectives*

These articles do not, in the main, compare living trust planning to will-planning/probate and reach definitive conclusions on which is the better planning vehicle. They pick away at the living trust as compared to some utopian standard and, in so doing, dwell on those areas where it falls short of utopian perfection. The bulk of these attacks focus on a very few categories, including after-death income tax planning, avoidance of certain creditors, perceived funding problems, and congressional legislation.

They do not compare will-planning/probate to living trusts on an apples-to-apples basis. If they did, they would lose the argument. A probate lawyer can contrive a situation where living trust planning may not be appropriate. We acknowledge that living trusts are not perfect; they are just better than the will-planning/probate alternative in an overwhelming number of planning situations.

The Attempt to Dismiss Living Trust Planning by Sweeping Generalizations

Some professional writers make generalizations that dismiss the living trust out of hand. They make sweeping statements in a few pages that raise issues the reader does not understand and the writer does not explain. The superficiality of these articles creates unfounded fears that prey upon the reader's lack of knowledge. These articles emphasize the exceptions rather than the rules. They make mountains out of molehills and distort the truth with generalities. It appears that these writers are using their articles to perpetuate the will-planning/probate bias.

Some professional writers treat the living trust with contempt and sarcasm. Their writings impugn the professionalism and integrity of living trust lawyers and, by association, the living trust. This kind of writing attempts to use parody and satire as a means of dismissing out of hand legitimate complaints and criticisms of wills and probate.[3]

Articles That Attack Living Trusts Because of Perceived Overselling and Promotion

One legal writer lambasted living trusts because he took exception to the way they were being marketed to the public in his area.[4] The arguments he raised in his article, and the answer they deserve, can be best summarized in excerpts from a letter to the editor of the journal in which the article appeared:

> *[The author's] critical analysis of revocable trusts in the September 1990 issue seems to reflect his professional revulsion to blatant promotion by lawyers. It is obvious that the newspaper advertisements for living trust seminars at the end of his article were the catalyst for the criticisms which preceded it.*
>
> *Certainly [the author] is not too young to recall the promotional efforts which the organized Bar has expended over many years to encourage the execution of Wills by everyone. The justification has been that intestate [dying without a Will] is a bad way to die. If you leave this world without a professionally drafted Will, the advertisements argue, you are leaving the disposition of your property to the state legislature. Remember those ads? Those promotions were blatant and clearly fee producing, but were sincerely directed toward encouraging a better legal service. The fact that lawyers promote their services is not an argument against that service.*
>
> *[The author] should not be distracted by the evil "straw man" of living trust seminars. If a revocable living trust is a better plan for our clients, we should all recommend it forcefully. . . .*
>
> *What [the author] fails to address in his article is the unavoidable fact that the general public does not find our existing testamentary and probate system to be economical, efficient or humane. That disapproval was around long before the recent promotion of living trusts and is based, at least in part, on the fact that Wills are invariably*

written strictly in the lawyer's language and reflect the lawyer's standard disposition strategies. Fees and costs of probated estates are too often outrageously high. Delays abound because the process does not seek to achieve speed or efficiency.

The Bar cannot simply refuse to recognize that some services we are now providing are regarded as burdens rather than solutions. Instead of clinging to our "tried and true" methods, the Bar must welcome those innovators who are willing to actively promote new ideas. It is facile to respond that public acceptance of living trusts is merely the result of hype and salesmanship. There are unnecessary costs and delays in transferring property at death. The existing public response to living trusts indicates that their needs have not been addressed. Let's not blame the innovators who have merely identified deficiencies in our existing systems.[5]

Does the Controversy Involve More Than Money?

Probate and after-death administration put control over decedents' estates and their heirs in the hands of lawyers and the courts. This is an awesome responsibility that provides an attorney prestige and power as well as meaningful remuneration. If lawyers discharge this responsibility with skill and dignity and enjoy the perquisites that go with it, there would be no reason for them to believe that probate should be avoided.

A major part of the great debate involves a determination of who will control the process that is going to pass the trillions of dollars of wealth to the next generation.

Both the will-planning/probate and living trust approaches require the services of an attorney. The will-planning/probate approach puts the power and control over this wealth in the hands of probate lawyers. The living trust approach places control in the hands of surviving beneficiaries who will use the services of lawyers and other professionals only on an "as needed" basis.

There is no question that probate lawyers enjoy the power and control that the probate process gives them as much as the fees it generates.

Do Probate Lawyers Attack Living Trust Companies and Living Trust Forms as a Method of Undermining the Use of Living Trusts?

An example of the way probate lawyers protect the status quo can be seen in the way the organized bar of some states views companies that offer forms for estate planning. A growing number of commercial businesses are selling trust forms directly to the consumer. In addition, commercial companies for years have also made form wills and do-it-yourself will kits available to the public. These companies advertise both locally and nationally on radio and television and in the newspapers. There has been quite an outcry lately by the legal profession over the sale of trust forms, but the sale of will forms either is unnoticed or is tacitly approved.

The refusal of the probate bar to convert to living trust planning has created an environment conducive to the proliferation of businesses that sell living trusts directly to the public without the traditional attorney-client relationship. These companies exist because the public is demanding what they are selling. It is apparent that the public has lost faith in will-planning/probate and has turned elsewhere for help.

Nonlawyer entrepreneurs have recognized that the public wants to avoid probate. These entrepreneurs mass-produce trust forms for sale directly to the public. Some of the companies that sell complete living trusts sell their forms through life insurance agents or financial planners, some through direct mail. In most of these schemes, no attorney is involved; the forms are filled out by the agent or financial planner who makes the sale. Sometimes, the forms are completed by the consumer. On occasion, these companies try to legitimize their activities by hiring a lawyer (who never meets the client) to "review" the documents and rubber stamp them as "legally correct."

Most of the living trust companies advertise heavily. The advertisements stress the expense and inconvenience of probate and tout many of the same advantages of living trusts that are recommended by estate planning attorneys.

The organized bar has taken very strong exception to these living trust form companies, and they have been investigated by bar associations or other government agencies in several states.[6] In at least one state, the attorney general has taken action against these companies for deceptive and misleading representations to consumers.[7]

What is all too revealing about the attacks on living trust companies is that the criticisms by probate lawyers, government agencies, and others frequently do not focus on the most dangerous aspect of these commercial activities, the fact that they sell "one-size-fits-all" legal forms without the guidance of a lawyer and without any planning. In many cases, these companies are engaging in the unlicensed practice of law. They very well may be preparing living trusts that will not be effective for the purchaser, for one reason or another. The focus of the outcry by the organized bar and others, however, is that sellers of trust forms are making unfounded criticisms about the drawbacks of probate and are making *false* claims about the benefits of living trusts.

We strongly believe that in most instances these companies are injuring the public because they are circumventing some of the most important elements of estate planning. This is not the focus of the criticisms, however! Here are some examples of some reasonable claims made by living trust companies that have been labeled "unfair" or "deceptive"[8]:

- That living trusts are markedly superior to a will for the estate planning needs of most persons
- That the costs of probating a will may consume a significant portion of a decedent's estate
- That living trusts are valid under state law
- That living trusts are difficult to challenge in court
- That living trusts can provide tax advantages
- That probate is expensive and time consuming

The investigating agencies have unquestionably been concerned with protecting the public from misleading and fraudulent practices. It appears, however, that these agencies have also been getting the bulk of their information from aggressive and vocal probate lawyers.[9] The statements listed here are true statements in all respects and have nothing to do with the sale of living trust documents by nonlawyers. Attacks upon the validity of these statements are not just attacks against nonlawyer companies, they are direct and inappropriate attacks on the validity of the living trust as a legally valid method of estate planning.

There is every appearance that probate lawyers use these companies as convenient scapegoats for attacking the legitimate uses of living trust planning by practicing professionals, and have even convinced some state governments to make unwarranted attacks on living trusts.[10] These attacks confuse the public even more and make it that much more difficult for legitimate living trust professionals to communicate proper living trust information to consumers. What is even more egregious is that general practitioners read this inaccurate information and often reach the same erroneous conclusions as the public.

It is ironic that, while the bar considers the promotion of living trust forms unaccceptable, it has no such criticism of will forms. To date, we are not aware of any prosecution or investigation of companies selling will forms. In fact, the organized bar *promotes* the use of form wills. The National Conference of Commissioners on Uniform State Laws drafted a Uniform Statutory Will Act in 1984, which has been adopted in Massachusetts.[11] Three other states, California, Maine, and Wisconsin, have statutory wills that provide actual forms as a part of the statutes. The California statutory forms even allow the creation of a trust within the will. People who use these forms are not likely to use the services of a lawyer.

The public's use of will forms apparently is not disturbing to probate lawyers. The reason is not difficult to grasp. Such form wills, whatever their shortcomings for the family involved, will yield the traditional result for lawyers: more probates. Lawyers lose very little income by the proliferation of form wills, because they generally charge minimal fees for writing wills anyway.

It is regrettable that the criticisms of the living trust which have been made by attorneys who are opposed to the use of living trust planning are diametrically opposed to the assessments of acknowledged scholars and estate planning leaders and well-known treatises about trust law. These authorities have for years encouraged and approved lawyers' use of living trusts.

If probate lawyers, newspaper reporters, and government officials would take the time to review the estate planning literature, they would find statements such as these:

> The purposes for which trusts can be created are as unlimited as the imagination of lawyers. There are no technical rules restricting the creation of trusts. The trust can be, and has been, applied as a device

for accomplishing many different purposes. One of the most important is and has always been the making of family settlements. 1 A. Scott and W. Fratcher, *The Law of Trusts* § 1, 2 (4th ed. 1987)

[The revocable living trust is] a major tool for estate planning purposes. Report of the Committee on Tax and Estate Planning of the American Bar Association, "The Revocable Living Trusts an Estate Planning Tool," 7 *Real Property, Probate and Trust Journal* 223 (1972)

[An estate planning approach that] throughout the seven hundred or so years of its history . . . has shown itself adaptable to many ends. Brantley, "Use of the Trust to Manage Property of the Elderly or Disabled," 42 *Arkansas Law Review* 713 (1989) [The writer is a chancellor and probate judge in Arkansas.]

Those who claim that criticism of probate is unfounded and unjustified will also find that criticisms of the probate system are in no way limited to commercial living trust companies. Thoughtful practitioners and scholars have criticized probate for years. In a very recent debate over the use of the living trust, a Connecticut practitioner who supports living trust planning candidly stated:

There is legally no reason why the bulk of the estate assets must be held for twelve to twenty months pending tax audits. But the fact is that assets are so held in many, if not most, cases. The track record of executors with respect to prompt asset distribution is abysmal, whether because of lawyer or banker procrastination or because prompt distribution makes the job look easy and makes fees based upon percentage of assets held look excessive.[12]

This frank assessment sounds as if not much has changed since Professor Bostick stated in 1968, that "A . . . serious deficiency of probate is that it suffers from the ailments of old age—a sort of arteriosclerosis of method that renders it both philosophically and functionally unable to cope with the insistent demand of modern society."[13]

The will-planning/probate system involves a complex set of factors that encompasses entrenched legal paradigms, prestige, and power. The will-planning/probate infrastructure is massive and ubiquitous. Dismantling it will not be easy. The living trust faces a significant uphill battle, not over whether it presents a better and less expensive planning alternative to the public but rather because it challenges the professional status quo. Because the living trust presents the better alternative, the estate planning paradigm is changing, but it is not likely to change overnight. Only a concentrated effort by concerned consumers and estate planning professionals will expedite this change.

The living trust reflects the changing needs and attitudes of the American public. It is time to change the way America plans.

APPENDIX A

Analysis of the After-Death Income Tax Issues

Income Splitting and the Throwback Rules

Questions for Discussion

- What is income splitting and what is its significance?
- What are the throwback rules and how do they affect the income taxation of trusts?
- Is income splitting a beneficial after-death income tax planning technique?

For a number of years, will-planning/probate advocates have emphasized that because a probate estate is a separate taxpaying entity, it has the ability to split income between its tax bracket and those of the decedent's heirs. Will-planning/probate advocates claim that by splitting this income, after-death income tax savings can be achieved. They argue that living trusts do not have this ability because they are subject to an elaborate set of income tax rules called *throwback rules*, which effectively prevent a trust from income splitting with its beneficiaries.

The Reality of Income Splitting

In spite of the propensity of will-planning/probate advocates to emphasize income tax splitting as a significant will-planning/probate benefit, its impact is minimal in most cases. The Tax Reform Act of 1986 (TRA 86) radically changed the progressive nature of our income tax system. Prior to TRA 86, there were a wide range of income tax brackets for individuals, trusts, and probate estates. Because of the numerous brackets and the liberal deductions and credits that existed prior to TRA 86, income splitting made sense. It was advantageous to spread income over several taxpaying entities and then shelter that income by "investing" in tax shelters and taking generous depreciation allowances and other deductions and credits that were not necessarily economically viable, but were established purely for tax saving motives.

There are now only three income tax brackets, and Congress has substantially curtailed deductions and credits. The income tax rates and bracket amounts for trusts and probate estates for 1992 are as follows[1]:

Income Tax Rates for Trusts and Probate Estates

Taxable Income	Income Tax
$0–$3,600	15%
Over $3,600 through $10,900	$540 plus 28% on the excess over $3,600
Over $10,900	$2,584 plus 31% on the excess over $10,900

The amount of trust and probate estate income that is subject to the 15 percent bracket is minimal. This is equally true of the amount of income subject to the 28 percent bracket. In 1992, any income over $10,900 was subject to the maximum 31 percent bracket.

Contrast the tax bracket amounts of trusts and estates to the 1992 bracket amounts for single individuals and married couples[2]:

Single Individuals

Taxable Income	Income Tax
$0–$21,450	15%
Over $21,450 through $51,900	$3,127.50 plus 28% on the excess over $21,450
Over $51,900	$11,743.50 plus 31% on the excess over $51,900

Married Individuals Filing Joint Returns

Taxable Income	Income Tax
$0–$35,800	15%
Over $35,800 through $86,500	$5,370 plus 28% on the excess over $35,800
Over $86,500	$19,566 plus 31% on the excess over $86,500

For a single individual, taxable income must exceed $51,900 to be subject to the 31 percent bracket. For married individuals filing joint returns, taxable income has to exceed $86,500 before the 31 percent bracket takes effect.

Since a greater amount of individual income is taxed at lower bracket amounts, it is much more advantageous for a probate estate or a trust to distribute its income to beneficiaries so that it will be taxed in their lower brackets. This result is exactly the opposite of the will-planning/probate advocates' position on this issue!

Will-planning/probate lawyers advocate leaving income in a probate estate so that it will be taxed at the estate's bracket rather than at the heirs' brackets. This may have been a major planning device in the past, but it is not of significance any longer.

The insignificance of income splitting in estates and trusts can be summarized in the words of the authors of a noted treatise on the federal income taxation of trusts, speaking on the changes made in TRA 86:

> The moderate two-rate schedule for all taxpayers discourages expectations of great savings from income splitting. Furthermore, the comparatively low threshold for loss to the trust and estate entities of the benefit of the lower rate actually deters accumulation at the entity level [FN 36 omitted]. Indeed, it will often be important to push the income through the entities immediately to secure more favorable income taxation at the beneficiary level.[3]

Here is an example that will clarify their analysis:

> *Assume that in 1992, an estate's beneficiaries were all in the 31 percent bracket, and that the estate's executor decides to retain the maximum amount of income possible to take advantage of income splitting, which is $10,900.*

> *The income tax on this amount of taxable income at the estate's bracket is $2,584. Had the executor distributed the income to the beneficiaries, the tax it would generate would be $3,379.*

> *At the most, income splitting can save $795.00 in federal income tax. This is hardly a massive tax savings!*

Income splitting is of little or no importance in the after-death income taxation of trusts and estates. The position of will-planning/probate proponents that income splitting is a major or even important advantage of a probate estate has not been valid since TRA 86 modified income tax rates.

The Throwback Rules

Part and parcel of income splitting is the propensity of will-planning/probate advocates to criticize living trusts as inadequate after-death income tax planning devices. They do so because of the application of an elaborate set of income taxation rules for trusts called the *throwback rules*.[4] The mere mention of these throwback rules has managed to strike fear into the hearts of practitioners for years because of their perceived complexity.

The truth of the matter is that the throwback rules are not as formidable as the press they receive seems to indicate, and they actually do no more than attempt to eliminate the use of income splitting in trusts.

Understanding the Throwback Rules

The key to comprehending the throwback rules is to understand that they are designed to make sure that any income retained in a trust that is later distributed to a beneficiary will be taxed in that beneficiary's tax bracket if it is higher than the trust's income tax bracket. The theory behind the throwback rules is that living trust income that is accumulated after the death of the maker should be eventually taxed in the higher of the trust's bracket or the beneficiary's bracket to discourage trust accumulations of ordinary income at a lower tax bracket. The underlying concept of throwback rules can be illustrated by a simple example:

> *Peter Jacobs set up a trust for his children. Each of his children is in the 31 percent personal income tax bracket.*

> *Peter's trust provides that his trustee can disburse income to his children or retain it in the trust for later distribution.*

> *Peter's trust is in the 28 percent bracket. Under the throwback rules, when the income is eventually distributed to the children, they must make up the difference between 28 and 31 percent as taxable income.*

There are a couple of basic elements to the throwback rules. The first is that income which is retained by a trust will be taxed initially in the trust's income tax bracket. Second, to the extent that there is a distribution from the trust in any trust year in excess of the trust's income for that year, the distribution will be subject to the throwback rules, but only if the trust has not distributed all its income in prior years.

Here is a simple example of how this works:

> *In 1987, a trust's distributable net income (DNI)[5] is $15,000. The trustee distributes only $5,000 to the beneficiaries. The remaining $10,000 is accumulated income and is taxed at the trust's income tax bracket.*

> *In 1988, the trust has DNI of $1,000, but the trustee again distributes $5,000. The $4,000 in excess of the current year's DNI is subject to the throwback rules because the trust has accumulated income in excess of the $4,000. The $4,000 amount is called an accumulation*

distribution for purposes of computing any tax that the beneficiary may owe because of the distribution.

In a year when a beneficiary receives an accumulation distribution, the beneficiary must make a computation to see whether any additional tax is due. The first step in the computation is to determine the number of years over which the income was earned by the trust on a first-in first-out basis. Assume the following:

A trustee makes an accumulation distribution of $40,000 in 1995. The trust was established in 1990 and had accumulated income as follows:

1990	$ 5,000
1991	$15,000
1992	$10,000
1993	$18,000
1994	$10,000

The accumulation distribution is attributable to four years, 1990 through 1993 and was earned at an average of $10,000 per year ($40,000 divided by four years). This income was previously taxed at the trust's bracket and the trust paid the tax on it.

Because of the throwback rules, the beneficiary looks to his or her last five years of income and eliminates the highest year of income and the lowest year.

The accumulation distribution is prorated among the three base years. In our example, $10,000 would be added to the beneficiary's taxable income in each of the three base years.

The beneficiary's income taxes are then recomputed for each of the three years. The average yearly increase in tax for the three years is determined. This average yearly increase in tax is multiplied by the number of years to which the accumulation distribution relates, which would be four years in our example.

This amount is then offset by a credit for any taxes paid by the trust in those years. Any remaining tax is payable by the beneficiary in the year that the accumulation distribution was made.

If the credit for taxes paid by the trust is greater than the amount the beneficiary owes, then no refund is payable.

While this illustration is a broad summary of the throwback rules, it demonstrates how the throwback rules turn out to be equitable if the beneficiaries are in lower tax brackets than the trust is. However, this is unlikely because of our compressed federal income tax brackets. These rules allow a trust to accumulate income but ensure that the tax on the income will be approximately the same whether the trust's income is paid to the beneficiary the year the trust earns it or whether it is retained by the trust and paid out in later years.

There is an important exception to the throwback rules that will-planning/probate advocates rarely mention when discussing after-death income tax planning. The throwback rules do not apply to beneficiaries who are under the age of twenty-one.[6] This exception allows the use of the trust for income splitting where there are younger beneficiaries!

The throwback rules involve a degree of complexity in tax computations. But this complexity is not a burden to individual trustees who have accountants and to professional trustees who use tax computation software packages which make the calculations.

The intent of the throwback rules is to tax beneficiaries as if they had received trust income in the year that it was earned so that the effect of income splitting is minimized. Since income splitting is now of minimal importance anyway, the throwback rules do not have a significant effect on after-death income tax planning and do not make a living trust disadvantageous.

Trapping Distributions

A rather esoteric advantage that probate estates have over trusts is the ability for estates to make trapping distributions that are exempt from the throwback rules.[7] A *trapping distribution* is a distribution of principal that carries with it the distributable net income of the distributing estate. If an estate makes a distribution to a trust which is required to distribute all of its income, called a simple trust,[8] then the distribution by the estate to the simple trust "traps" the DNI so that any future distributions by the trust are not subject to the throwback rules.

Not all trust property can be distributed in this manner,[9] but some practitioners use this technique to reduce or eliminate DNI for purposes of after-death income tax planning.

It has been suggested that a trust can take advantage of trapping distributions if it is used in conjunction with a probate estate and there is proper drafting in both the trust and the will.[10] This technique involves creating a probate estate and a continuing trust for administrative purposes as part of the living trust–centered plan. The two entities are used together to delay distributions of distributable net income.[11]

A trust, in conjunction with a probate estate, can be used

to take advantage of this after-death planning technique if it becomes important in a specific planning situation.

In the main, the use of trapping distributions presents an intellectual exercise for a handful of practitioners and legal scholars. Because of the compression of income tax brackets for trusts and estates, this exercise is mostly theoretical. The decision on whether to use living trust planning versus will-planning/probate will never turn on the issue of trapping distributions.

The Revocable Living Trust as a Separate After-Death Income Tax Entity

Although will-planning/probate advocates often claim that income splitting is exclusive to probate estates, a living trust also can be a separate after-death income tax entity for purposes of income splitting. This income tax splitting opportunity arises when a living trust is used in lieu of a probate. For example, the traditional revocable living trust that is designed to accomplish federal estate tax planning for married couples is divided into a marital trust and a family trust on the death of its maker. This division is supposed to occur, at least by the terms of most living trust documents, immediately on the death of the trust maker. Living trust documents that do not include federal estate tax planning or that are for unmarried individuals commonly create subtrusts for various beneficiaries on the death of the trust maker. These subtrusts, much like marital and family trusts, are also supposed to be funded immediately on the death of the trust maker.

In reality, the funding of subtrusts does not take place immediately on the death of the trust maker, and this is true even if the living trust was fully funded during its maker's lifetime. Because of valuation issues, after-death income tax issues, and issues relating to federal estate tax, there is sometimes a lag between the death of the maker and the actual funding of these subtrusts. In the interim, the original living trust functions much as an estate does.[12]

Because this "continuing living trust" functions as an estate does, it is subject to the same income tax rules as a probate estate. The continuing trust has its own federal identification number[13] and is treated as a separate taxpaying entity until such time as it is possible to fund any subtrusts or to distribute all of its assets to beneficiaries. The continuing trust ends when the subtrusts are funded. During the time that the continuing living trust is in existence, it is fully capable of income splitting, just as an estate is. Under these circumstances, a probate estate has *no* income splitting advantages over a living trust!

Capital Gain Treatment
of Living Trusts and Probate

Capital gains have lost much of their significance since the Tax Reform Act of 1986. Prior to 1987, when a taxpayer realized a long-term capital gain on the sale of a capital asset, only 40 percent of the gain was taxable. Since the top income tax bracket at that time was 50 percent, the maximum capital gains tax was 20 percent before 1987.

The 1986 act repealed the special tax treatment for capital gains and made the full capital gain subject to taxation at ordinary income tax rates. These rates were as high as 31 percent. The Revenue Reconciliation Act of 1990 reduced the maximum bracket for capital gains to 28 percent, even though the top income tax bracket for ordinary income is 31 percent.[14]

While capital gains are less important now than they were prior to 1987, they do have some importance in the income taxation of trusts and probate estates. The lower maximum capital gains bracket, coupled with some special accounting rules applicable to trusts, affords some after-death income tax planning possibilities for living trusts that compare favorably with the income taxation of probate estates.

The Trust as a
Separate Capital Gains Taxpayer

In trust accounting, it is usual and ordinary practice to allocate capital gain income to the trust principal rather than to the trust income.[15] A trustee excludes the capital gain from the computation of the trust income that is distributable to its beneficiaries.

The Internal Revenue Code states that capital gains are not included in a trust's distributable net income unless they are actually paid, credited, or required to be distributed.[16] Essentially, this means that most trusts are separate taxpayers for purposes of capital gain income and that such income is not subject to the throwback rules.

A trust, as a separate capital gains taxpayer, offers after-death income tax planning possibilities. Even though separate income tax brackets are not especially important because of their abbreviated number, a trust has the ability to use what little advantage there is in income splitting:

Cynthia is a beneficiary of a trust; she is in the maximum 31 percent bracket. Her trust is in the 15 percent bracket.

If Cynthia's trustee sells a trust asset for a profit—a capital gain—the profit will be taxed at the trust's income tax bracket rather than Cynthia's maximum capital gain rate of 28 percent.

Because capital gains income is not generally included in the computation of a trust's distributable net income, it is not usually subject to the throwback rules. This allows the trustee to make later distributions of the capital gains as nontaxable distributions of principal rather than as income.

The Probate Estate as a Separate Capital Gains Taxpayer

A probate estate is taxed as a separate taxpayer for capital gain income. It too can use income splitting for capital gains.

From a tax perspective, the treatment of capital gains is the same for a probate estate and a trust. However, in order for the probate estate to take advantage of the capital gains comparison, the probate estate must remain open. The cost of probate may very well be significantly greater than the income tax savings that are realized. Probate's other disadvantages make this saving even more insignificant.

Our Conclusion

Federal tax legislation has significantly reduced the impact of income splitting. It is no longer a planning technique that gives will-planning/probate any advantage over living trust–centered planning.

The Ability to Choose a Fiscal Year

Questions for Discussion

- What is a fiscal year?
- Can both a living trust and a probate estate have a fiscal year?
- Does a fiscal year save after-death income tax?

Will-planning/probate advocates often contend that an advantage a probate estate has over a trust is that a probate estate is able to choose a fiscal year, while a trust cannot.[1] A *fiscal year* is any tax period that is different than a calendar year. A calendar year is from January 1 through December 31. An example of a fiscal year is the tax period from June 1 through May 31. Prior to Tax Reform Act of 1986, both estates and trusts could elect a fiscal year, but now the Internal Revenue Code generally requires trusts to report income on a calendar year.[2]

An estate's ability to choose a fiscal year does not necessarily give a probate estate a meaningful income tax planning advantage over a living trust.

The Practical Benefit of an
Estate's Ability to Choose a Fiscal Year

The ability of the estate's executor to choose the probate estate's fiscal year has theoretical income tax advantages:

Assume a decedent with a probate estate dies on June 1, 1990. On the basis of this date of death, the executor has the choice of electing any fiscal year as long as it ends by May 31, 1991. In the first year after the decedent's death, the fiscal year can be less than 365 days. This is called a short fiscal year. However, after the first year the fiscal year must be the full 365 days.

Now, let's assume that the executor chooses a fiscal year ending January 31—February 1 through January 31 —and all of the decedent's heirs are calendar year taxpayers.

In terms of our assumptions, the heirs will not have to report any taxable distributions made to them from June 1, 1990, through December 31, 1990, in their 1990 income tax returns.

They will, however, have to report all of the income they received in 1990 and in January 1991 on their 1991 income tax returns; they will not have to pay income tax on these amounts until April 15, 1992.

On its face, using a fiscal year to defer income tax payable on distributions to heirs looks attractive. A closer examination reveals serious flaws.

One problem with deferring income into later tax years is that eventually past pleasures turn into current sins. A probate estate must eventually be closed. Research has shown that most estates remain open for less than two years. When an estate is closed, all of its income must be distributed to the heirs. This tends to cause what tax attorneys and accountants call *income bunching,* an accumulation of income all in one tax year to the heirs. Let's continue with our example:

Let's further assume that the estate is open until September 30, 1992, a total of twenty-eight months.

On April 15, 1992, the heirs paid tax on all the income deferred from 1990 and from January 1991. On April 15, 1993, they will pay the taxes on all the income generated from February 1, 1991, through January 31, 1992.

When the estate closes in 1992, all income earned from February 1, 1991, through September 30, 1992, will be included in the heirs' income for 1992. This is in addition to the heirs' income from February 1, 1991, through January 31, 1992.

On April 15, 1993, the heirs have their day of reckoning. All deferral stops, and the piper must be paid. Because of income bunching, the ultimate tax consequences may be worse than if no income deferral was used.

Several factors can exacerbate the bunching of income. The income deferred in the initial fiscal year of administration is often low because the first fiscal year is usually less than twelve months long. In addition, a number of estate expenses are generated early on, and the initial taxable income is often low because of these expenses. The estate's assets are more likely to be nonliquid early in the probate proceeding and often do not generate meaningful income until such time as they are reduced to cash or cash equivalents. In subsequent fiscal years, expenses are likely to be lower and income higher. These factors can result in much greater income taxes in the year the estate is closed, thereby reducing or eliminating any advantages of deferral.

If taxable distributions are paid from an estate, they may not have to be reported on the recipient's income tax return until a later date. However, what advocates of the fiscal year concept sometimes overlook is that the heirs may have to make quarterly estimated tax payments on the amounts that they receive.[3] These estimated tax payments vary on the basis of the amount of income distributed in prior years and the income tax situation of a recipient, but they may well dilute the effectiveness of the fiscal year technique, because the tax will have to be paid prior to the due date of the return.

Our Conclusion

The perceived benefits of deferring income by choosing a fiscal rather than a calendar year in will-planning/probate are illusory.

Personal Exemptions
for Trusts and Estates

Questions for Discussion

- What is the difference in the personal exemptions for a trust and for a probate estate?
- Is the difference meaningful?

Perhaps the greatest nonissue in the continuing after-death income tax debate between trusts and estates is the personal exemption that each is granted. A personal exemption is simply a deduction from gross income. The amount of the exemption is an arbitrary amount set by Congress. Advocates of will-planning/probate invariably argue that the larger personal exemption granted to a probate estate gives it an advantage over living trust planning.

Personal Exemptions for Trusts and Estates

A trust has a smaller personal exemption than an estate. An estate is allowed a personal exemption of $600. A complex trust, which is a trust that is not required to distribute all of its income currently, is allowed an exemption of $100. A simple trust is allowed a $300 exemption.[1]

An estate's personal exemption is $500 greater than that of a complex trust. Assuming the worst case scenario, where an estate and a complex trust are in the 31 percent income tax bracket, the estate can save a total of $155 per year. If the estate is in existence for three years, the total savings is $465.

Our Conclusion

The difference between a probate estate's personal exemption and a living trust's exemption is insignificant.

Estimated Tax Payments

Question for Discussion

• Do both probate estates and trusts have to make quarterly estimated income tax payments?

Prior to 1986, neither trusts nor probate estates were required to make quarterly estimated income tax payments.[1] One of the goals of the Tax Reform Act of 1986 was to reduce the incentive to use estates and trusts for the deferral of income tax; as a result, one provision requires probate estates and trusts to begin making quarterly estimated income tax payments.[2] An exemption was granted, however, to probate estates for the first two taxable years after the decedent's death.[3] This probate estate advantage was soon extended to certain trusts[4] but is still mentioned by probate advocates as a benefit belonging exclusively to a probate estate.

Estimated Tax
Payments for Trusts and Estates

The Technical and Miscellaneous Revenue Act of 1988 extended the two-year exemption for the payment of quarterly estimated income tax payments to trusts "to which the residue of the decedent's estate will pass under his will. . . ."[5] This means that revocable living trusts that receive assets from pour-over wills are also exempt from quarterly payments of estimated taxes for a two-year period.

In the Revenue Reconciliation Act of 1989, the two-year rule was applied to trusts that are "primarily responsible for paying debts, taxes, and expenses of administration," and where no will is admitted to probate.[6] This amendment was intended, at least in part, to apply to fully funded revocable living trusts.

The law now puts probate estates and revocable living trusts on equal footing for purposes of estimated taxes. The most noteworthy aspect of this legislative history is that there is a clear indication that Congress recognizes that a probate estate and a revocable living trust are comparable income tax entities.

Our Conclusion

Probate estates and living trusts are treated the same for purposes of estimated income tax payments.

The Separate Share Rule

Questions for Discussion

- What is the separate share rule?
- What is its impact on a probate estate?
- What is its impact on a trust?
- Does a living trust have an advantage over a probate estate under the separate share rule?

The separate share rule is income tax law that affects distributions of income and principal from a trust. Will-planning/probate advocates contend that a probate estate has an income tax advantage over a living trust because the separate share rule does not apply to probate estates. On the other hand, living trust proponents claim that the separate share rule provides a benefit—rather than a detriment—for living trust–centered planning.

What Is the Separate Share Rule?

The separate share rule states that if a trust instrument creates separate and distinct shares for its beneficiaries, then those shares will be treated as separate trusts for income tax purposes.[1] An example of a situation that triggers the separate share rule follows.

> *Stuart's revocable living trust provides that after his death, his trustees are to hold his trust property in a single trust. The income from the trust assets is to be divided into four equal shares for the benefit of his four children. Each child's share of the income is to be accumulated until that child reaches twenty-one years of age. After a child is twenty-one, the trustee can make discretionary distributions of income and principal to the child.*
>
> *Stuart died while all of his children were under the age of twenty-one. Melanie, his oldest child, turned twenty-one several years after Stuart's death. On Melanie's twenty-first birthday, the trustees distributed $40,000 to her. The trust's total income for the year in which the distribution to Melanie was made was $20,000.*

Under the separate share rule, each child's share is treated as if it were a separate trust, and the income is divided for tax purposes equally among the beneficiaries. Therefore, in this situation, Melanie's taxable income (her distributable net income) is $5,000, one-fourth of $20,000.

The separate share rule does not apply to a trust in which the trustee has discretion over distributions of trust income or principal. A situation that does *not* trigger the separate share rule is the following:

> *Stuart's revocable living trust provides that after his death, his trustees are to hold his trust property in a single trust. The trustees are given the discretion to distribute income and principal to Stuart's four children for their health, education, maintenance, and support. There is no requirement that distributions be made equally among*

the children. When Stuart's youngest child reaches the age of thirty-five, the trust is to be divided into equal shares for his children.

Stuart died while all of his children were under the age of thirty-five. Melanie, his oldest child, turned twenty-one several years after Stuart's death. On Melanie's twenty-first birthday, the trustees distributed $40,000 to her. The trust's total income for the year in which the distribution to Melanie was made was $20,000.

In this situation, the separate share rule will not apply. Melanie's distributable net income, on which she will pay income tax, is $20,000. Melanie will not have to pay income tax on the remaining $20,000.[2]

This same result would occur if Melanie received her distribution of $40,000 from her father's probate estate. An heir who receives a distribution from a probate estate is treated as receiving the net income of the estate to the extent that it has taxable income. Any distributions an heir receives in excess of the estate's taxable income will be treated as distributions of principal to the heir for income tax purposes.

Will-planning/probate advocates contend that because an heir who receives taxable income from the estate pays the income tax on that income, additional after-death income tax can be saved if the executor distributes the income *first* to an heir who is in the lowest income tax bracket. For example:

Assume that Melanie's three brothers make a great deal of money and Melanie makes none.

In this situation, the executor would make distributions first to Melanie. If the probate estate made $20,000 of

*income in 1992, and it was all distributed to Melanie,
she would pay income tax on the probate estate's entire
$20,000 of income at her lower income tax bracket.*

Will-planning/probate advocates say this ability to shift income to lower brackets is a benefit of a probate estate. Their position is questionable. The process of shifting income may create unequal distributions among an estate's heirs. The possibility that one heir may pay all of the tax on the estate's income may not be what the decedent intended. If that is what the decedent intended, the same result could be achieved with a discretionary trust.

The important point to consider is that the separate share rule never applies to a probate estate. This puts the control over which heir will pay income tax on distributions at the sole discretion of the executor.

A living trust does not suffer from this disadvantage because its terms can be drafted to meet the precise desires of the trust maker. If a trust maker wants the separate share rule to apply, the trust document will create separate trust shares. If the trust maker does not want the separate share rule to apply, then the trust document can be written so that separate shares are not created.

Our Conclusion

The separate share rule gives a living trust–centered estate plan a planning advantage over will-planning/probate.

Amounts Permanently Set Aside for Charity

Questions for Discussion

- Does a probate estate have special rules for amounts set aside for charity?
- Do these special rules give will-planning/probate a meaningful advantage over living trusts?

The rules for charitable gifts made by probate estates and trusts after the death of their makers are straightforward. Outright charitable gifts are fully deductible for federal estate tax purposes for both trusts and wills.[1] In addition, an estate or a trust can exclude from its taxable income any income that is paid to a charity.[2] Unlike charitable gifts by individuals, there are no deduction limitations for an estate or a trust on the amounts that can be given to charities.

A will or a trust may provide that certain dollar amounts of the probate estate or the trust property are to be set aside for charitable purposes. Any of the income generated by the amounts set aside for charity which is then paid to a charity is excludable from the taxable income of the probate estate or trust.

There is, however, a difference between the tax treatment of an estate and a trust if a capital gain is generated on the amounts permanently set aside for charity if that gain is *not* paid to the charity. Following is an example of how this works in a probate estate:

> *Let's assume that under will-planning/probate, the decedent leaves a portfolio of income-producing securities which is permanently set aside for a charity.*
>
> *If some of the securities are sold at a profit by the estate's executor, the estate will not have to pay income tax on any long-term capital gain. This is true whether or not the capital gain is distributed to the charity.*

If a trustee permanently sets aside amounts for charity, the capital gain income *must* be paid to the charity or the capital gain income will be taxable to the trust.[3] Will-planning/probate advocates view this different tax treatment as an advantage that probate estates have over living trusts.

The Practical Effects of the Charitable Set Aside Difference

Commentators rarely explain the ramifications of this issue. This difference in the income tax treatment of amounts permanently set aside for charity is only applicable while an estate is in probate. Since a probate estate is not supposed to be "permanent," this rule is only applicable for a limited period of time.

As a practical matter, people who want to make continuing gifts to charity use a trust to accomplish their objective. Continuing trust gifts, whether made from a living trust or from a testamentary trust, are subject to the same charitable rules. Any capital gains that are generated by a trust are subject to income taxation if they are not paid to charity. In our experience, trust capital gain income is almost always paid to charity, thus avoiding the problem.

Our Conclusion

A probate estate avoids income tax on capital gains generated from amounts permanently set aside for charity that are not paid to charity; a trust does not.

S Corporation Stock

Questions for Discussion

- Can a revocable living trust own S corporation stock during the maker's lifetime?
- Can a living trust own S corporation stock after the maker's death?

A revocable living trust can hold S corporation stock during the lifetime of the trust maker and after the maker's death. The public and a number of professionals often confuse the Subchapter S rules as they apply to revocable living trusts and mistakenly believe that living trusts are not effective in holding and distributing S corporation stock.

A Trust Maker's Death Does Not Have to Affect S Corporation Stock Adversely

A revocable living trust can hold S corporation stock for two years after a trust maker's death without disqualifying a corporation from Subchapter S status.[1] During this two-year period, a corporation's income is taxable to the maker's estate rather than the trust.[2] This occurs despite the fact that the S corporation distributions are paid to the trust.

A probate estate does not have to be opened solely for the purpose of paying the income tax on S corporation distributions when a living trust owns the stock. When a living trust acts in lieu of a probate estate, the trust will be treated as an estate for the purpose of reporting the Subchapter S income.[3]

Will-planning/probate advocates state that a probate estate has an advantage over living trusts in that a probate estate can hold S corporation stock until the estate is closed—"which often will exceed two years."[4] However, if a will creates a testamentary trust to hold the S corporation stock, the law expressly provides that the two-year rule does not apply to a testamentary trust. If S corporation stock is transferred to a testamentary trust, the trust can only hold the stock for sixty days if it is not a qualified Subchapter S trust.[5]

S corporation stock may be retained in trust for longer than two years as long as the stock is held in a qualified Subchapter S trust.[6] The rules for qualified Subchapter S trusts make the following provisions:

> During the life of the current income beneficiary, there shall be only one income beneficiary of the trust who must be a citizen or resident of the United States;
>
> Principal distributed during the life of the income beneficiary may be distributed only to that beneficiary;
>
> The income beneficiary's income interest in the trust shall terminate on the earlier of the beneficiary's death or the termination of the trust; and
>
> Upon the termination of the trust during the income beneficiary's life, the trustee shall distribute all the trust's assets to the beneficiary.[7]

Perhaps an example will make these rules more understandable:

> *John had an S corporation. He left a living trust that created separate trusts on his death for his children. Each child's separate trust contained terms that provided that all of the trust's income must be paid to the child and that only the child could receive trust principal.*

> *John's trusts for his children also provided that all of his children were to receive all of their separate trust's principal on their thirty-fifth birthday, and if they died before that time that they could leave the proceeds to anyone they wanted.*

> *John's trusts for his children are qualified Subchapter S trusts.*

A living trust can hold the S corporation stock for two years after the maker's death regardless of its terms or beneficiaries. Prior to the end of the two-year period, the S corporation stock must either be distributed directly to beneficiaries or be transferred to subtrusts that are qualified Subchapter S trusts.[8] If an income beneficiary dies while the trust is in existence, the Subchapter S stock can pass to another qualified trust or the original trust can remain in existence for a successor beneficiary.

A marital deduction trust that gives a spouse a general power of appointment can be a qualified Subchapter S trust.[9] Likewise, a qualified terminable interest property (QTIP) trust may be a qualified Subchapter S corporation trust.

Subchapter S stock cannot be held in a trust that has more than one income beneficiary. The commonly used family, credit shelter, or residuary trust does not qualify as a Subchapter S trust if the trust names more than one beneficiary. However, a family trust can be a qualified Subchapter S trust if it is properly written.

Our Conclusion

A properly drafted living trust can hold Subchapter S stock, as can a probate estate.

The Nonrecognition of Losses Between a Trust and Its Beneficiaries

Questions for Discussion

- Does a probate estate recognize losses that are not available to a trust?
- In what situations are losses between a trust and a beneficiary not recognized?
- What planning techniques can be utilized to avoid the impact of the nonrecognition of losses by a trust?

Probate advocates claim that the nonrecognition of losses between a trust and a beneficiary under Section 267 of the Internal Revenue Code is a weakness that does not exist in a probate estate. We believe that this issue is a relevant factor in after-death income tax planning that must be taken into consideration and that it can be successfully addressed and circumvented in a majority of trust planning situations. We agree with the noted estate planning attorney and scholar Frederick R. Keydel:

Aside from the purely technical (and usually solvable) Section 267 disallowance . . . , this author can identify only one possible disadvantage of using the revocable trust . . . as the *customary* approach to client estate plans generally.

This possible disadvantage is the risk of a negative initial client response to an estate plan that relies on a [trust] document other than a Will.[1]

Situations in Which Losses Between a Trust and a Beneficiary Cannot Be Recognized

Unless a special election is made to the contrary, a probate estate must report both gains and losses on sales or exchanges of its property between it and its heirs on the estate's income tax return.

When a person dies, all of his or her property receives "a step-up" in basis. For example:

> *If a person purchases a fine antique for $5,000 and, at his or her death, it has a fair market value of $6,000, the $1,000 in appreciation is not subject to federal income tax. If the antique is sold after the owner's death for $6,000, there is no taxable gain.*

The step-up in basis rules apply to every asset in an estate, and the rules apply whether or not any federal estate tax is paid.

A loss can be generated between a probate estate and one of its heirs if property that is distributed to the heir has decreased in value between the date it was valued and the date of its distribution. For example:

> *Assume that probate property with a stepped-up basis of $20,000 is valued at $15,000 on the date it is distributed to an heir. There will be a capital loss of $5,000. The probate estate's executor will be able to report that loss on the probate estate's income tax return.*

A loss can also be generated between a probate estate and one of its heirs if estate property is sold at a loss to an heir. Any gains on distributions or sales to an heir are also reported by the probate estate on its income tax return.

For trusts, the rules are different. Unlike a probate estate, a trust cannot recognize losses on its income tax return for sales and exchanges between the trust and its beneficiaries. And unless the trustee makes a special election, any gains realized on sales or distributions of trust property from a trust to its beneficiaries are reported on the trust's income tax return.[2] An example of how the rules for losses that are applied to living trusts are different from the rules for losses that are applied to probate estates is the following:

> *Assume that property held in a living trust after the trust maker's death has a stepped-up basis of $20,000 but is valued at $15,000 on the date it is distributed to a beneficiary. There will be a capital loss of $5,000. Because of Section 267 of the Internal Revenue Code, the living trust will not be able to deduct that loss at the time the property is distributed to the beneficiary.*

For whatever the reason, transactions between trusts and their beneficiaries are considered to be "transactions between related taxpayers."[3] Similar transactions between a probate estate and its heirs are not considered to be transactions between related taxpayers, yet there is no discernable difference between the two types of transactions.

Generally, a *pecuniary distribution* is a type of distribution that falls under the nonrecognition of gain or loss rules.[4] An example of a pecuniary distribution is "Upon my death, distribute the sum of $20,000 to my sister." This language instructs the executor or trustee to pay that amount in cash. The terms of some pecuniary distributions allow them to be paid either in cash or in specific property of equal value. An example of such a distribution is "Upon my death, distribute the sum of $20,000 to my sister, which can be paid in cash or in kind." If an executor or trustee paid the $20,000 in the form of an automobile, for example, the distribution of the car would be considered as an in-kind satisfaction of a pecuniary distribution.

If the value of the property that is used to satisfy the pecuniary distribution is either greater or lower than the basis of the property, then there is a gain or loss. For example:

> *If a pecuniary distribution was satisfied with property having a stepped-up basis of $15,000 but is valued at $20,000 at the time it is distributed, then a probate estate or trust will realize a $5,000 gain.*

What if a pecuniary distribution is satisfied with property that had a stepped-up basis which is greater than its value at the date the pecuniary distribution is made? If property with a stepped-up basis of $17,000 is valued at $15,000 on the date it is used to satisfy a pecuniary distribution, the trust or estate sustains a $2,000 loss. An estate can report the $2,000 loss on its income tax return. A trust cannot!

This loss is not entirely lost. On a subsequent disposition of the property by a trust beneficiary, the loss can be used to offset any gain at that time.[5] For example:

Louise's living trust calls for a specific distribution to her sister, Meg, of $45,000 in cash or in kind.

Meg decides that she would like to receive Louise's vacation home, which has a stepped-up basis of $50,000 but is currently valued at $45,000.

When the trust distributes the vacation home to Meg, the trustee cannot take an income tax deduction for the $5,000 loss.

Meg later sells the home for $60,000. Since Meg's basis is $50,000,[6] the potential gain is $10,000.

However, since the trust could not use the loss that was sustained when the property was distributed to Meg, she can now use that loss to offset her gain.[7]

Therefore, Meg can shelter the $10,000 gain with the $5,000 loss; her taxable gain will be only $5,000 ($10,000 − $5,000).[8]

What if Meg later sold the property for a loss instead of a gain?

Assume that Meg later sells the home for $40,000. Since Meg's basis is $50,000, her loss is $10,000, which she can report on her income tax return.

If Louise had used a will instead of a living trust, her probate estate could have taken the $5,000 loss when the property was distributed to Meg. Of course, if Meg later sold the home for a profit, she would have to recognize the full gain at that time.[9] This concept is illustrated in the following example:

Louise's will calls for a specific distribution to her sister, Meg, of $45,000 in cash or in kind.

Meg decides that she would like to receive Louise's vacation home, which has a stepped-up basis of $50,000 but is currently valued at only $45,000.

When the vacation home is distributed to Meg, the probate estate can take an income tax deduction for the $5,000 loss.

Meg later sells the home for $60,000. Meg's stepped-up basis is $50,000, so she must now report the full $10,000 gain on her income tax return.

In this example, the estate recognized the loss. Meg did not; she recognized a $10,000 gain when she sold the property.

When a probate estate suffers a loss on its income tax return because of the in-kind satisfaction of a pecuniary distribution, the heir who receives the property does not receive the exclusive benefit of the loss. The loss shelters the probate estate's income and therefore benefits all of the heirs in direct proportion to their interest in the decedent's estate.

When a loss is sustained between a trust and a beneficiary, the loss benefits that beneficiary. The loss is not shared with beneficiaries who had no interest in the transaction.

Thus, if a trust beneficiary sells "loss property" at a later time, the result may be more equitable than if the loss was taken by the trust. While every situation is different, it would appear that from a beneficiary's point of view a deduction against personal income would be more valuable than a loss against trust income.

In some situations, a trust or a will may call for a number of pecuniary distributions, or a single pecuniary distribution may be satisfied with a number of different types of property. For example:

> *Louise's will calls for a specific distribution to her sister, Meg, of $45,000 in cash or in kind.*

> *Meg decides that she would like to receive Louise's car. Its stepped-up basis is $18,000, but it is currently valued at only $15,000.*

> *Meg would also like a sculpture that has a stepped-up basis of $25,000 and is currently valued at $30,000.*

> *When the car and sculpture are distributed to Meg, the probate estate has a $3,000 loss and a $5,000 gain. They can be offset against each other so that the estate has a net taxable gain of $2,000.*

An in-kind distribution from a living trust that creates a loss cannot be offset against gains created by other in-kind distributions. In this situation, the trust would have a taxable gain of $5,000. The $3,000 loss could only be used by Meg when she subsequently sold the car at a gain.

The Pecuniary Formula Clause

Most federal-estate-tax-oriented estate plans use a formula clause to maximize the federal estate tax benefits of a decedent's $600,000 exemption equivalent amount and the maker's unlimited marital deduction. A *formula clause* generally creates two subtrusts, one for the marital deduction property and the other for the exemption equivalent property.

There are three basic kinds of formula clauses: a pecuniary clause, a fractional share of the residue clause, and a minimum worth clause.

A *pecuniary formula clause* is a type of pecuniary distribution. It is a distribution of a specific dollar amount that can be satisfied in cash or in kind. Any in-kind distribution in satisfaction of a pecuniary formula is taxable to a trust to the extent that the value of the in-kind property as of the date of distribution exceeds its basis[10]:

> *Assume that the stepped-up basis of a house is $100,000 and that the value of the house is $110,000 on the day that it is distributed to a family subtrust. The $10,000 difference is treated as a gain.*

A probate estate must also recognize any gains realized when satisfying a pecuniary distribution.[11]

A *loss* sustained in satisfaction of a pecuniary formula is not allowed to a trust but is allowed to a probate estate. A probate estate can recognize losses on its income tax return and can offset them against any gains. A trust cannot offset gains with losses incurred in the in-kind satisfaction of a pecuniary formula clause. When there is a trust loss, the benefit of the loss can be taken by the beneficiary when the property is subsequently sold.

The Fractional Share of the Residue Formula

The *fractional share of the residue formula* clause is used to avoid recognition of gains and losses. The distribution of assets through a fractional share formula is not an event that triggers gain or loss in trusts or estates.[12]

A fractional share formula creates a percentage allocation of each asset to the marital trust and the family trust. For example, the result of a fractional share formula may be that 55 percent of each asset belongs to the marital trust and 45 percent to the family trust. Each subtrust would then own an undivided share of each asset.[13]

The Minimum Worth Formula

A formula that is used instead of the pecuniary and fractional share formulas is the minimum worth formula. It too can be used to minimize or avoid capital gains and losses when making allocations of trust property.[14] A *minimum worth formula* allows a fiduciary to satisfy distributions either in cash or in kind, partly in cash and partly in kind, or on a pro rata basis. Under the terms of a minimum worth formula, the trustee can, to a great extent, control the extent of gains and losses. It can eliminate capital gain and loss problems and some of the administrative problems associated with fractional share formulas.[15]

Sales to Third Parties

Another method for avoiding the nonrecognition of losses in sales or exchanges by a trust to a beneficiary is for the trustee to sell the loss assets to an unrelated third party, take the loss on the trust income tax return, and distribute the cash proceeds to the beneficiary. This works well when there are assets that have no sentimental value or where the asset is readily available for sale. This simple solution is often overlooked.

The Impact of the Nonrecognition of a Loss by a Trust

The potential benefit of losses that are realized upon the distribution to a heir or beneficiary in satisfaction of an in-kind distribution are frequently limited because they are capital losses rather than ordinary losses and there are restrictions on their use. Under the capital loss rules, a capital loss must first be used to offset any capital gains generated in the same taxable period.[16] Any capital losses in excess of capital gains can be deducted at the rate of only $3,000 per year.[17] As a result, the losses lose their value over time.

Our Conclusion

Probate estates have preferential after-death income tax benefits that generate immediate capital losses. Living trust beneficiaries can only take these losses when the property is sold.

Ordinary Income on the Sale of Depreciable Property

Questions for Discussion

- Does a probate estate recognize capital gain income on a sale or exchange of depreciable property between it and its heirs?
- What is the impact of ordinary income treatment on the sale of depreciable property between a trust and a beneficiary?

Any gain on the sale or exchange of depreciable property between related parties is ordinary income rather than capital gain income.[1] A trust and its beneficiaries are related parties for purposes of the Internal Revenue Code, but an estate and its beneficiaries are not.[2] This different treatment offers an estate a small advantage over a living trust.

The Impact of Ordinary Income Treatment on the Sale of Depreciable Property

When a depreciable asset is sold for a price greater than its depreciated cost basis, the depreciation taken must be recaptured, as is illustrated in the following example:

Alyce, owner of a sole proprietorship, buys a truck for $10,000. She depreciates the truck at the rate of $2,000 each year. At the end of three years, the cost basis of the truck is $4,000 ($10,000 cost less three years of depreciation at $2,000 per year).

At the beginning of the fourth year, Alyce sells the truck for $5,000. There is a taxable gain of $1,000 (the $5,000 purchase price less the depreciated cost basis of $4,000).

Because Alyce was able to deduct $6,000 for depreciation, she must recapture the depreciation as ordinary income. Therefore, her $1,000 gain is not a capital gain; it is an ordinary gain.[3]

Let's suppose that Alyce bought an old car for $10,000 and used it as part of her trade or business. She depreciates the car at the rate of $2,000 each year. At the end of three years, the cost basis of the car is $4,000 ($10,000 cost less three years of depreciation at $2,000 per year).

Alyce then sells the car for $12,000 when she finds out that it is a valuable antique. Alyce has $6,000 of ordinary

> *income representing all of the depreciation she took and $2,000 capital gain income, which is the difference between her original cost basis and the sales price.*

Capital gains can only be taken after all depreciation deductions are recaptured. Similar rules also apply to depreciable real estate, although there is less exposure to depreciation recapture than there is with personal property.[4]

The Impact of Ordinary Income Treatment on the Sale of Depreciable Property Between a Trust and a Beneficiary

The maximum tax rate for capital gains is 28 percent, while the maximum tax rate for ordinary income is 31 percent.[5] Any gain on the sale or exchange of depreciable property between a trustee and a beneficiary is taxed as ordinary income rather than as capital gain income. However, if the gain is taken by the executor of a probate estate, it is capital gain income. Thus, under current income tax rules, the loss of capital gains treatment by the trust may cost the trust or its beneficiaries a maximum of 3 percent of the taxable gain.

If a trustee desires to sell depreciable property to a beneficiary or use depreciable property to satisfy a pecuniary bequest, the trustee can avoid current income tax on any gain. If the trustee makes a special election not to recognize the gain, the beneficiaries will recognize the gain when they later sell the property.[6] An executor can make the same election.

Our Conclusion

Just like a probate estate, a trust does not have to recognize gain on a sale or exchange of depreciable property between it and its beneficiaries. If, however, the trustee chooses to recognize the gain, the trust will pay, at most, 3 percent more tax than a probate estate will pay.

Rental Real Estate
Income Tax Deductions

Questions for Discussion

- To what extent can a probate estate use rental real estate income tax deductions?
- To what extent can a trust use rental real estate income tax deductions?
- How can a living trust maximize its rental real estate income tax deductions?

A probate estate can take rental real estate deductions for the first two taxable years after death as long as the decedent actively participated in the rental activity before his or her death.[1] This benefit is not extended to trusts. This advantage can be significant in some planning situations.

An Estate's Ability to Use
Rental Real Estate Deductions

Rental real estate losses are disallowed to the extent that the losses turn the activity into a tax shelter. Generally, rental real estate activity losses can only be deducted to the extent of the income earned from the rental real estate, and to the extent that the taxpayer has gains from other passive activities.[2] However, an individual taxpayer, including a fully funded revocable living trust, who has at least a 10 percent interest in a rental real estate activity in which he or she actively participates may offset up to $25,000 of losses incurred each year against other taxable income from active sources.

The $25,000 deductible amount is reduced by 50 percent of the amount by which the taxpayer's adjusted gross income for the year exceeds $100,000 and is totally eliminated when the taxpayer's adjusted gross income is $150,000 or more.[3] The $25,000 offset is subject to a number of other complex requirements.

Probate estates can continue to take rental real estate deductions for the first two taxable years after the date of death.[4] If the decedent is married, the $25,000 amount is reduced by the amount allowable to the surviving spouse within an estate's tax year. The loss treatment is limited to the first two taxable years of probate. If the executor chooses a fiscal year that creates a relatively short first taxable year, then the full benefit of this provision may not be realized because the two-year period may be as short as thirteen months. The amount not used in the first year can be carried over to the next taxable year of the estate,[5] but only a maximum of $25,000 can be deducted in that second year.

If the surviving spouse has rental real estate, the probate

estate will not receive the full $25,000 write-off. This can occur when the property is held in joint tenancy, as is very common, or when each spouse owns assets in his or her own name.

Rental Real Estate and Revocable Living Trust Planning

After the death of their makers, trusts are not allowed to take rental real estate deductions. However, rental real estate losses that cannot be deducted by a trust do not disappear; they are added to the basis of the property immediately before the property is distributed to a trust beneficiary.[6] While certainly not as advantageous as a current income tax deduction, it will save income tax when the property is subsequently sold.

Our Conclusion

A probate estate can recognize rental real estate activity losses for two years; a living trust cannot.

The Deductibility of Administrative Expenses

Question for Discussion

• Are after-death administrative expenses deductible by a trust for federal estate and income tax purposes?

Probate advocates at times suggest that a trust may not be able to take the same federal estate and income tax deductions as a probate estate. However, the Internal Revenue Code regulations specifically state that administration expenses incurred by a trust are deductible for federal estate tax purposes to the extent that such expenses are allowable in a decedent's probate estate.[1] These amounts include trustees' fees where the fees are generated in performing services that would normally be performed by the executor of an estate.[2]

For both probate estates and trusts, administration expenses are only deductible to the extent that they relate to the settlement of the estate. Expenses are not deductible if the services performed are for the personal benefit of the beneficiaries or heirs.[3]

In those states where the assets in the living trust are not subject to the claims of creditors the deductibility of administrative expenses is more restrictive. Those expenses that are related to the maker's death and incurred in vesting title to the beneficiaries, including the preparation of federal and state death tax returns, and are paid within three years of the due date of the federal estate tax return are deductible by a trust for federal estate tax purposes.[4]

Any expenses not allowable as federal estate tax expenses are almost always deductible on the trust's income tax return. Where no federal estate tax is due, this is an important benefit.

Our Conclusion

Administrative expenses incurred by a fully funded revocable living trust are generally subject to the same rules as those for a probate estate.

The Sixty-five-Day Rule for Trusts

Questions for Discussion

- What is the sixty-five-day rule?
- Can both trusts and probate estates take advantage of this rule?

The "sixty-five-day rule" only applies to trusts. This rule gives the trustee the ability to distribute income and principal to trust beneficiaries for sixty-five days after the close of the trust's tax year.

Under the sixty-five-day rule, a trustee can elect to treat distributions made within the first sixty-five days following the end of a trust's tax year as having been distributed on the last day of the trust's previous tax year.[1] The amount to which the election applies cannot exceed the previous year's undistributed trust income.[2]

This rule does not shift trust income to a different tax year of a beneficiary.[3] For example, if both the trust and its beneficiaries have as their tax years the calendar year and a sixty-five-day rule distribution is made by the trust to the beneficiaries on February 15, 1992, the beneficiaries must include the amounts in income in their 1991 income tax returns.

The sixty-five-day rule helps a trustee to gather all tax information and to make the correct tax decisions by giving the trustee an additional sixty-five days. Executors of probate estates do not have this luxury. By the end of the typical probate estate's tax year, all distribution decisions must be made and all income and deductions computed. This puts a heavy burden on the executor and often makes it impossible for the executor to maximize tax planning strategies.

Our Conclusion

The sixty-five-day rule is an after-death income tax advantage that a living trust has over a probate estate.

The Status of a Trustee as a Statutory Executor

Question for Discussion

- Can a trustee make the same after-death federal tax elections as an executor?

Will-planning/probate advocates occasionally assert that a trustee of a revocable living trust cannot make certain important tax elections under the Internal Revenue Code after the death of the trust maker. They argue that a probate estate may have to be opened so that an executor can be appointed to perform these functions.[1]

The Status of a Trustee as a Statutory Executor for Making Tax Elections

The Internal Revenue Code defines the term *executor*, when used in relation to the federal estate tax, as "the executor or administrator of the decedent, or, if there is no executor or administrator appointed, qualified, and acting within the United States, then any person in actual or constructive possession of any property of the decedent."[2] The Tax Court has affirmed, and the IRS has acquiesced, that a trustee *is included* in this broad definition of an executor.[3]

A trustee, acting in the capacity of a statutory executor, can make certain federal estate tax elections such as alternate valuation,[4] special use valuation,[5] qualified terminable interest property,[6] and installment payment of federal estate tax.[7] For these very important elections, the trustee and the statutory executor are treated the same.

Personal Liability

In general, an executor and a trustee are not personally liable for federal estate taxes.[8] However, distributions to beneficiaries that would jeopardize the collection of federal estate taxes may very well create personal liability to both an executor and a trustee. While the extent of this liability is sometimes not clear,[9] the Internal Revenue Code gives trustees the ability to obtain a release from personal liability.[10] The procedure parallels that for executors.[11]

Signing Joint Income Tax Returns

An area where an executor and a trustee are not treated in the same manner is in the signing of a joint federal income tax return filed by a decedent's surviving spouse. Apparently, only an executor or administrator has the authority to join with the surviving spouse in the signing of a joint return.[12] Generally, this does not present a problem because the surviving spouse may file the joint return even when there is no executor or administrator.[13]

A potential problem may arise, however, if an executor or administrator is later appointed. Either may disaffirm the joint return.[14] If this disaffirmation occurs, the income tax elections made with respect to the estate will no longer be valid, and the surviving spouse is treated as filing a separate return. This executor or administrator must then also file a separate return. In our experience, the chance that this administrative inconvenience will occur is remote.

The Spousal Gift Splitting Election

The broad definition of an executor only applies to the federal estate tax provisions of the Internal Revenue Code. It does not necessarily extend to the gift tax provisions. Because of this, a trustee taking the place of an executor may not be able to consent to a split gift election on the surviving spouse's gift tax return. The regulations specify that a decedent's executor or administrator can consent to a split gift election.[15] If a husband and a wife make a split gift, and one of them dies before the gift tax return has been filed, the regulations do not preclude a trustee from signing the gift tax return.[16] As a practical matter, it appears that if no executor has been appointed, a trustee could sign the gift tax return.

The Existence of Both a Trustee and an Executor

While a trustee is accorded statutory executor status when acting in lieu of an executor of an estate, some confusion may arise if there are both a trustee and an executor. This can occur in several ways. A probate estate may be necessary because the trust was not fully funded at the maker's death or a will may be necessary to appoint the personal guardian for a decedent's minor children. Sometimes, a nominal probate is created for after-death income tax reasons or for cutting off of claims of creditors under probate nonclaim statutes. (See Chapter 8, "Protection from Creditors.")

An executor takes precedence over a trustee for purposes of making elections and serving as the statutory executor under the Internal Revenue Code.[17] For example, a trustee can apply for release of personal liability only after an executor has been discharged.[18]

The problem that commentators writing on this issue have traditionally wrestled with is the confusion that may exist where there are both a trustee and an executor. The fear is that if the trustee and the executor cannot act in concert, then chaos will ensue. Proper living trust–centered planning has specific drafting in the living trust and the pour-over will that coordinates the activities of the trustee and the executor of the pour-over will to prevent this problem.

More important, the executor named in a will should generally be a trustee of the living trust, and the alternate executors named in the will also should be successor trustees of the trust. If the same fiduciary is serving in both capacities, there should be no conflict between the two.[19]

Our Conclusion

Trustees of living trusts are treated as executors under the Internal Revenue Code for most purposes; where they are not, a pour-over will gives a living trust–centered plan the same after-death federal tax elections as a probate estate.

APPENDIX B

1991 Probate Survey of Four States

Parameters of
Our 1991 Probate Survey
of Four States

To corroborate what we read, heard, and experienced over the past twenty years, we conducted a survey of four states, each of which represents the four types of probate administration systems, as follows:

Iowa	Percentage-fee statute
New York	Traditional nonsimplified process
Oregon	"Simplified" statute
Texas	Modified Uniform Probate Code

We engaged a consultant to devise a scientific research method. Our consultant was Michael Jacroux, Ph.D., statistics department chair, Washington State University.

The objectives of our survey were:

1. To corroborate or disprove the results of several earlier surveys
2. To determine the average attorney and executor fees in the surveyed states
3. To determine the average time it takes to probate estates in the surveyed states

The criteria established for the surveyed files were:

1. They must have been closed during 1989.
2. They must be from both urban and rural areas.
3. They must be for decedents' estates only; conservatorship and guardianships were not to be included.

To make it possible to study the differences in probate fees and delays between rural and urban counties within each state, the counties within each state were classified as being urban or rural by the U.S. Bureau of the Census definitions of urban and rural as found in the *1987 Statistical Abstract of the United States*, pages 4 and 888.

Dr. Jacroux determined the number of urban and the number of rural counties we would have to survey in each state to give us a statistically valid sampling of the state's population:

Iowa	two urban, three rural
New York	three urban, three rural
Oregon	two urban, two rural
Texas	three urban, three rural

Next we randomly selected the specific urban and rural counties in each state to meet those numbers. We then contacted either the court administrator of each state or the clerks of the selected probate courts to obtain the total number of decedents' estates closed during 1989. From those numbers, Dr. Jacroux again determined the actual number of files we had to survey to give us a statistically valid sampling. We then hired researchers who selected those numbers of files from the 1989 closed files in each probate court.

We conducted the survey during March and April 1991 in twenty-one counties in the four states. The majority of our researchers were the probate court clerks who had access to and knowledge of the files. The data gathered by our researchers were organized and compiled by Dr. Jacroux.

We encountered two problems during the course of the survey that led us to report our findings in median terms as well as in average terms. Many of the files did not contain the information that directly answered our questions, and in some instances aberrant amounts skewed the results. For example, in Texas, there was one file in which the executor's fee was $500,000, 34 percent of the gross estate. In New York, one file caused the average of attorneys' fees to be over $100,000 and the length of time to be over four years.

Glossary

Adjudication of Mental Incompetency
A proceeding in probate court to determine whether a person is sufficiently competent to manage his or her personal and financial affairs. If the judge makes a finding of incompetency, generally the judge will appoint a *guardian* and a *conservator* (see below).

Ancillary Administration
An additional probate proceeding that is conducted in a state other than the home state of the decedent, usually because the decedent owned real property outside his or her state. Ancillary administration is required for real property owned by a decedent outside his or her home state because each state has jurisdiction over the real property in that state. Ancillary administration is sometimes required when a decedent owns personal property that is located outside the home state.

Conservator
A financial guardian appointed by a probate judge to manage the financial affairs of a person who has been adjudicated incompetent. A conservator has authority over all of the incompetent's property. The conservator may be the same person as the personal *guardian* (see below).

Conveyance
Transferring ownership of property from one owner to another.

Domicile
A person's legal home. Regardless of how many residences a person has, he or she can have only one domicile. Domicile is determined by where a person is living and his or her intention to remain there permanently. Some of the factors that the courts or officials may look at to determine domicile are place of employment, location where the family resides, place where post office boxes are maintained, and location of bank accounts and burial plots. The state of a person's domicile determines what state taxes a person pays and also where a decedent's estate will be probated.

Durable Power of Attorney
The same as a *power of attorney* (see below), except that a durable power of attorney continues to be valid after its maker's disability. In some states, when the maker is declared mentally incompetent by a court, the durable power of attorney is invalid. A durable power of attorney can be established for general purposes or it can be limited to specific purposes such as funding or health care.

Durable Power of Attorney for Health Care
A special type of limited *durable power of attorney* in which the maker gives another person the authority to make health care decisions when the maker is unable to make decisions because of illness or injury.

Executor
The person or institution who is named in a will and approved by the probate court to act as the representative of a decedent's estate. In some states, a female executor is

called an executrix. When a person dies intestate, the proper term for the executor is administrator (*administratrix,* if female). Many states use the term *personal representative* rather than *executor* or *administrator.*

Guardian

A guardian is an agent appointed by the court to manage the personal and financial affairs of a person who has been adjudicated incompetent. The personal guardian is charged with caring for the incompetent person in a role similar to that of a parent. A financial guardian, sometimes called a *conservator,* manages the incompetent's property and financial affairs. The same person can be appointed to serve as personal guardian and financial guardian, or the court can assign the responsibilities to different persons.

Intestacy

Dying without a will. If a person dies intestate, his or her property will go through probate unless the property passes by valid will-substitutes such as a fully funded living trust, joint tenancy property, or beneficiary designation property. Property that passes by intestacy passes to heirs who are specified in the state law governing intestacy.

Irrevocable Trust

A trust that cannot be changed once it has been signed by its maker except by court action in a proceeding called *reformation.*

Joint Tenancy

A form of property ownership in which two or more owners each own 100 percent of the same property. It is similar to *tenancy in common* (see below), except that an owner is not able to pass on his or her property at death. A deceased joint tenant's ownership rights pass by law to the surviving joint owners or owner.

Living Trust

A living trust, also called *inter vivos* trust, is created while the maker is alive and is effective immediately. The trust maker is frequently a beneficiary of his or her living trust. Most living trusts are *revocable* (one that can be changed) but sometimes for estate planning purposes a maker may create an *irrevocable trust* (one that cannot be changed).

Living Trust–Centered Planning

Estate planning that is based on a fully funded revocable living trust and encompasses other necessary documents to plan properly. A living trust–centered estate plan should take into account the hopes, fears, dreams, and ambitions of an individual and be tailored to his or her needs.

Living Will

A document that provides instructions to physicians, health care providers, family, and courts as to what life-prolonging procedures are desired if a person should become terminally ill or in a persistent vegetative state and unable to communicate his or her wishes.

Personal Property

All property other than land, buildings that are attached to land, and certain oil, gas, and mineral interests.

Per Stirpes

A legal term that means that if a person dies, his or her inheritance will pass to his or her heirs in equal shares. For example, if a mother leaves her property to her three children, *per stirpes*, and one of her children has died leaving two children of her own, the deceased child's one-third share will be equally divided between the deceased child's two children.

Power of Attorney

A written instrument in which a principal (maker) gives someone (agent) the authority to act on his or her behalf. A power of attorney ends when it is revoked by the principal and when the principal is incompetent or dies. A power of attorney for general purposes is a general power of attorney, and a power of attorney for specific purposes is a limited power of attorney.

Probate

In the narrow, technical sense, a legal proceeding to determine the validity of a will. However, most professionals now consider the term to indicate not only the process of determining the validity of the will but the administration of a decedent's estate. This includes notifying and paying creditors, paying taxes, and transferring the title of property to heirs.

Probate Court

The court that is in charge of probate and administration, and also guardianship.

Real Property

Property that is land, buildings attached to land, and interests in minerals, oil, and gas.

Recording

Placing a document in the public records (usually in the office of the clerk of the court), where it is indexed and is available for review by the public. Examples of documents that are recorded are deeds for real property and mortgages.

Revocable Trust

A trust that can be changed by the trust maker if the maker changes his or her mind about its provisions.

Tenancy by the Entirety

In some states, *joint tenancy* (see above) between married persons. It is more restrictive than joint tenancy because both the husband and the wife must agree to a transfer of an interest in the property. Generally, creditors of one spouse cannot reach tenancy by the entirety property.

Tenancy in Common

Ownership of property by two or more persons in which each person owns a percentage of the property. Each owner is able to sell or give away his or her share. Each owner can also pass on his or her share at death.

Testacy

Dying with a valid will. All property controlled by the will passes through the probate process.

Testamentary Trust

A trust that is created in a valid will.

Ward

A person whose financial or personal affairs, or both, are placed under the control of a guardian, in a proceeding in the probate court. Persons who may become wards are children under the legal age who lose their parents and adults who become incompetent or severely disabled.

Will

A legal document that is used to pass property to heirs at a person's death. A will is only effective on the death of its maker.

Will Planning/Probate

Our term for those lawyers who prefer to use a will as the foundation or main planning document for estate planning.

Will-Substitutes

Any legal document or form of ownership of property that passes property on death without going through probate or without being controlled by a will. Living trusts, joint tenancy ownership, and beneficiary designations such as those ordinarily used for life insurance and employee benefit plans are common will-substitutes.

Authors' Note

Consumers and estate planning professionals have told us they need more and better information and education about estate planning. We established the National Network of Loving Trust® Attorneys to meet this demand for increased knowledge and expertise in estate planning. The network is an educational and practice resource that enables a limited number of attorneys to provide proper estate planning productively and profitably to their clients. Attorneys who belong to the network embrace the Loving Trust® principles of effective counseling, active listening, and relationship-building with clients and other professionals alike.

Members of the network have access to some of the finest estate planning reference materials, technical support, seminars, and marketing and practice aids that are available. They are educated in the theory and practice of estate planning and thoroughly trained in using the Loving Trust® estate planning system. They use state-of-the-art computer software and documentation in their practices. Loving Trust® Inc. provides technical support and issues periodic bulletins to all members. To keep current in the law, Loving Trust® Inc. offers network members Practical Skills and Advanced Skills seminars that are held frequently throughout the United States.

Attorneys who are members of the network range from board certified estate planners to general practitioners. They have an interest in serving their clients' estate planning needs and see themselves as practitioners who are expanding their horizons to secure a satisfying, rewarding, and enriching way of practicing law.

If you are an attorney and would like more information about the National Network of Loving Trust® Attorneys, call (800) 638-8681 and ask for a brochure.

Notes

Introduction

1. Farnham, *The Windfall Awaiting the New Inheritors*, FORTUNE, May 1990, at 72.
2. Gottschalk, *Revocable Living Trusts Become Popular Option in Estate Planning*, Wall Street Journal, Feb. 4, 1987, at 33, col. 4.
3. Gottschalk, *Living Trust Hoopla Bears a Close Look*, Wall Street Journal, Feb. 11, 1991, at C1.
4. Faltermayer, *The (Financially) Perfect Death*, FORTUNE, Feb. 1991, at 131.

Chapter 1

1. Casner, *Estate Planning—Avoidance of Probate*, 60 COLUMBIA L. REV. 108 (1960).
2. N. DACEY, HOW TO AVOID PROBATE! (1966).
3. Leetham, *Probate Concepts and Their Origins*, 9 WHITTIER L. REV. 763, 764–65 (1988).
4. Langbein, *The Nonprobate Revolution and the Future of the Law of Succession*, 97 HARVARD L. REV. 1108 (1984).
5. BLACK'S LAW DICTIONARY 1365–66 (4th ed. 1968).
6. The Court Statistics Project, STATE COURT CASELOAD STATISTICS: ANNUAL REPORT 1988, Table 2. Unpublished Data. Williamsburg, Va.: National Center for State Courts in cooperation with the Conference of State Court Administrators, 1989.
7. In their law practice, the authors have personally reviewed a number of estates that were in probate for over two decades.
8. PUBLIC POLICY INSTITUTE, AMERICAN ASSOCIATION OF RE-

TIRED PERSONS (AARP), CHEAPER, QUICKER AND SIMPLER PRO-
BATE ADMINISTRATION: A POLICY OVERVIEW 2 (1989).

9. T. E. ATKINSON, HANDBOOK OF THE LAW OF WILLS 540 (1937).

10. For example, HOW TO AVOID PROBATE! by NORMAN F. DACEY
(see *supra* note 2) was a national bestseller for months.

11. W. FRATCHER, PROBATE CAN BE QUICK AND CHEAP: TRUSTS
AND ESTATES IN ENGLAND (1968).

12. Wellman, *The Lawyer's Stake in Probate Reforms*, 47 MICHIGAN
BAR JOURNAL 10, 11, and note 1 (1968), citing to figures published in Bauer, *Legal Fees in Probate*, 105 TRUSTS & ESTATES
850, 851–53 (1966).

13. See, *e.g.*, GROVE, HANDLING THE SMALL ESTATE, THE PRAC-
TICAL LAWYER'S MANUAL ON WILLS AND PROBATE NO. 1, 133,
134, American Law Institute and the American Bar Association
(1974), advising that to determine the fee for handling an estate
the attorney should look to the "[fee] schedule of the local bar
association." The article cautioned that the schedule might be
"inadequate" and the "rule of thumb" for a fee is 5 percent of
a gross estate less than $10,000 and from 3 to 5 percent for a
larger estate.

14. *E.g.*, Wellman, *Uniform Probate Code: A National Necessity*, TRIAL
Aug./Sept. 1970, at 22. "Probate courts are simply not the right
agencies to control the way this important area of professional
service is organized to serve clients," and Probate Judge William
Treat called for probate reform and attorney reform in *Through
the Probate Canal with Gun and Camera: A View from the Bench*, 113
TRUSTS & ESTATES, July 1974, at 24.

15. IRC § 6018(a) (1972).

16. Alabama, Alaska, Arizona, Colorado, Florida, Hawaii, Idaho,
Maine, Michigan, Minnesota, Montana, Nebraska, New Jersey,
New Mexico, North Dakota, South Carolina, Texas, and Utah.

17. Anderson, *The Influence of the Uniform Probate Code in Nonadopting
States*, 8 UNIVERSITY OF PUGET SOUND L. REV. 599, 600 (1985).

18. UNIFORM PROBATE CODE art. 6, prefatory note, 8 U.L.A. 280
(West Supp. 1991).

19. See generally, Langbein, *supra* note 4.

20. G. TURNER, REVOCABLE TRUSTS § 2.01 (2d ed. 1991).

21. MCGOVERN, KURTZ, & REIN, WILLS, TRUSTS & ESTATES 592
(1988). The exception to administration as a needless expense,
according to this source, is when the estate is insolvent or when
debts that are owed to the decedent must be collected. However,

even in these cases, we question the need for administration if a living trust–centered plan is used.

22. Gergen, *America's Legal Mess*, U.S. NEWS & WORLD REPORT, Aug. 19, 1991, at 72.

23. See MCGOVERN, KURTZ, & REIN, *supra* note 21, at 592–93.

24. Richardson & Muehleck, *Avoiding Probate with Revocable Trusts: Advantages and Disadvantages*, 5 JOURNAL OF TAXATION OF INVESTMENTS 294, 295 (1988).

25. For example, see Cantwell & Rhodes, *Standby Trusts: Spare Tires for Late-Life Trips*, COLORADO LAWYER, May 1990, at 851.

26. AARP, A REPORT ON PROBATE: CONSUMER PERSPECTIVES AND CONCERNS (1990).

27. *Id.* at 14, citing Topolnicki, MONEY MAGAZINE, Oct. 1987, at 84.

28. *Id.* at 14, citing Kroll, *Matters of Life and Death—Are Living Trusts Making Probate Practice a Dying Field?* CALIFORNIA LAWYER, Jan. 1989, at 28.

29. *Id.* at 6.

30. Trusts date from very early periods in English law and have been widely used by lawyers for a variety of purposes. 1 A. Scott & W. FRATCHER, THE LAW OF TRUSTS, §§ 1, 1.3 (4th ed. 1987); see also, G. BOGERT, TRUSTS, §§ 1, 2, and 6 (1987).

31. RESTATEMENT (SECOND) OF TRUSTS § 2 (1957).

32. *Id.* at §§ 17, 100.

33. Meyer, *The Revocable Trust as a Will Substitute—A Coming of Age*, 39 UNIVERSITY OF COLORADO L. REV. 1, 2 (1967).

Chapter 2

1. See McLane v. Russell, 131 Ill. 2d 509, 546 N.E. 2d 499 (1989), *affirming* 159 Ill. App. 3d 429, 512 N.E. 2d 366 (3d Dist. 1987), where an attorney was successfully sued for malpractice when he prepared a will but left property in joint tenancy.

2. AARP, A REPORT ON PROBATE, 14.

3. ABA, Committee on Significant New Developments in Probate and Trust Law Practice, *Developments Regarding the Professional Responsibility of the Estate Planning Lawyer: The Effect of the Model Rules of Professional Conduct*, 22 REAL PROPERTY, PROBATE AND TRUST JOURNAL 1, 5 (1987).

4. See, for example, Jones, *Putting Revocable Trusts in Their Place*,

129 TRUSTS & ESTATES 8, 20–22 (1990); Richardson & Muehleck, 294, 295–96.

5. The results of the study are found in G. TURNER, § 2.02. Mr. Turner also cites a second study with similar results, but it is unclear as to the scope of the second study.

6. *Id.* at 2–5 note 4.

7. 1 KESS & WESTLIN, FINANCIAL AND ESTATE PLANNING ¶ 2580 (1983) (updated monthly).

8. G. TURNER, § 2.02, at 2–3 note 2.

9. The UNIFORM PROBATE CODE, OFFICIAL 1990 TEXT AND COMMENTS in §§ 3-1201 & 3-1202 provides for transfer of personal property by affidavit in small estates of $5,000 or less, on certain conditions; §§ 3-1203 and 3-1204 provide for summary administration by the personal representative when the net value of the estate is not greater than the value of the exempt property, certain allowances, and costs. FLORIDA STATUTES ch. 735, part II (1989) provides for summary administration for estates of $25,000 or less, minus the value of property exempt from creditors. CALIFORNIA PROBATE CODE §§ 6600-6615 (West 1990 Supp.) provide for setting aside by the court for the small estate of $20,000 (over and above liens and encumbrances). The small estate exemption in Illinois is $7,500, ILLINOIS ANNOTATED STATUTES ch. 110 1/2, §§ 25-1, et seq. (Smith-Hurd 1978, 1990 Supp.). New York's is $10,000, or less, exclusive of setoff property, New York Surrogate's Court Procedure Act §§ 1301–1309 (McKinney 1967, 1990 Supp.). A majority of the states have some type of small estate exemption.

10. Filing fees are generated by revocable living trusts in one state. In Connecticut a succession tax return must be filed with the probate court irrespective of whether there is a will or a trust. See Bearns, *The Case Against the "Living Trust" Hucksters*, ESTATES AND PROBATE NEWSLETTER, March 1990, at 3.

11. One writer who tends to advocate will-planning/probate has acknowledged that living trusts may well be better for people with modest estates. Miller, *Update on Whether to Consider Using a Funded Living Trust to Avoid Probate*, 16 ESTATE PLANNING 140, 141 (1989).

12. IRC § 1014(b). The value is as of date of death, but can, under certain circumstances, be the value as of six months after the date of death. IRC § 2032(a).

13. Keydel, *"Funding" the Revocable Trust—Pros, Cons, and Caveats*, 14 PROBATE NOTES 98, 105 (1988).

14. Arkansas, California, Delaware, Hawaii, Iowa (in Iowa the percentage fee is supposed to be the maximum fee and the fee must be reasonable as determined by the probate court), Missouri, Montana, New Mexico, Pennsylvania, Utah, and Wyoming.

15. Examples are Montana, MONTANA CODE ANNOTATED §§ 72-3-631 & 72-3-633, and Iowa, IOWA PROBATE CODE §§ 633.197, 633.198.

16. At least one state, Missouri, has a statutory percentage schedule that is the *minimum* fee. MISSOURI REVISED STATUTES § 473.153 (1989).

17. California Law Revision Commission Staff, *California Probate Attorney Fees Study* #L-1036, Nov. 11, 1989 (hereinafter *Calif. Prob. Fee Study*).

18. *Id.* at 11, 12-18.

19. Miller, 142; G. TURNER, § 2.02, at 2–4; *Calif. Prob. Fee Study*, 12–19.

20. G. TURNER, at § 2.03. Jurisdictions vary as to the types of services eligible for treatment as extraordinary services, but this list is indicative of those services. See also *Calif. Prob. Fee Study*, 14–19; H.WEINSTOCK, PLANNING AN ESTATE: A GUIDEBOOK OF PRINCIPLES AND TECHNIQUES § 6.7 (3d ed. 1988) (updated periodically); and Miller, 142.

21. G. TURNER, § 2.02, at 13.

22. The results of the study were published in the AARP REPORT ON PROBATE.

23. *Id.* at 18.

24. *Id.* at 17.

25. DELAWARE CODE ANNOTATED, CHANCERY COURT RULE 192 (1974).

26. See *Association Adopts Principles Regarding Probate Practices and Expenses*, 62 ABA JOURNAL 348 (1976).

27. See Stein & Fierstein, *The Role of the Attorney in Estate Administration*, 68 MINNESOTA L. REV. 1107, 1173–75 (1984), for an analysis of the ABA position on fees.

28. These states are Alaska, Arizona, Colorado, Connecticut, Florida, Georgia, Idaho, Illinois, Indiana, Kansas, Kentucky, Maine, Michigan, Minnesota, Mississippi, Nebraska, Nevada, New Hampshire, New Jersey, New York, North Carolina, North Dakota, Oklahoma, Oregon, Rhode Island, Tennessee, Texas, Vermont, West Virginia, Wisconsin, and the District of Columbia. Statutes in South Carolina, South Dakota, Virginia, and Washington make no provision for attorneys' fees. In Alabama, the

courts set attorneys' fees. From AARP, A REPORT ON PROBATE, 16 note 21.

29. These are the standards in the COLORADO PROBATE CODE, cited in W. SCHMIDT, JR., HOW TO LIVE—AND DIE—WITH COLORADO PROBATE 13 (1985).

30. *Id.* The ABA standards are found in ABA, MODEL RULES OF PROFESSIONAL CONDUCT, Rule 1.5(a) (1989).

31. Maximum Fee Guidelines and Schedule for Supervised Estates of the Hamilton Superior Court, No. 2, 24th Judicial Circuit, Noblesville, Ind.; distributed to attorneys, June 28, 1990. See also *Calif. Prob. Fee Study*, 44 note 98.

32. In Goldfarb v. Virginia State Bar, 421 U.S. 773, 95 S. Ct. 2004, 44 L. Ed. 2d 572 (1975), minimum fee schedules for legal services having a connection with interstate commerce were found to be in violation of the Sherman Antitrust Act. Even though the connection with interstate commerce was slight, minimum fee schedules for all legal services were soon dropped. (See the reference to *Goldfarb* in the 1976 ABA STATEMENT OF PRINCIPLES ON PROBATE FEES, *Calif. Prob. Fee study*, 348.)

33. AARP, A REPORT ON PROBATE, 25.

34. See Stein & Fierstein, part IV, "Attorney Fee Charging," at 1172–92, and *Calif. Prob. Fee Study*, 37, 38 (based upon CALIFORNIA PROBATE CODE §§ 901 and 902, in force in 1987).

35. The *Calif. Prob. Fee Study* shows that federal estate taxes and the filing of a federal estate tax return have little or no bearing on the size of the probate fees, and that state death taxes have little, if any, effect on fees. The California study confirms that attorneys' fees average in the 3 percent range. It also reflects two other significant points that bear repeating. The first is that these fees were estimated on estates with no complications and no federal estate tax issues. The second is that attorneys' fees are consistently the same regardless of what type of fee schedule is in effect and notwithstanding the type of probate statute under which they were calculated.

36. Our statistics consultant was Dr. Michael Jacroux, chairman of the department of mathematics at Washington State University. For a description of the study design and methods, please see Appendix B.

37. Texas has "independent administration," which is similar to unsupervised probate under the Uniform Probate Code. Under independent administration, the executor (personal represent-

ative) does not have to file the attorney's fee with the court. Thus our information in Texas may not be totally accurate. However, we conducted an informal survey among a number of attorneys in Texas, and it appears that at least in the urban areas, probate fees are consistent with the averages that we see nationwide.

38. See Fanning, *Fee-busting*, FORBES, Sept. 7, 1987, at 64; see also the discussion of fees in SUCCESSION OF BENTON, 354 So. 2d 721 (La. Ct. App. 1978).

39. American College of Probate Counsel, FEES OF EXECUTORS, ADMINISTRATORS, AND TESTAMENTARY TRUSTEES (1985) (currently American College of Trust and Estate Counsel, Los Angeles, Calif.).

40. For example, 1981 New York Laws Ch. 803 provides that the fee is to be calculated as follows: one half of the allowed percentage rate is taken on the value of the property received and one half on the value of the property distributed. More than one full commission may be paid for estates of $100,000 or more in principal.

41. H. WEINSTOCK, § 6.7, at 125.

42. AARP, A REPORT ON PROBATE, 13.

43. Technical Advisory Memorandum 8838009. Some courts agree with the IRS. For example, see Estate of DeWitt, 54 TCM 759, TC Memo. 1987-502, CCH Dec. 44,238(m) (1987).

44. George Turner gives an example of this dual probate problem. He estimates that on a $500,000 estate the combined probate fees for both estates, assuming no appreciation in the value of the estate assets between the deaths of the spouses, to be $62,000, which is 12.4 percent of the entire estate. G. TURNER, § 3.06.

45. When we refer to titling property in the name of the trust, it is with the full awareness that legal title is held in the name of the trustees. The phrase "titling in the name of the trust" is used merely for convenience.

46. For example, Richardson & Muehleck, 296, state that the attorney's fee for a trust is much higher than the fee for preparing a will in large part because of the transfer process.

47. The concept of professionals working together has been written about by R. ESPERTI & R. PETERSON in the HANDBOOK OF ESTATE PLANNING xii–xiii (3d ed. 1991) and in LOVING TRUST 269–79 (1988).

48. Charles Schwab has created a trust marketing division that will transfer client securities into a trust at no charge as long as the

account is created at that company. They have several brochures touting the living trust in their facilities and are now being copied by other brokerage firms.

49. This figure is a product of the authors' collective experience. It represents the highest figures that have been quoted by their colleagues from around the nation. It is potentially too high, but represents an attempt to give every possible edge to the will-planning/probate bar in making the necessary comparisons in areas where there is no hard data or evidence.

50. IRC § 212(c).

51. IRC § 67.

52. For a detailed discussion of professional trustees and their fees, see G. TURNER, §§ 10.01–10.04.

53. See, for example, Richardson & Muehleck, 296; see also Bearns, 3, 10; Jones, 20.

54. G. TURNER, § 2.02; AARP, A REPORT ON PROBATE, 17.

55. See LAWYERS AND CERTIFIED PUBLIC ACCOUNTANTS: A STUDY OF INTERPROFESSIONAL RELATIONS, a statement issued by the National Conference of Lawyers and CPA's, distributed jointly by the AICPA and the ABA. The study contains a Statement of Principles on Estate Planning, which sets forth some broad guidelines as to the delineation of the roles of the CPA and the lawyer in the estate planning process.

56. Sometimes trustees charge extraordinary fees for complex or unusual transactions, but this is not common. If a corporate fiduciary that charges a termination fee is named, the distribution process will also generate that fee. However, under the instant analysis, this is not likely, since distribution is occurring immediately rather than after a period of years or decades.

57. For example, Richardson & Muehleck, 295, cite some probate filing fees for various jurisdictions. The fees range from a low of $90 to a high of $800.

58. One of the few writers who has tackled this comparison states that while there are costs that are common to both trust and probate administration, it is reasonable to assume that the charges for the after-death trust services "will amount to 70 per cent of the statutory or customary fee" of the costs of probate administration (H. WEINSTOCK, 126).

Chapter 3

1. G. TURNER, § 4.06, at 4–14.
2. H. WEINSTOCK, 52.
3. Bayles & McCartney, AP series on *Guardians of the Elderly*, parts 1–5, Sarasota Herald Tribune, Sept. 20–24, 1987.
4. *20/20:* "When You Have No Rights," ABC television broadcast, Mar. 4, 1988.
5. Zartman, *Planning for Disability*, 15 PROBATE NOTES 11, 14 (1989).
6. These odds have been stated as: at age 42, the odds are 3.01 to 1; at age 52, the odds are 2.28 to 1; Rattiner, *Disability Income: The Forgotten Insurance*, JOURNAL OF ACCOUNTANCY, Dec. 1990, viii, citing to VIII JOURNAL OF THE AMERICAN SOCIETY OF CHARTERED LIFE UNDERWRITERS, no. 1 (1958).
7. AARP, TOMORROW'S CHOICES: PREPARING NOW FOR FUTURE LEGAL, FINANCIAL, AND HEALTH CARE DECISIONS (1988).
8. *Id.*, at 41.
9. *Id.*
10. *Revocable Living Trust as an Estate Planning Tool*, 7 REAL PROPERTY, PROBATE AND TRUST JOURNAL 223, 224 (1972). See also Billings and Englebrecht, *Bypassing the Probate Process*, BEST'S REVIEW, Dec. 1987, at 28, 39.
11. For an overview of problems with state guardianship systems in general, and recent efforts at study and reform, see Gottlich and Wood, *Statewide Review of Guardianships: The California and Maryland Approaches*, 23 CLEARINGHOUSE REVIEW 426 (1989).
12. 3 AMERICAN JURISPRUDENCE 2d *Agency* § 23 (1986).
13. *Id.*
14. See UNIFORM PROBATE CODE art. 5, pt. 5, prefatory note, 8 UNIFORM LAWS ANNOTATED 511, 512 (1989), stating that the only earlier known statutes similar to the durable power of attorney concept as it appears in the UPC were certain provisions of the Code of Virginia dating from 1950.
15. UNIFORM PROBATE CODE §§ 5-501 and 5-502, 8 UNIFORM LAWS ANNOTATED 513, 514 (1989).
16. G. BOGERT, TRUSTS, § 16.
17. Zartman, at 14.
18. It was approved by the National Conference of Commissioners on Uniform State Laws in 1979, and has been adopted in 26 states and the District of Columbia. Uniform Durable Power of

Attorney Act historical note, 8A UNIFORM LAWS ANNOTATED 275 (1983) (Supp. 1991 at 88). A number of other states have enacted statutes influenced by the UPC. Uniform Durable Power of Attorney Act prefatory note, 8A UNIFORM LAWS ANNOTATED 276 (1983) The Uniform Act is identical to art. 5, pt. 5, of the Uniform Probate Code.

19. 3 AMERICAN JURISPRUDENCE 2d *Agency* § 57 (1986), citing to RESTATEMENT (SECOND) OF AGENCY § 123.

20. FLORIDA STATUTES § 709.08 (1991).

21. COLORADO REVISED STATUTES ANNOTATED § 15-14-501(1) (1989).

22. For example, the court in Rice v. Floyd, 768 S.W. 2d 57, 60-61 (Ky. 1989), held that "the durable power of attorney is not a substitute for the appointment of a guardian. The existence of a durable power of attorney cannot prevent the institution of guardianship proceedings."

23. *E.g.,* FLORIDA STATUTES § 709.08 (1991) authorizes appointment of an agent with health care powers within the general durable power of attorney statute, and a separate procedure for designating a "health care surrogate" is found in FLORIDA STATUTES ch. 745 (1991). As of July 1991, thirty-eight states and the District of Columbia had statutes authorizing a health care power of attorney (from tables provided by the Legal Counsel for the Elderly, AARP).

24. *E.g.,* IRC § 6012 requires each individual to file an income tax return, and Treas. Reg. §§ 1.6061-1 and 1.6012-1(a)(5) specify when an agent may file an income tax return. See also 26 CODE OF FEDERAL REGULATIONS § 601.504, re designating an agent as the taxpayer's representative.

25. Brantley, *Use of the Trust to Manage Property of the Elderly or Disabled*, 42 ARKANSAS L. REV. 619 (1989).

26. Martin & Roush, *Revocable Trusts*, 51 JOURNAL OF THE KANSAS BAR ASSOCIATION, Spring 1982, at 8.

27. Brantley, 622, note 7.

28. Zartman, 15.

29. Brantley, 621, 630.

30. AARP, TOMORROW'S CHOICES, 39.

Chapter 4

1. For example, B. R. Stock, in her book IT'S EASY TO AVOID PROBATE AND GUARDIANSHIPS, states that based on a survey of five hundred estates in nine states, the average length of probate is sixteen months.
2. G. TURNER, § 2.04, at 2–10.
3. Gergen, 72.
4. Our four-state probate sampling conducted in 1990 indicates that probate lasts from four to fifteen months. The average length of time estates stayed in probate in Iowa was 239 days for urban counties and 341 days for rural counties; in New York it was 174 days for urban counties and 354 for rural ones; in Texas it was 121 for urban counties and 118 for rural ones, and in Oregon it was 394 days for urban counties and 470 days for rural counties.
5. An irrevocable agency results from a power coupled with an interest, or given as security, and does not end at death. 3 AMERICAN JURISPRUDENCE 2d *Agency* §§ 63, 64.
6. For a survey of these statutes, see R. ESPERTI & R. PETERSON, HANDBOOK, 265, appendix C.
7. COLORADO REVISED STATUTES § 15-11-403 (1989); FLORIDA STATUTES § 732.403 (1989); MARYLAND STATUTES § 3-201.
8. R. ESPERTI & R. PETERSON, HANDBOOK, 265, appendix C.
9. H. WEINSTOCK, 127; G. TURNER, § 2.04, at 2–9.
10. *E.g.*, IRC § 6324(a)(2) imposes personal liability for federal estate tax.
11. For example, see CALIFORNIA PROBATE CODE § 9100; New York Surrogate's Court Procedure Act § 1802; NEW JERSEY REVISED STATUTES TITLE 3B, c.22, Section 4; and OHIO REVISED CODE ANNOTATED 2113.08.
12. Keydel, *"Funding,"* 98, 104.
13. See, *e.g.*, Terrill, *Revocable Trusts: Panacea or Placebo?* BEST'S REVIEW, Aug. 1989, at 62.
14. Miller, *Update on Whether to Consider Using a Funded Living Trust to Avoid Probate*, 16 ESTATE PLANNING 140, 141–42 (1989).
15. 1 A. CASNER, ESTATE PLANNING 327 (4th ed. 1980, & Supp. 1983).
16. BERALL, CAMPFIELD, and ZARITSKY, 468-2ND Tax MANAGEMENT SERIES, REVOCABLE INTER VIVOS TRUSTS A-20 (1991).
17. Antonucci, *Advantages of the Funded Revocable Trust in Estate Plan-*

ning, ESTATES AND PROBATE NEWSLETTER, Connecticut Bar Association, March 1990, at 1.

18. IRC § 2204 establishes liability and IRC § 6501 is the statute of limitations.
19. IRC § 2002, IRC § 2203; DeNiro v. United States, 561 F.2d 653 (6th Cir. 1977).
20. Treas. Reg. § 20.2002-1.
21. *E.g.*, Richardson & Muehleck, 294, 299.
22. 6 MERTENS, LAW OF FEDERAL GIFT AND ESTATE TAXES, ch. 43.02–43.12 (1960).
23. IRC § 2204. Originally, this section applied only to executors. In 1970, Section 2204(b) was added to include trustees and other fiduciaries. See R. STEPHENS, G. MAXFIELD, S. LIND, AND D. CALFEE, FEDERAL ESTATE AND GIFT TAXATION ¶ 8.03[2] and note 25 (6th ed. 1991).
24. 48 STATUTES AT LARGE 760 (1934), 31 UNITED STATES CODE SERVICE, ch. 6, § 192 (1958).
25. AARP, CHEAPER PROBATE ADMINISTRATION.
26. *Id.*, This figure was confirmed by employees of the Internal Revenue Service.
27. IRC § 6018(a). For nonresidents who are not U.S. citizens, if the gross estate exceeds $60,000, a return must be filed.
28. See generally IRC §§ 2205, 6324(a), and 6901 (dealing with transferee liability).
29. IRC § 6501.
30. IRC § 6905; Keydel, *"Funding"* 113.
31. IRC § 6905(a) allows the discharge for executors. IRC § 6905(b) defines an executor as an executor or an administrator duly appointed in the United States, leading one to conclude that trustees are excluded from this treatment. However, § 6905(c) cross-references to § 2204, which refers to, and includes, a trustee under its provisions.
32. Treas. Reg. § 1.641(b)-3.

Chapter 5

1. 1 J. SCHOENBLUM, MULTISTATE AND MULTINATIONAL ESTATE PLANNING § 16.05.2 (1982).
2. One article succinctly sums up the problem by stating, "[e]ager investors are excited by the potential return on their investments and the status gained by owning property, but few consider the

potential burden on their heirs of complex ancillary proceedings necessary to clear title to these various out-of-state assets. McDonnell, Harris, & Cantwell, *The Final Game: Ancillary Administration Proceedings Under the Uniform Probate Code and in Non-UPC Jurisdictions*, 6 PROBATE L. J. 211 (1985).

3. Sometimes, a state's statute allows the acceptance of a will probated in the domiciliary state, but this is not common. 79 AMERICAN JURISPRUDENCE 2d *Wills* § 831 (1975).

4. *Id.* § 1057.

5. RESTATEMENT (SECOND) OF CONFLICT OF LAWS § 321 (1) (1971); UNIFORM PROBATE CODE §§ 4-201 to 4-207, 8 UNIFORM LAWS ANNOTATED 421–24 (1983).

6. McDonnell, Harris, & Cantwell, 225.

Chapter 6

1. Dobson & Barwick, LIVING TRUST: LOVE IT OR LEAVE IT, an outline of a debate presented to the national convention of the International Association for Financial Planning, September 21, 1990, at New Orleans, La.

2. Terrill, 62, 66.

3. R. ESPERTI & R. PETERSON, LOVING TRUST, 51–52.

4. PRINCE, *Targeting the Affluent Family Business*, 129 TRUSTS AND ESTATES 39, 46 (1990).

5. See, *e.g.*, FLORIDA STATUTES § 709.08 (1990).

6. FLORIDA STATUTES § 737.405 (1991).

7. *E.g.*, the Connecticut Probate Court Administrator's 1986 TECHNICAL RECOMMENDATION states that access to the returns, and one would hope to any attachments to it such as the trust, should be limited to only those persons with a direct economic interest in the return. This select group includes heirs and beneficiaries as well as " 'persons whose economic interests may be diminished by the information in this return' TR 86-360" (Bearns, 311).

Chapter 7

1. Jaworski, *The Will Contest*, 10 BAYLOR L. REV. 87, 88 (1958).

2. Florida's probate laws are typical and demonstrate how potential litigants are invited into the probate process. FLORIDA STATUTES § 733.212 (1991 Supp.) requires publication of notice for admin-

istration and service of personal notice on the surviving spouse and beneficiaries, and permits personal notice to be served to legatees or devisees under a **prior will**. Also, under FLORIDA STATUTES § 733.109 (1991), any "interested person" may petition for revocation of probate of a will up until the time the administrator is discharged if they did not receive personal notice, as long as the petition is filed within specified time periods.

3. D. M. Schuyler, in his 1974 article *Revocable Trusts—Spouses, Creditors, and Other Predators*, University of Miami Eighth Institute on Estate Planning, ¶ 74.1304, at 13–35, predicted that the more revocable living trusts are used, the more contests there are likely to be. There is no evidence that this has occurred.

4. *E.g.*, 80 AMERICAN JURISPRUDENCE 2d *Wills* § 905; TEXAS PROBATE CODE ANNOTATED SECTION 3(r) (Vernon 1980).

5. Johanson, *The Use and Misuse of Revocable Trusts: Possibilities and Problems*, from outline of presentation of paper at the Southwestern Legal Foundation's 29th Annual Institute on Wills and Probate, University of Texas at Austin (May 4, 1990).

6. Note, *Will Contests on Trial*, 6 STANFORD L. Rev. 91, 92 (1953).

7. Davis v. Hunter, 323 F. Supp. 976, 979 (D. Conn. 1970).

8. Estate of Wagner, 220 Neb. 32, 367 N.W.2d 736, 738 (1985).

9. See Estate of Peter C., 488 A.2d 468, 470–71 (Me. 1985); the guardian is a fiduciary to his ward and must put the interests of his ward above his own.

10. Johanson, 27.

11. Davis v. Hunter, 323 F. Supp. at 979, 980.

12. 1 A. CASNER, ESTATE PLANNING 60 (1st ed., 1953).

13. 79 AMERICAN JURISPRUDENCE 2d *Wills* § 71.

14. 1 A. SCOTT & W. FRATCHER, § 18.

15. 79 AMERICAN JURISPRUDENCE 2d *Wills* § 76.

16. Schuyler, ¶ 74.1303 B., at 13–26.

17. 79 AMERICAN JURISPRUDENCE 2d, *Wills* § 389 and 4 A. SCOTT & W. FRATCHER, §§ 331.1, 333.2, and 333.3.

18. See generally 79, 80 AMERICAN JURISPRUDENCE 2d *Wills*.

19. 76 AMERICAN JURISPRUDENCE 2d *Trusts* § 41 (1975).

20. See 76 AMERICAN JURISPRUDENCE 2d *Trusts* § 34; RESTATEMENT (SECOND) OF TRUSTS § 2.

21. Johanson, 21.

22. *Id.*, at 23; Professor Johanson is the Fannie Coplin Regents Professor of Law at the University of Texas at Austin.

23. RESTATEMENT (SECOND) OF TRUSTS § 57.

24. *E.g.*, at least forty-nine states and the District of Columbia have

adopted statutes dealing with the pouring-over of property by will into pre-existing trusts (6 A. SCOTT & W. FRATCHER, § 54.3). According to Scott and Fratcher, thirty-one of these states have adopted the Uniform Testamentary Additions to Trusts Act. Louisiana has a statute that permits an inter vivos trust to incorporate by reference any or all of the terms of an existing trust.

25. G. BOGERT, TRUSTS, § 22.
26. 76 AMERICAN JURISPRUDENCE 2d *Trusts* § 36.
27. *Id.* § 115.
28. See generally 2 A. SCOTT & W. FRATCHER, § 99; see also Annotation, *Trusts: Merger of Legal and Equitable Estates Where Sole Trustees Are Sole Beneficiaries*, 7 AMERICAN LAW REPORTS 621 (4th ed. 1981).
29. Mathias v. Fantine, No. 89AP080063 (Ohio Ct. App., 5th Dist., Mar. 1, 1990) (Lexis, 1990 Ohio App.) [not reported].
30. 79 AMERICAN JURISPRUDENCE 2d *Wills* § 951.
31. UPC § 3-407; UNIFORM PROBATE CODE PRACTICE MANUAL § 8.13, at 111, 112.
32. Warnick, *The Ungrateful Living: An Estate Planner's Nightmare—The Trial Attorney's Dream*, 2 LAND AND WATER L. Rev. 401, 415 (1989).
33. Keydel, *"Funding,"* 98, 104; see also the Report of the Committee on Estate and Tax Planning, *The Revocable Trust as an Estate Planning Tool*, 7 REAL PROPERTY, PROBATE AND TRUST L. J. 223, 227 (1972).
34. Schuyler, at ¶ 74.1303, at 13–28 & 13–29.
35. *Id.* ¶ 74.1303, at 13–29 & ¶ 74.1304.

Chapter 8

1. Falender, *Notice to Creditors in Estate Proceedings: What Process Is Due?* 63 NORTH CAROLINA L. Rev. 659, 667–68 (1985).
2. *Id.* 664–72.
3. Tulsa Professional Collection Services v. Pope, 485 U.S. 478, 108 S. Ct. 1340 (1988).
4. *Id.* at 1347.
5. Reutlinger, *State Action, Due Process, and the New Nonclaim Statutes: Can No Notice Be Good Notice if Some Notice Is Not?* 24 REAL PROPERTY, PROBATE AND TRUST JOURNAL 433, 435, *cf.* note 6. The applicable statute of limitations is the shorter of the non-

probate nonclaim statutory period or the statute of limitations for the particular type of claim made. For example, if the non-probate nonclaim statutory period is three years, but the statute of limitations for an action under a contract is two years, the shorter period would apply.

6. Miller, 140, 145.

7. *E.g.*, see Andrews, *Creditors' Rights Against Nonprobate Assets in Washington: Time for Reform*, 65 WASHINGTON L. REV 73, 85 (1990).

8. 2A A. SCOTT & W. FRATCHER, § 156. RESTATEMENT (SECOND) OF TRUSTS § 156.

9. Report of Probate and Trust Division Committee D-3 on Special Problems of Fiduciaries, *Creditors' Rights Against Trust Assets*, 22 REAL PROPERTY, PROBATE AND TRUST JOURNAL 735, 750 (1987).

10. Jones v. Clifton, 101 U.S. 225, 230 (1880).

11. RESTATEMENT (SECOND) OF TRUSTS, § 330 comment o.

12. See 4 A. SCOTT & W. FRATCHER, § 330.12.

13. *Creditors' Rights Against Trust Assets*, 750.

14. In re Kovalyshyn's Estate, 136 N.J. Super. 40, 343 A.2d 852 (1975); State Street Bank and Trust Co. v. Reiser, 7 Mass. App. 633, 389 N.E.2d 768; Johnson v. Commercial Bank, 284 Or. 675, 588 P.2d 1096 (1978). *E.g.*, in New York, see Estates, Powers and Trusts Law § 10–10.6 (McKinney 1967); MICHIGAN STATUTES ANNOTATED § 26.155 (118) (Supp. 1973); CALIFORNIA PROBATE CODE §§ 19001 and 19012 (1992).

15. The erosion of the rule that a trust maker's creditors are cut off after the maker's death has been caused, in part, by the inconsistency between two significant legal treatises issued by the American Law Institute. The American Law Institute is an organization that is charged with compiling treatises on the current state of the law in several different areas. These treatises are called *Restatements of the Law*. They are the product of the work of legal scholars, judges, and lawyers who do extensive research as to the status in a particular area of the law. *Restatements* are widely accepted by both lawyers and courts as definitive pronouncements of the law. From time to time, *Restatements* are updated. When they are, they are denoted as such by calling them *Restatement (Second)*.

Under the *Restatement (Second) of Trusts*, creditors of the maker of a revocable living trust cannot reach the trust assets after the death of its maker. This was consistent with the first *Restatement of Property*. However, under the *Restatement (Second) of Property*, it appears that creditors of the maker of a revocable living trust can reach trust assets after the death of the maker. This inconsistency has created some uncertainty regarding the rights creditors have as to revocable living trusts after the death of their makers.

16. See generally Schuyler, ch. 13 ¶ 74.1302.
17. 37 AMERICAN JURISPRUDENCE 2d *Fraudulent Conveyances* § 28 (1968); see also 4 A. SCOTT & W. FRATCHER, § 330.12.
18. *Creditors' Rights Against Trust Assets*, 737–38.
19. MISSOURI REVISED STATUTES § 456.610 (1983); for trust assets of makers who die on or after January 1, 1992, CALIFORNIA PROBATE CODE §§ 19000–19403 (West 1992).
20. Exceptions would be secured creditors, or when the maker has made conveyances that defraud creditors.
21. Langbein, 1108, 1120; see general discussion *Id.* 1120–1125.
22. *Id.* 1124.
23. Wellman, *Lawyer's Stake*, 10, 12. Wellman said, "The time-honored remedy of filing a claim against an estate seems to be useful principally to undertakers and disappointed heirs." Now, there is evidence that even funeral directors no longer rely on the probate process. A recent AARP report on probate questions whether creditors still rely on probate. It cites a finding by a funeral industry publication that funeral directors prefer to bill family members (even arranging financing) rather than look for payment from the decedent's estate. AARP, A REPORT ON PROBATE, 29, citing to Hast, MORTUARY MANAGEMENT (October 1989), at 15.

Chapter 9

1. 1 J. SCHOENBLUM, § 14.03.
2. See RESTATEMENT (SECOND) OF CONFLICT OF LAWS, § 11(2).
3. A 1988 article in FORBES provided a long list of the factors that state taxing agencies and tax courts are said to look at in determining domicile for the purposes of state taxation. Some of these factors are: the place of your employment or business activities; the reasons that you changed your address or have more than one address; whether your homes are leased or owned; whether you have more than one home; where you are registered to vote; where you have a driver's license; where your car is registered;

where you have bank accounts; the location in which you signed
your will; where your family lives and your children attend
school, and the states in which you have mailing addresses. Flan-
agan, *Border Games*, FORBES, June 13, 1988, at 112–13.

4. 1 J. SCHOENBLUM, § 14.02.

5. *Id.*

6. 5A A. SCOTT & W. FRATCHER, § 652, citing to RESTATEMENT
(SECOND) OF CONFLICT OF LAWS, at §278.

7. See G. BOGERT, TRUSTS, § 182, at 728–29.

8. *Id.* at 731–32.

9. According to 5A A. SCOTT & W. FRATCHER, § 601, this technique
may not always be successful. Public policy considerations, such
as protection of a spouse, may be considered in a determination
of which law applies.

Chapter 10

1. 42 UNITED STATES CODE SERVICE 1396 (Law. Co-op. 1985)
(Social Security Act, title XIX, Grants to States for Medical Assistance Programs).

2. AARP, TOMORROW'S CHOICES; see also H. GORDON, HOW TO
PROTECT YOUR LIFE SAVINGS FROM CATASTROPHIC ILLNESS
AND NURSING HOMES 19 (1990).

3. 42 US CODE SERVICE 1396a(a)(17) (Law. Co-op. Supp.1991).

4. The types of assets and values may vary from state to state, but
this list is representative of those exempt assets in most states.
See H. GORDON, 123–24, 164, and 168.

5. IRC § 2503(b) allows gifts of present interests to be gift-tax free
as long as they do not exceed $10,000 per year per recipient.
IRC § 2010(a) allows a credit against taxable gifts until they
cumulatively reach $600,000. This unified credit amount can be
used during lifetime or at death under the federal unified estate
and gift tax system. For federal purposes, gifts in excess of the
$10,000 annual exclusion and which are not sheltered by the
unified credit exemption equivalent amount of $600,000, will
be subject to federal transfer tax.

6. See 42 US Code Service § 1396a(k) (Law. Co-op. Supp. 1991).

7. It is possible to create an irrevocable trust that allows the community spouse to receive income that does not affect the Medicaid eligibility of the institutionalized spouse. However, if at any
time the community spouse would like to qualify for Medicaid,

the income will count. This is one reason that irrevocable trusts must be used with great care. REGAN, TAX, ESTATE AND FINANCIAL PLANNING FOR THE ELDERLY, § 10.08[1] (1991).

8. The $10,000 exclusion is lost because gifts made to an irrevocable trust are gifts of future interests which do not qualify for the annual exclusion under IRC § 2503(b).

9. 42 US CODE SERVICE 1396p(c)(1) (Law. Co-op. 1985 & Supp. 1991).

10. 42 US CODE SERVICE 1396p(c)(2)(B) & (C) (Law. Co-op. 1985 & Supp. 1991).

11. See 42 US CODE SERVICE 1396p (Law. Co-op. 1985); but the law extends certain protections to a surviving spouse and family members.

12. IRC §§ 2056(a) and (b)(7)(B).

13. See 42 US CODE SERVICE 1396a(k)(2) (Law. Co-op. Supp. 1991).

Chapter 11

1. See generally, IRC § 671–79, subtitle A., ch. 1J, part IE (1986).
2. IRC § 671.
3. Treas. Reg. § 1.671-4.
4. Treas. Reg. § 301.6109-1(a)(2).
5. Revenue Ruling 57-51, 1957-1 CUMULATIVE BULLETIN 171.
6. See generally Keydel, *"Funding,"* 98, 99–104; see also Cantwell & Rhodes, 859.
7. G. BOGERT, TRUSTS, § 25, at 70.
8. See generally RESTATEMENT (SECOND) OF TRUSTS § 156 and 4 A. SCOTT & W. FRATCHER, § 330.12; see also G. BOGERT TRUSTS, § 40.
9. In Chapter 8, "Protection from Creditors," the issues of creditors' claims are addressed.
10. When a trust maker transfers his or her residence to a living trust, federal law prohibits a lender from exercising a due-on-sale clause as long as the property is a residential property of less than five dwelling units and the borrower retains the right to occupy the residence. The lender should be notified prior to transfer. Garn–St. Germain Depository Institutions Act of 1982, Pub. L. No. 97–320, 96 Stat. 1469, 1505, Sec. 341; codified at 12 US CODE SERVICE § 1701j-3 (Law. Co-op. 1991 Supp.). See also the implementing regulations issued by the Office of Thrift Supervision, 12 CODE OF FEDERAL REGULATIONS § 591.1 (1991).

11. See J. PESCHEL & E. SPURGEON, FEDERAL TAXATION OF TRUSTS, GRANTORS AND BENEFICIARIES, ¶ 12.07[C] (2d ed. 1990).
12. See Meyer.
13. For a precise income tax reporting outline for nominee partnerships, see L. W. SCHMIDT, A PRACTICAL GUIDE TO THE REVOCABLE LIVING TRUST, F-51 (1990).
14. Keydel, *How to Take Title to Trust Property Including a Simple Way to Convert Joint Property into Revocable Trust Property*, 13 PROBATE NOTES 230 (1988).
15. In Colorado, for example, Colorado Bar Association REAL ESTATE TITLE STANDARD No. 3.2.1 (Rev'd Jan. 1987) is a title standard specifically establishing a presumption in favor of the validity of an unrecorded deed. Unrecorded deeds are not allowed in some states, so before using them it is important to ascertain their validity before using them.
16. UNIFORM PROBATE CODE, rev. art. 6, pt. 2 (1989); UNIFORM PROBATE CODE, OFFICIAL 1990 TEXT AND COMMENTS, 435–57.
17. A Uniform Transfer on Death Security Registration Act (TOD Security Act) was promulgated in 1989 and has been adopted by two states, Colorado and Wisconsin [8A UNIFORM LAWS ANNOTATED 243 (West Supp. 1991)]. The Act has been adopted as part of the UNIFORM PROBATE CODE Revised art. 6, pt. 3 (1989 rev. Code). See also, Wellman, *Transfer-on-Death Securities Registration: A New Title Form*, 21 GEORGIA L. REV. 789 (1987).
18. There are differences in planning between community property states and noncommunity property states. For purposes of this illustration, they can be ignored.

Chapter 12

1. IRC § 6166.
2. Treas. Reg. §§ 1.6166A-3(e)(3) and 1.6166A-3(e)(4) state that a distribution, sale, exchange, or other disposition of an interest in a closely held business by a trustee to whom the decedent transferred the interest during lifetime is not a disposition for purposes of accelerating the federal estate tax if the business interest was included in the decedent's estate under IRC §§ 2035 through 2038, or § 2041. Even though IRC § 6166A was repealed by Public Law No. 97-34, IRC §§ 6166 and 6166A are similar in language and application.

3. IRC § 6312 (1954) was repealed as to securities issued after March 3, 1971, by Pub. L. No. 92-5.
4. TREASURY DEPARTMENT CIRCULAR No. 300, 4th Rev., § 306.28(b), 38 FEDERAL REGISTER 7083.
5. General Counsel Memorandum 19347, 1938-1 Cumulative Bulletin 218, was declared obsolete on other grounds in REVENUE RULING 73-209, 1973-1 Cumulative Bulletin 614.
6. IRC § 1223(11).
7. IRC §§ 453 and 453A.
8. IRC § 453B. A disposition of an installment obligation includes the sale or other transfer of the obligation in any manner not approved by IRC § 453B.
9. IRC §§ 453(e) and 453(f)(1).
10. REVENUE RULING 74-613, 1974-2 CUMULATIVE BULLETIN 153.
11. See PRIVATE LETTER RULING 7943063 and PRIVATE LETTER RULING 8011060.
12. REVENUE RULING 76-100, 1976-1 CUMULATIVE BULLETIN 123.
13. Unless the installment obligation is transferred in a satisfaction of a pecuniary bequest, the transfer of the obligation to a beneficiary is not a disposition that will accelerate the gain. IRC § 453B(c).
14. The Omnibus Budget Reconciliation Act of 1990, Public Law No. 101-508, § 11521(a), repealed the rule prohibiting the transferee of proven oil and gas properties from claiming the percentage depletion allowance for all transfers after October 11, 1990. Even before this law was effective, transfers of proven oil and gas properties to revocable living trusts were allowed without adversely affecting percentage depletion. IRC § 613A(c)(1); PRIVATE LETTER RULING 8104202; REVENUE RULING 84-14, 1984-1 CUMULATIVE BULLETIN 147; Treas. Reg. § 1.613A-3(i)(1)(ii) example 15; IRC 613A(c)(9)(B)(i) [now repealed]; PRIVATE LETTER RULING 8248065; PRIVATE LETTER RULING 8417045; PRIVATE LETTER RULING 8337023 and REVENUE RULING 84-14, 1984-1 CUMULATIVE BULLETIN 147.
15. IRC §§ 743 and 754; REVENUE RULING 79-84, 1979-1 CUMULATIVE BULLETIN 223.
16. See also ANNOTATION, provision for postmortem payment or performance as affecting instrument's character and validity as a contract, 1 AMERICAN LAW REPORTS 1178, 1265–69 (2d edition 1948).
17. In Uniform Probate Code states, a partnership interest may be transferred at the death of a partner by an after-death assign-

ment. The partnership interest will avoid probate without adverse income tax consequences. For those states that prohibit nonprofessional partners in a professional partnership, these methods are ideal for purposes of funding a revocable living trust.

18. IRC § 1034.
19. REVENUE RULING 66-159, 1966-1 CUMULATIVE BULLETIN 162.
20. IRC § 121.
21. PRIVATE LETTER RULING 8007050.
22. REVENUE RULING 85-45, 1985-1 CUMULATIVE BULLETIN 183, citing REVENUE RULING 66-159; PRIVATE LETTER RULING 8007050. In addition, an individual whose real estate is involuntarily converted can defer any gain created by the conversion (IRC § 1033). The IRS has ruled that these involuntary conversion benefits likewise apply to property held in a revocable living trust. PRIVATE LETTER RULING 8729023.
23. Treas. Reg. § 1.454-1(a)(1)(iii), REVENUE RULING 58-2, 1958-1 CUMULATIVE BULLETIN 236, and PRIVATE LETTER RULING 7826024.
24. See PRIVATE LETTER RULING 7729003.
25. IRC § 1361(c)(2)(i).
26. Proposed Treas. Reg. § 1.1361-1A(h)(3); IRC § 1361(c)(1).
27. IRC § 2032A.
28. IRC § 2032A(a)(2).
29. IRC § 2032A(e)(9).
30. See PRIVATE LETTER RULING 8109073.
31. One commentator has stated that it is not feasible for a living trust to hold title to sole proprietorships. His reason is that a sole proprietorship is not an identifiable entity, but rather an amalgamation of assets and liabilites organized as a business. Technically, he is correct, a sole proprietorship is an amalgamation of assets; practically, the problem is easily overcome. Miller, 140, 144.
32. J. PESCHEL & E. SPURGEON, ¶ 3.02.
33. Treas. Reg. § 301.7701-4(a).
34. IRC § 302.
35. IRC § 302(b)(3).
36. IRC § 318(a).
37. Siblings do not fall under the attribution rules in IRC 318(a)(1). Therefore, Mike is only considered as owning what his parents own.
38. IRC § 302(c)(2).

39. IRC § 302(c)(2)(C).
40. REVENUE RULING 83-121, 1983-2 CB 74.
41. Employee Retirement Security Act of 1974, Public Law No. 93-406, 88 Statutes at Large 829 (codified as amended at 29 US CODE SERVICE §§ 1001 et seq. (Law. Co-op. 1990).
42. IRC §§ 401(a)(11) and 417(a)(2); Treas. Reg. § 1.401(a)-20.
43. IRC § 402(e).
44. IRC §§ 401(a)(9)(B)(ii),(iii), and (iv).
45. IRC § 401(a)(9)(B)(iii); Proposed Treas. Reg. § 1.401(a)(9)-1, Q&A C-3(a).
46. IRC §§ 402(a)(7) and 408(d)(3)(C)(ii)(II).
47. IRC § 401(a)(9)(B)(i).
48. Proposed Treas. Reg. § 1.401(a)(9)-1, Q&A D-2A(b).
49. Proposed Treas. Reg. § 1.401(a)(9)-1, Q&A D-2.
50. Proposed Treas. Reg. § 1.401(a)(9)-1, Q&A D-2A(a).
51. See generally Proposed Treas. Reg. § 1.401(a)(9)-1.
52. Proposed Treas. Reg. § 1.401(a)(9)-1, Q&A D-2A(b). Obviously, if the participant has died, his or her life expectancy is short. The life expectancy is computed by taking the participant's age at his or her date of death and determining life expectancy as if the participant were alive.
53. Proposed Treas. Reg. § 1.401(a)(9)-1, Q&A D-2A(b).
54. Proposed Treas. Reg. § 1.401(a)(9)-1, Q&A D-5.
55. These exceptions relate to transitional rules found in the Tax Equity and Fiscal Responsibility Act of 1982 (TEFRA), the Deficit Reduction Act of 1984 (DEFRA), and the Tax Reform Act of 1986. For an explanation of these rules, see AMERICAN COLLEGE OF TRUST AND ESTATE COUNSEL HANDBOOK ON DISTRIBUTIONS FROM QUALIFIED RETIREMENT PLANS AND INDIVIDUAL RETIREMENT ACCOUNTS (ACTEC Study #20) (1990).
56. IRC § 2039(a).
57. IRC § 2056(b)(7).
58. IRC § 2056(a).
59. Keydel & Wallace, *The Revocable Trust—Disclaimer Method for Integrating Qualified Plan and IRA Death Benefits into an Estate Plan*, 13 PROBATE NOTES 158, 163–65 (1987).
60. See R. STEPHENS, G. MAXFIELD, S. LIND, & D. CALFEE, ¶ 5.06[7][b].
61. Keydel and Wallace, 163–65.
62. Keydel states in another article, "Attempting to a name a person's testamentary trust as beneficiary raises the question of which testamentary trust (marital or non-marital) the person should

name as beneficiary of what benefits and amounts (considering the goal of avoiding over qualification of the marital deduction" Keydel, *"Funding,"* 98, 103.

63. IRC § 4980A(d).
64. IRC § 4980A(d). In general, the excess accumulation is calculated as follows: The value of a person's total interest in all retirement plans at the date of his death reduced by the present value of a single life annuity with annual payments equal to the greater of $150,000 or $112,500 (in 1986 dollars) adjusted annually for inflation, payable for the life expectancy of the person using his date of death age. IRC §4980A(d)(3). For example, a person dies at age 70 with $2,000,000 in a qualified retirement plan. In his year of death $150,000 is greater than $112,500 indexed for inflation. The person's life expectancy at age 70 is 6.0522 years using IRS tables. The present value of a single life annuity is $907,830 (6.0522 × $150,000). Thus the excess accumulation subject to the 15 percent excise tax is $1,092,170 ($2,000,000 - $907,830). Treas. Reg. §54.4981A-1T(d) Q&A d-9.

A limited edition to the general method of calculating the excess accumulation applies to individuals who had accrued retirement plan benefits in excess of $562,500 on August 1, 1986, and who filed a special election on their individual tax return prior to 1989. An explanation of this exception is beyond the scope of this book.
65. IRC § 691(c)(1)(C).
66. IRC § 2053(c)(1)(B).
67. IRC § 4980A(d)(5).
68. IRC § 691(c).
69. IRC § 691(a).
70. Treas. Reg. § 1.691(a)-4(b).
71. See Fullerton, *When Can a Fiduciary Disclaim Property on Behalf of Another?* 17 ESTATE PLANNING 272, 274 (1990); see also PRIVATE LETTER RULING 9016026 and PRIVATE LETTER RULING 9016067.
72. Keydel & Wallace, at 161.

Chapter 13

1. *E.g.,* CALIFORNIA CORPORATIONS CODE § 13406; New York Business Corporation Law § 1507. State statutes many times apply to professional partnership interests as well. The same

logic that is applied to professional corporation stock is applied to partnership interests.

2. Michigan Opinion of Attorney General No. 5190 (1977).
3. Miller, 140, 144.
4. Florida Constitution art. VII, § 6.
5. Florida Constitution art. X, § 4.
6. Oklahoma Opinion of Attorney General No. 71-133 (June 11, 1971).
7. IRC § 1244(b).
8. IRC § 1212(b).
9. IRC § 1211(b).
10. IRC § 172(b).
11. Treas. Reg. § 1.1244(a)-1(b)(2).
12. IRC § 1244(d)(4).
13. See SCHOENFELD, 98-4th Tax Management Series SMALL BUSINESS STOCK—SECTION 1244.
14. A proposal of the Individual Members of the Estate and Gift Taxes Committee of the Section of Taxation, and of the Section of Real Property, Probate and Trust Law of the American Bar Association, entitled Tax Simplification Proposal No. 1, dated March, 1991, sent to Robert J. Leonard, Esquire, Chief Counsel, Staff Director, House Ways and Means Committee, United States Congress, on March 26, 1991, contains suggested legislation that would correct this needless disqualification for § 1244 stock when transferred to a living trust or to an estate.
15. IRC §§ 422, 422A, 423, and 424. The Omnibus Budget Reconciliation Act of 1990 repealed IRC § 422 for any transaction after November 5, 1990. There is a grandfather provision. Former IRC § 422A was revised and renumbered as § 422. IRC § 424 was repealed for any transaction after November 5, 1990. There is also a grandfather provision for it.

Sections 422 and 424 have limited application. Section 422, dealing with qualified stock options, applies to options granted after December 31, 1963, and before May 20, 1976. It was replaced by § 422A. Section 424 applies to options granted after February 26, 1945, and before December 31, 1964. Stock and options under these provisions rarely occur, but for those to whom these sections still apply should be cognizant of these rules.

16. IRC § 421(a).
17. IRC § 424(c).
18. A qualified stock option has a three-year holding period begin-

ning on the day after the day the stock is transferred to the individual [Former IRC § 422(a)(1)]. The holding periods for incentive stock options, employee stock purchase plans, and restricted stock options are two years from the date the option was granted and one year after the transfer of the stock to the individual. Former IRC §§ 422A(a)(1), 423(a)(1), and 424(a)(1).

19. IRC § 424(c).
20. Treas. Reg. § 1.425-1(c)(2).
21. Former IRC §§ 422(b)(6), 422A(b)(5), 423(b)(9), and 424(b)(2).
22. IRC § 421(c)(1).
23. It is interesting to note that the language dealing with wills is the same in each section of the Internal Revenue Code dealing with stock options and purchase plans, leading one to believe that this provision was added in the original legislation and copied into subsequent legislation without a great deal of thought or consideration.

Chapter 14

1. Revenue Act of 1932, § 803(a), 47 STATUTES AT LARGE 169, 279; in 1950 the three-year rule was added.
2. Public Law No. 94-455, § 2001(a)(5), 90 STATUTE 1520, 1848 (1976).
3. See IRC § 2035(d)(2).
4. These transfers are transfers that, had they been retained by the decedent, would have increased the decedent's gross estate under IRC §§ 2036, 2037, 2038, or 2042.
5. IRC §§ 2035 and 2038; Technical Advisory Memorandum 8609005.
6. Technical Advisory Memorandum 9018004, Technical Advisory Memorandum 9010004, and Technical Advisory Memorandum 9010005; these rulings are discussed in Keydel, *Gifts Made from Revocable Trusts*, 4 PROBATE AND PROPERTY, Sept./Oct. 1990, at 51.
7. Technical Advisory Memorandum 9010004; Technical Advisory Memorandum 9010005.
8. Keydel, *Gifts*, 53.
9. The Tax Simplification Bill of 1991 (H.R. 2777, S. 1394, 102 Cong., 1st Sess. (1991)) introduced into the House and the Senate on June 26, 1991, contained legislation that would eliminate the gift in contemplation of death problems associated with living

trusts. Although the provisions relating to gifts from living trusts are not controversial, they were not enacted. We expect these provisions will be introduced again.

10. In PRIVATE LETTER RULING 8635007, the IRS held that when a trustee of a revocable living trust distributed property to an attorney-in-fact acting under a durable power of attorney for the purpose of having the attorney-in-fact make gifts, neither the trustee nor the attorney-in-fact had the power to make such gifts. Under state law, the trustee could only make gifts if authorized by the trust, and the attorney-in-fact could only make the gifts if authorized by the durable power. Since neither instrument authorized the gifts, the IRS determined that the gifts must be included in the decedent's gross estate under § 2038 as revocable transfers.

11. This power would be a general power of appointment. See IRC § 2041.

12. See Keydel, *"Funding,"* 98, 107.

13. *Id.*

Chapter 15

1. In 1993, the top rate is scheduled to drop to 50 percent [IRC § 2001(c)(2)]. For estates exceeding approximately ten million dollars, the estate tax rate is increased by 5 percent until the estate exceeds $21,040,000 ($18,340,000 for decedents dying after 1992) [IRC § 2001(c)(3)].

2. For example, employer-paid annuities going directly to beneficiaries, employer-created death-benefit-only plans, social security payments to dependents, and life insurance proceeds *only* for policies you do not own or control (R. ESPERTI & R. PETERSON, HANDBOOK, 48).

3. IRC § 2010(a).

4. IRC § 2056.

5. The authors wrote about how tax planning for them can be accomplished in The IRREVOCABLE LIFE INSURANCE TRUST (1992).

6. Report, Committee on Significant New Developments in Probate and Trust Law Practice, ABA, *Developments Regarding the Professional Responsibility of the Estate Planning Lawyer: The Effect of the Model Rules of Professional Conduct*, 22 REAL PROPERTY, PROBATE AND TRUST JOURNAL 1, 5 (1987).

7. Testamentary trusts have their own drawbacks and are discussed in Chapter 23, "Comparing Testamentary and Living Trusts."
8. AARP, A Report on Probate, 10.
9. IRC § 2518.
10. IRC § 2518(b).
11. Treas. Reg. §25.2518-2(c)(4).
12. Kennedy v. Com., CA-7, 86-2 USTC ¶13,699, rev'g TC Memo. 1986-3; Gladys L. McDonald, 89 TC 293, CCH Dec. 44,118 (1987); Dancy, CA-4, 89-1, USTC ¶13,800; Estate of E. O'Brien, 55 TCM 977, CCH Dec. 44,813(M), TC Memo. 1988-240 (1988).
13. See IRC §§ 2036(a), 2036(c), Treas. Reg. § 20.2036-1(b)(3); IRC § 2038(a), Treas. Reg. § 20.2038-1(a)(3).
14. IRC § 2038(a).
15. Keydel, *"Funding,"* 98, 99, 100.

Chapter 16

1. In the states that allow an independent or unsupervised probate and administration, the court has less direct intervention in the management of a business. The executor is still the manager of the business, and is subject to all of the rules of the probate statute.
2. Casner, *Estate Planning—Avoidance of Probate*, 108, 134.
3. *Id.*

Chapter 17

1. The most recent survey of the effect of state spousal election laws as they affect both probate and property not passing through probate was published in 1985 by the American College of Probate Counsel, now named the American College of Trust and Estate Counsel. This study, entitled *Surviving Spouse's Right to Share in Deceased Spouse's Estate*, provides an analysis of the spousal election laws in all of the states and the District of Columbia in effect for the years 1983 or 1984. The survey reported that 22 states protect a spouse from being disinherited through nonprobate transfers such as with a living trust. Twenty-five states and the District of Columbia have laws which do not protect a spouse from living trust or other nonprobate transfers. At the time of the report the law was unclear on the rights of a

surviving spouse in Connecticut, Mississippi, and Ohio. We believe that there have been few changes in these laws since this study was made.

2. BLACK'S LAW DICTIONARY, 580.

3. *Id.* at 459.

4. See R. ESPERTI & R. PETERSON, HANDBOOK, 145–48; GEORGIA CODE ANNOTATED § 53-2-9 (1982).

5. For example, in Florida, a surviving spouse can elect to take 30 percent of the deceased spouse's property that is subject to administration. FLORIDA STATUTES §§ 732.206 & 732.207 (1991). In Wyoming the elective share applies to all property subject to disposition under the will. WYOMING STATUTES § 2-5-101 (1977, rev. 1980).

6. *E.g.*, Colorado, Minnesota, New York, New Jersey.

7. See R. ESPERTI & R. PETERSON, HANDBOOK, 265–83, Appendix C, Spouses Have Rights Too, for a summary of spousal statutory rights in the fifty states and the District of Columbia.

8. The community property states are Arizona, California, Idaho, Louisiana, Nevada, New Mexico, Texas, and Washington. The quasi-community property state is Wisconsin.

Chapter 18

1. 42 US CODE SERVICE §§ 9601 et seq. (Law. Co-op. 1989 and Supp. 1991).

2. See discussions in the following articles: Adams, *Clean Hands in a New Context: Environmental Hazards for Fiduciaries,* 1991 Philip E. Heckerling 25th Institute on Estate Planning ¶ 1300; Dribin, *Fiduciaries Need to Be Aware of Liability for Environmental Violation,* 16 ACTION LINE 1 (newsletter of the Real Property, Probate and Trust Law Section of the Florida Bar), Jan./Feb. 1991; Shi and Moxley, *New Hazards for Fiduciaries, Environmental Liability,* 4 PROBATE AND PROPERTY, Nov./Dec. 1990, at 37, 38; Vaughn, *Environmental Dangers for Fiduciaries,* 16 AMERICAN COLLEGE OF TRUST AND ESTATE COUNSEL NOTES, Fall 1990, at 77.

3. See sources cited in *supra* note 2.

4. 42 US CODE SERVICE 9601(35)(A)(ii)(Law. Co-op. 1989).

5. 42 US CODE SERVICE §§ 9601 (35)(A) and 9607 (b)(3)(a) & (b)(1989).

6. 42 US CODE SERVICE 9601(35)(A)(i)(Law. Co-op. 1989).

7. These issues were raised but were not decided in United States

v. Estate of Forster, No. 88-70613 (E.D. Mich. 1988). In another case, City of Phoenix, Arizona v. Garbage Service Company, No. CIV 89-1709 PHX PGR (D. Arizona, Apr. 4, 1991), a bank that was an executor of an estate and later a trustee of a testamentary trust held legal title to contaminated property for sixteen years. The court ruled that the bank was not liable as an owner, but could be held liable as an operator. This case is still in litigation.

8. S.651 was introduced by Senator Jake Garn, and H.R. 1450 was introduced by Representative John La Falce. CONGRESSIONAL RECORD, March 19, 1991, at E-987.

Chapter 19

1. See the Judge Advocate General's School, U.S. Army, ACIL-ST-262, LEGAL ASSISTANCE WILLS GUIDE (January 1989), published as the ALL-STATES WILLS AND ESTATE PLANNING GUIDE, by the American Bar Association (1990).
2. 5A A. SCOTT & W. FRATCHER, §§ 558, 559.
3. With regard to nonresident testamentary trustees, see 1 J. SCHOENBLUM, § 17.06.2.
4. 5A A. SCOTT & W. FRATCHER, § 557.

Chapter 20

1. The law of at least one state has the same provision for living trusts as for wills. FLORIDA STATUTES § 737.106 (1991) provides that, unless otherwise provided in the trust instrument, a divorced spouse is treated as having predeceased the maker of the trust upon the entry of judgment for divorce.
2. Wyoming, Kansas, and the District of Columbia are the only jurisdictions in the nation that do not have some form of pretermitted heir statute. Warnick, *The Ungrateful Living: An Estate Planner's Nightmare—The Trial Attorney's Dream*, 24 LAND AND WATER L. Rev. 401, 410 (1989).
3. See generally BERALL, CAMPFIELD, and ZARITSKY, A-25.
4. *Id.*
5. In some states, the courts will apply the pretermitted heir statutes to revocable living trusts. New Hampshire and Illinois are examples: In Re Estate of Came, 129 N.H. 544, 529 A.2d 962 (1987); Harris Trust and Savings Bank v. Donovan, 203 Ill. App.

3d 259, 148 Ill. Dec. 578, 560 N.E. 2d 1175 (1st. Dist., Ill. App. 1990) rehearing denied (Oct. 16, 1990).

6. 2 A. SCOTT & W. FRATCHER, § 112.3.

7. The Washington State Supreme Court applied the state's anti-lapse statute to a revocable living trust in Re Estate of Button, 79 Wash. 2d 849, 490 P.2d 731 (1971).

Chapter 21

1. Letter from Jere D. McGaffey, Chair, Section of Taxation, ABA, to Robert J. Leonard, Esq., Chief Counsel, Staff Director, House Ways and Means Committee, United States Congress March 26, 1991. The letter was accompanied by a proposal of the Individual Members of the Estate and Gift Taxes Committee of the Section of Taxation, and of the Section of Real Property, Probate and Trust Law of the ABA, entitled Tax Simplication Proposal No. 1, dated March 1991 [hereinafter Tax Proposal].

2. Tax Proposal, *supra* note 1, at 1-1.

3. H.R. 2777, S. 1394, 102 Cong., 1st Sess. (1991).

4. H.R. 2777 § 441.

5. Tax Proposal, *supra* note 1 at 1-5.

Chapter 22

1. 1A A. SCOTT & W. FRATCHER, § 54.3 and Supp. 1990; and Uniform Testamentary Additions to Trusts Act, Table, 8A UNIFORM LAWS ANNOTATED 240 (West Supp. 1991 Pocket Part); see also G. BOGERT, TRUSTS § 22, at 61.

2. Uniform Testamentary Additions to Trusts Act § 1, 8A UNIFORM LAWS ANNOTATED 603 (West, 1983); for a listing of the states that have adopted the Uniform Act see 8A UNIFORM LAWS ANNOTATED 240 (West Supp. 1991).

3. Sutton, *The Use of Pour-Back Provisions in a Revocable Trust*, ESTATE, GIFTS AND TRUST JOURNAL, May/June 1980, at 4.

4. William D. Kirchick, Esq., of the Boston law firm of Bingham, Dana and Gould, in a letter to the authors dated June 3, 1991.

5. MOORE, THE ADVANTAGES OF PROBATE, University of Miami 10th Institute on Estate Planning, ch. 4, ¶406, ¶416.2 (1976). Report, Committee on Taxation of Trust Income, *Post Mortem Income Tax Aspects of the Living Trust*, 4 REAL PROPERTY, PROBATE

AND TRUST LAW JOURNAL 339, 352 (1969); HILKER, POST-
MORTEM PROBLEMS OF REVOCABLE TRUSTS, University of
Southern California Law Center Tax Institute, ch. 17, ¶ 1708.3.

Chapter 23

1. The first eight reasons are explained in detail in Keydel, *"Funding,"* 98, 99–103.
2. For example, see Cantwell & Rhodes, 851.
3. See G. TURNER, § 3.08.
4. "Because of the usual requirement of administration of the testator's probate estate, the [testamentary] trust may not be fully funded until the probate administration has been completed several years after the testator's death." G. BOGERT, TRUSTS AND TRUSTEES § 1031 (rev. 2d ed. 1988).
5. G. BOGERT, TRUSTS § 180, at 719.
6. *Id.*
7. 1 KESS & WESTLIN, FINANCIAL AND ESTATE PLANNING, ¶ 1380.15.
8. See 19B J. APPLEMAN, INSURANCE LAW AND PRACTICE §§ 11241 & 11242 (rev. ed., 1982).
9. 1 J. SCHOENBLUM, § 14.02.
10. See G. BOGERT, TRUSTS § 181; RESTATEMENT OF TRUST § 269 (SECOND) comments g and h (1983).
11. Keydel, *"Funding,"* 99–100.
12. A testamentary trust is subject to the throwback rules. It must choose a calendar year. It has the same personal exemption allowance as a living trust. The separate share rule applies, as do the rules with regard to the taxation of capital gains for property permanently set aside for charities. S corporation stock can be held in a testamentary trust only if the trust is a qualified S corporation trust just like a living trust.

    There is no recognition of losses in transactions between a testamentary trust and a beneficiary. However, when property is distributed to the trust from the probate estate, losses can be recognized. There is ordinary income treatment on the sale of depreciable property between a testamentary trust and a beneficiary.

    The rules for rental real estate deductions and deductions for low-income housing are the same. The sixty-five-day rule applies equally to each.

13. G. TURNER, § 3.08, at 3–9.
14. BLEDSOE & LUSTIG, TEXAS LIVING TRUST, THE ULTIMATE ES-
TATE PLANNING TECHNIQUE FOR THE 1990'S (1991).

Chapter 24

1. In some states joint tenancy between spouses is called tenancy by the entirety.
2. Professor Wellman, one of the innovators and primary advocates of the Uniform Probate Code, refers to joint tenancy as "[t]he most desired and most criticized form of co-tenancy." Wellman, *Securities Registration,* 789.
3. IRC § 2040(b).
4. IRC §§ 2040(a) and (b).
5. IRC § 1014(b)(9). If the decedent acquired his or her interest in the property within one year from date of death, this rule does not apply. IRC § 1014(e).
6. The cost basis of property can vary because of depreciation, capitalized costs, and other factors. This example is simplified for illustration purposes.
7. Arizona, California, Idaho, Louisiana, Nevada, New Mexico, Texas, Washington, and, for most purposes, Wisconsin.
8. IRC § 1014(b)(6).
9. PUBLIC POLICY INSTITUTE, AARP, PROBATE ADMINISTRATION, 40; AARP, A REPORT ON PROBATE, 10.
10. AARP, A REPORT ON PROBATE, 10.
11. Michael J. Berger in his article *How Title to Assets Is Held Can Determine Whether Probate Is Avoided,* 18 ESTATE PLANNING 98, 100 (1991), states, "Probably the best method to avoid the entanglements of probate is to use a living trust."
12. IRC § 2523. When joint tenancy is created between spouses, there is a gift to the extent that one spouse has made contributions toward the acquisition of the property in excess of the contributions made by the other spouse. For example, if a spouse purchases property with his or her own funds, but the property is titled in joint tenancy, that spouse has made a gift to the other spouse. The amount of the gift is one half of the value of the property at the time it is put in joint names. Because of the unlimited marital deduction for gifts between spouses, the gift is not taxable. A transfer out of joint tenancy from both spouses to one spouse is not a taxable event either, because it too is

sheltered by the gift tax unlimited marital deduction. REVENUE RULING 83-178, 1983-2 CUMULATIVE BULLETIN 171.

13. Treas. Reg. § 25.2511-1(h)(5); REVENUE RULING 78-362, 1978-2 CUMULATIVE BULLETIN 248. The creation of most joint bank accounts, the purchase of U.S. savings bonds in joint names, and the creation of joint brokerage accounts are transfers for purposes of the gift tax. However, for these types of property, there is not a gift until the noncontributing tenant actually uses the funds. Treas. Reg. § 25.2511-1(h)(4); REVENUE RULING 68-269, 1968-1 CUMULATIVE BULLETIN 399.

14. Treas. Reg. § 25.2511-1(g)(1).

15. IRC § 2503(b).

16. IRC § 2502(a).

17. Use of the exemption equivalent is mandatory and automatic; it is applied to taxable gifts until such time as it has been fully depleted. REVENUE RULING 79-398, 1979-2 CUMULATIVE BULLETIN 338.

18. June may be able to use a qualified disclaimer planning depending upon the law in effect in her federal jurisdiction.

19. Bolton Roofing Co. v. Hedrick, 701 S.W. 2d 183 (Mo. Ct. App. 1985).

Chapter 25

1. O. W. HOLMES, *The Autocrat of the Breakfast-Table* (1858), as quoted in Budish, *The Multipurpose Trust*, MODERN MATURITY, Aug./Sept. 1991, at 44.

Chapter 26

1. Curran, Report: Survey of the Public's Use of Legal Services, *Two Nationwide Surveys: 1989 Pilot Assessments of the Unmet Legal Needs of the Poor and of the Public Generally* 55, 69 (1989).

2. S. R. COVEY, THE SEVEN HABITS OF HIGHLY EFFECTIVE PEOPLE 23 (1989).

3. See, *e.g.*, Herold, *Living Trust Lore: Fact or Fiction?* N. J. L. J., March 28, 1991, at 12; and also Bearns.

4. Jones, *Putting Revocable Trusts in Their Place*, 129 TRUSTS AND ESTATES, 1990, at 8.

5. Mankoff, Letter to the Editor, 129 TRUSTS AND ESTATES, December 1990, at 12.
6. Specifically, these states are Nebraska, Iowa, Wisconsin, and Washington. See *Attorneys: Beware of Living Trust Documents*, The Star (Dane County, Wisconsin), May 2, 1991, at 1.
7. See, for example, State of Nebraska, Department of Justice, press release dated November 20, 1990, Lincoln, Nebraska.
8. *Id.*
9. There is ample documentation to suggest that the organized probate bar is opposed to methods of avoiding probate. For example, a recent newsletter of the Indiana Bar Association stated that "the section has formed a committee to collect information regarding the selling of probate avoidance schemes." 10 PROBATE, TRUST, PROPERTY AND DEATH TAX NEWSLETTER 1 (1991).
10. For example, *supra* note 7.
11. Uniform Statutory Will Act prefatory note, 8A UNIFORM LAWS ANNOTATED 205 (West Supp. 1991).
12. Antonucci, *Advantage of the Funded Revocable Trust in Estate Planning*, ESTATES AND PROBATE NEWSLETTER OF THE CONNECTICUT BAR ASSOCIATION, March 1990, at 1, 2.
13. Bostick, *The Revocable Trust: A Means of Avoiding Probate in the Small Estate?* 21 UNIVERSITY OF FLORIDA L. Rev. 44, 47 (1968).

Appendix A

Income Splitting and the Throwback Rules

1. REVENUE PROCEDURE 91-65, 1991-50 INTERNAL REVENUE BULLETIN 12. Each year, the bracket amounts are indexed for inflation.
2. *Id.*
3. J. PESCHEL & E. SPURGEON, ¶ 6.03[B][1], at 6–11.
4. IRC §§ 665 through 668.
5. DNI is defined in IRC § 643(a). DNI is not necessarily the same as accounting income, and is basically the taxable income of the trust. The effect of the concept of DNI is to give income beneficiaries the benefit of all trust deductions even though some of them may be attributable to trust principal, not to trust income.
6. IRC § 665(b). This rule does not apply when there are multiple trusts.

7. See Cornfeld, *Trapping Distributions*, 1980 University of Miami 14th Institute on Estate Planning, ch. 14, ¶¶ 1400–1407.
8. IRC § 651(a).
9. Treas. Reg. § 1.665(e)-1(b).
10. *Id.;* see also Keydel, *"Funding,"* 98, 120; Sutton, 4.
11. See HILKER, ch. 17, ¶ 1708.2, for a more complete explanation of this technique.
12. Treas. Reg. § 1.641(b)-3(b). See also REVENUE RULING 55-287; 1955-1 CUMULATIVE BULLETIN 130 and Commissioner v. First Trust and Deposit Company, 118 F.2d 449 (2d Cir. 1941).
13. REVENUE RULING 64-99, 1964-1 CUMULATIVE BULLETIN 482.
14. IRC § 1(h) [formerly § 1(j); amended 1990].
15. 3A A. SCOTT & W. FRATCHER, § 233.1 and note 2; RESTATE-MENT (SECOND) OF TRUSTS § 233 comment b, "Profits on the sale or exchange of principal are ordinarily principal."
16. IRC § 643(a)(3).

The Ability to Choose a Fiscal Year

1. IRC §§ 441 and 645(a); Treas. Reg. §1.443-1(a)(2).
2. IRC § 645(a).
3. IRC § 6654.

Personal Exemptions for Trusts and Estates

1. IRC § 642(b).

Estimated Tax Payments

1. I.R.C § 6654(k)(1954).
2. J. PESCHEL & E. SPURGEON, ¶ 3.06[B].
3. Tax Reform Act of 1986, Public Law No. 99-514, § 1404(a); IRC § 6654(1)(2).
4. Technical and Miscellaneous Revenue Act of 1988, Public Law No. 100-647, §1014(d)(2); IRC § 6654(1)(2).
5. Public Law No. 100-647, § 1014(d)(2); IRC §6654(1)(2).
6. Public Law No. 101-239, § 7811(j)(6); IRC §6654(1)(2).

The Separate Share Rule

1. IRC § 663(c). Technically, the separate share rule deals with the computing of DNI for complex trusts.
2. Ordinarily, this amount would be subject to the throwback rules.

However, since Melanie just turned twenty-one, the throwback rules do not apply.

Amounts Permanently Set Aside for Charity

1. IRC § 2055.
2. IRC § 642(c)(1). This is not true for a simple trust.
3. IRC § 642(c)(2).

S Corporation Stock

1. This is true as long as the value of the trust is included in the estate of the trust maker for federal estate tax purposes. IRC § 1361(c)(2)(A)(ii); IRC § 2038.
2. IRC § 1361(c)(2)(B)(ii).
3. See HILKER, ch. 17, ¶¶ 17-41 to 17-42.
4. Becker, *Wills vs. Revocable Trusts, Tax Inequality Persists*, 3 PROBATE AND PROPERTY 17, 19 (1989).
5. IRC § 1361(c)(2)(A)(iii).
6. IRC § 1361(d).
7. IRC §1361(d)(3).
8. Where there is a single trust having more than one beneficiary, if the trust provides for substantially separate and independent shares for the different beneficiaries, then the shares are treated as separate trusts. IRC §1361(d)(3); PRIVATE LETTER RULING 8737038.
9. PRIVATE LETTER RULING 8415025.

The Nonrecognition of Losses Between a Trust and Its Beneficiaries

1. Keydel, *"Funding,"* 98, 103, 104.
2. IRC §§ 267(a) and 267(b)(6).
3. *Id.*
4. Treas. Reg. § 1.661(a)-2.(f)(1).
5. IRC § 267(d).
6. IRC § 267(d) does not affect the basis of property for determining gain. Treas. Reg. § 1.267(d)-1(c)(1); Meg's basis is the same as the stepped-up basis for federal estate tax purposes.
7. IRC § 267(d).
8. The examples assume that all income has been paid out previously.
9. Treas. Reg. § 1.661(a)-2(f)(3).

10. Suisman v. Eaton, 15 F. Supp. 113 (D. Conn. 1935), *affirmed* 83 F. 2d 1019 (2d Cir. 1936), *cert den* 299 U.S. 573; REVENUE RULING 56-270, 1956-1 CUMULATIVE BULLETIN 325; clarified by REVENUE RULING 60-87, 1960-1 CUMULATIVE BULLETIN 286; Treas. Reg. § 1.1014-4(a)(3).
11. IRC § 661(a).
12. REVENUE RULING 60-87, 1960-1 CUMULATIVE BULLETIN 286; TECHNICAL ADVISORY MEMORANDUM 8145026.
13. Fractional share formulas are being used more and more for reasons other than the nonrecognition of loss rules. For example, a primary use of the fractional share of the residue formula is to avoid the acceleration of income with respect to a decedent when the trust consists of qualified plan proceeds. Also, under REVENUE PROCEDURE 64-19, 1964-1 CUMULATIVE BULLETIN 682, a fractional share formula preserves the marital deduction by allocating a fair share of appreciation and depreciation to the marital and credit shelter trusts.
14. REVENUE PROCEDURE 64-19, 1964-1 CUMULATIVE BULLETIN 682.
15. See S. R. COVEY, MARITAL DEDUCTION AND CREDIT SHELTER DISPOSITIONS AND THE USE OF FORMULA PROVISIONS 95–98, 111 (1984).
16. IRC § 1212(b).
17. IRC § 1211(b).

Ordinary Income on the Sale of Depreciable Property

1. IRC § 1239(a).
2. IRC § 1239(b)(2).
3. IRC § 1245.
4. IRC § 1250.
5. IRC § 1(h).
6. IRC § 643(e).

Rental Real Estate Income Tax Deduction

1. IRC § 469(i)(4).
2. IRC § 469.
3. IRC § 469(i)(1).
4. IRC § 469(i)(4).
5. IRC § 469(i)(1).
6. IRC § 469(j)(12).

The Deductibility of Administrative Expenses

1. Treas. Reg. § 20.2053-1(a)(1).
2. Treas. Reg. § 20.2053-3(b)(3).
3. Treas. Reg. § 20.2053-8(b).
4. Treas. Reg. § 20.2053-8.

The Sixty-five-Day Rule for Trusts

1. IRC § 663(b).
2. Treas. Reg. § 1.663(b)-1(a)(2)(i). Computation of the income of a trust is described in Treas. Reg. § 1.643(b)-1 and the computation of DNI is described in Treas. Reg. §§ 1.643(a)-1 through 1.643(a)-7. It is not the purpose of this book to explain these accounting concepts in detail, so for a more complete description of the income taxation of trusts, see J. PESCHEL & E. SPURGEON.
3. Treas. Reg. § 1.663(b)-1.(a)(2)(ii).

The Status of a Trustee as a Statutory Executor

1. *E.g.*, Richardson & Muehleck, 294, 303.
2. IRC § 2203.
3. New York Trust Co. v. Commissioner, 26 TC 257 (1956), acq. 1956-2 Cumulative Bulletin 7; DeNiro v. United States, 561 F.2d 653, 657 (6th Cir. 1977).
4. IRC § 2032
5. IRC § 2032A.
6. IRC § 2056(b)(7).
7. IRC § 6166.
8. IRC §§ 2022 & 2204; Treas. Reg. § 20.2002-1; Hochberg & Silbergleit, *Recent Cases Narrow Scope of Executor's Personal Liability for Estate Taxes*, 7 ESTATE PLANNING 2 (1980).
9. See R. STEPHENS, G. MAXFIELD, S. LIND, & D. CALFEE, ¶ 2.02 & 8.03.
10. IRC § 2204(b).
11. IRC § 2204(a); If both an executor and a trustee are serving, the discharge of the executor is a prerequisite of the trustee's obtaining a discharge.
12. Treas. Reg. §§ 1.6013-1(a)(3)(d)(3) and 1.6013-4(c).
13. Treas. Reg. § 1.6013-1(a)(3)(d)(3).
14. Treas. Reg. § 1.6013-1(d)(5).
15. Treas. Reg. § 25.2513-2(c).
16. Treas. Reg. §§ 1.6012-3(b)(1) and 20.2203-1.

17. IRC § 2204(a).
18. IRC § 2204(b).
19. When William D. Kirchick, Esq., of the law firm of Bingham, Dana & Gould of Boston, Massachusetts, reviewed this chapter, he pointed out that "in some states, like Massachusetts, if the trustee is the same person as the executor, then it may be necessary to have a guardian-ad-litem appointed upon the allowance of the executor's accounts in order to avoid any unity of interest problem between the executor and trustee." However, this issue has never arisen in our experience.

Index